TOTAL
SURVEILLANCE

TOTAL SURVEILLANCE

INVESTIGATING THE BIG BROTHER WORLD OF E-SPIES, EAVESDROPPERS AND CCTV

JOHN PARKER

PIATKUS

⌘   **Visit the Piatkus website!**   ⌘

Piatkus publishes a wide range of exciting fiction and non-fiction,
including books on health, mind body & spirit, sex, self-help, cookery,
biography and the paranormal. If you want to:

- read descriptions of our popular titles
- buy our books over the internet
- take advantage of our special internet offers
- enter our montly competition
- learn more about your favourite
  Piatkus authors

visit our website at:

www.piatkus.co.uk

Published in the UK in 2000 by
Judy Piatkus (Publishers) Limited
5 Windmill Street
London W1T 2JA
e-mail: info@piatkus.co.uk

For the latest news and information on all our titles,
visit our website at www.piatkus.co.uk

The moral right of the author has been asserted
A catalogue record for this book is available
from the British Library

ISBN 0 7499 2033 5

This book has been printed on paper manufactured with respect for the environment using wood
from managed sustainable resources

Page design by Zena Flax

Typeset by Action Publishing Technology Ltd, Gloucester
Printed and bound in Great Britain by
Biddles Ltd, Guildford & King's Lynn
www.biddles.co.uk

CONTENTS

PROLOGUE

Surveillance: n. Close observation or supervision over a person, group etc. for an undefined period of time, esp. one in custody or under suspicion

THE WORD 'SURVEILLANCE' WAS once generally associated with police and intelligence agencies, and suspicion was indeed the motivation of the people watchers. Not any longer. The technology that blasted us into cyberspace in the late 1980s turned surveillance into an all-embracing scenario that few can escape. Suspicion often does not even enter the equation. You may have committed no criminal act. You are not spying for some foreign power. You do not belong to a gang of organised drug dealers, paedophiles or terrorists. Nor are you cheating the tax people or the welfare system. In fact, you may be pursuing a thoroughly normal, mundane or perhaps even reclusive existence. Whatever, we are all being subjected to increasing levels of surveillance of one kind or another: watched, filmed, listened in to, recorded, tracked, entered on to databases, put on lists. In short, the term 'private lives' is as dated as Noël Coward's charming little play.

Whether or not you possess a computer, and regardless of your age, social station, work, wealth or health, someone somewhere is interested in you – and indeed in anyone who lives in a half-civilised environment. We are the targets, million upon million of us, of eavesdroppers, government agents, special agents, private agents, security officers, law enforcement agencies, commercial database builders, cybersnoopers, computer hackers and surveillance specialists engaged in a large and daunting number of tasks. They maintain a watching brief over us, achieved by widespread monitoring and interception of global communications networks, national telephone and mobile phone systems, computer networks and the Internet, as well as mass and clandestine observation through various listening devices, closed circuit television cameras, vehicle tracking systems and other appliances directed against the public.

Their object is to obtain information that is often private, confidential, valuable or top secret. The greater danger is that it is all being entered on to huge databases that may be networked, sold, hacked into and generally put to clandestine use. Nothing is sacrosanct. Information obtained may range through topics as diverse as Joe Public's shopping habits or health records, a politician's clandestine sexual encounter with his secretary, the latest BMW engine designs or matters of the highest importance to the security of a nation.

There are thousands of these people in the supposedly legitimate side of the surveillance business scattered around the world. A large proportion of them are state-employed, but those numbers are being matched by privately run contingents employed by business, commerce and industry, a few power-hungry billionaires, and a rapidly expanding network of international crime syndicates and terrorists whose resources allow them to invest in the kind of technology that many governments would be pleased to possess.

What they all have in common is an array of electronic devices, powerful computers and sophisticated software. Much of it was originally created for the Star Wars era, or designed and invented for military use against Saddam Hussein or the IRA and the paramilitaries in Northern Ireland, or for top secret government surveillance operations, and is now in common usage. To these trinkets may be added the download facilities of assorted interception aids linked to a sky full of satellite technology that helped to shape the foreign policy and national security of the major powers in the latter half of the twentieth century and which can identify objects on Earth as small as six inches square. This technology allows the ordinary person to be monitored to an extraordinary degree.

The effects of the revolution in all forms of communication is both startling and worrying. Nation competes with nation – and especially with the disquieting supremacy of the United States – in the battles of post-modern warfare which are based upon the skills of computer wizards.

This upsurge in state and private surveillance is insidious. It has been carried along on the impetus generated by the demands for greater powers by government agencies and military machines in order to defend us against espionage, terrorism and crime. It came upon us almost unnoticed and with considerable ease.

I have had direct personal experience of the widespread powers of modern surveillance, beginning long ago during a period of undercover reporting while carrying out investigative work for *Life* magazine. I have also been monitored while working on my previous books, in which British civilian and military intelligence took a keen interest prior to publication. And it happened again while working on this book. In May 1999, for example, the intelligence agencies on both sides of the Atlantic became aware of my plans after receiving a tip-off from a former code-breaker employed by the American National Security Agency at a top secret spy station in Britain. Thereafter they kept track of my progress as my e-mails and telephone conversations floated about the ether. Those in my profession who write about matters relating to state or military enterprises expect and anticipate such observation.

Even so, a surprising experience occurred, appropriately enough, in 1984, the year that Orwell described so powerfully in his book of the same name. Surveillance emerged from a source that as a journalist I would have least expected – my own employer. In June that year, Robert Maxwell bought the *Daily Mirror*, where I was then night editor, and brought with him some electronic aids that were almost unheard of in the work environment. An unseemly period in British newspaper history began. Maxwell's employees were subjected to a form of worker surveillance, then probably unique in Britain.

One of his first acts was to install a new Ericsson telephone system. None of us knew at the time that the system was linked to Maxwell's private headquarters and lent itself to interception. Telephone calls and mail on the internal computer networks were all subject to his scrutiny whenever he wished. The irony was that Maxwell himself was being bugged – by British intelligence, the American National Security Agency, the CIA, the KGB, Mossad and Uncle Tom Cobley and all. For those of us drawn into that world of Maxwellian reality – not far from Orwellian fiction – his staff surveillance operations, which only became known about after his death in 1991, were an appalling discovery.

Yet less than a decade after that discovery, such surveillance activities are widespread. Surveys of global corporations and major businesses throughout the United States and the UK have shown that up to 60 per cent of the workforces of those two nations are being subjected to some form of electronic surveillance. But that is only part of the story. Jack Albright, a former American secret service agent, has in-depth knowledge of the world of surveillance. He was not far off describing Orwell's vision when he outlined to me the potential for being watched at the beginning of the twenty-first century:

> The side effect of advances in communications technology and miniaturisation was the opening up of an era of amazing ability for multi-faceted surveillance, interfaced and networked in global systems. Brought down to street level, it means that the 'theys' of this world (of which I am one) are capable of monitoring your telephone calls, watching your movements, opening your mail, reading your e-mails, scanning your faxes, taking a look in your computer files while you're on-line, keeping track of your car, keeping track of you, where you live, where you work, and for whom and why, what you get up to while you're there, what you say in your messages over company systems, and then on into once very private affairs like how much tax you pay, who you owe money to, what medication (or illicit drugs) you're on and pretty well every other damn thing . . . there is barely a corner of life in today's connected world that cannot be viewed by people outside of your normal domain, and who will not necessarily have any entitlement to do so.
>
> And that's where we hit the schizophrenia zone – trying to justify the fact that all of the above, all the surveillance, is vital and has only one way to go, in an upward spiral. This is not just to satisfy the prying tendencies of America's National

Security Agency, the CIA and the FBI, or Britain's MI5 and GCHQ, or any of the other international intelligence and law enforcement agencies. That exists, sure enough, supposedly to protect society from the ruthless, lawless people living among us and whose attacks, as each year passes, raise the level of wonderment that this could happen in a so-called civilised age. Equally empowered in the e-world, however, is private enterprise and particularly those employed in the growth industry of databasing – the facts of life that are being compiled, stored and utilised on every single one of us.

The speed with which mass surveillance against the public has gathered momentum has taken the overseers of both the law and human rights by surprise. A dramatic change occurred in little more than half a decade, and there was nothing on the statute books, or even established codes of practice, to control it. The implications are unknown; the courts have no precedent to call upon.

At the turn of the millennium civil liberties and privacy campaigners were marshalling their forces, armed with the evidence of decades of more traditional forms of abuse by the spy and law enforcement agencies. Much of it dated to times when the systems had but a fraction of today's sophistication. Then, it was a fairly straightforward issue: that 'society had to be watched for its own good'. Secrecy, combined with the clandestine operations of state agencies, was generally accepted. All that changed with the explosion of telecommunications, global computer networks and the Internet. Thousands of other interested parties, from state agencies to commerce and crime, have got into the act to the point where mass surveillance is now reaching a level which the famous silent majority may find unacceptable.

However, it is not just technological advances that have brought about the disturbing expansion in surveillance techniques. In 1989 there was a sudden and totally unpredicted upheaval in the political climate. The collapse of Communism meant that the vast manpower of rival intelligence agencies, who had been largely spying on each other needed new missions in order to survive. The KGB and the East German Stasi – the principal enemies of Western intelligence who between them employed more than a million spies and tens of thousands of agents and part-timers – were going out of business. When, as one optimist put it, 'the Russians came out with their hands up' at the turn of the 1990s, the spy business looked to be on the verge of vanishing into its own shadows. The Cold War had ended and the Communist administrations of the Soviet Union and the Eastern Bloc went down in the wake of the collapse of the Berlin Wall in 1989. A 'new world order' and the possible dissolution of NATO were predicted at the time by pundits in high places, and gloom descended upon the spy trade. There were immediate and quite hefty cuts in government security budgets; agents and operatives were called home and sacked. The world, it seemed, would soon be full of ex-spies.

Were they now to be herded off to the knacker's yard? Not a chance! Two factors were not foreseen. The first was that Russia, freed from its iron-fist constraints, began to descend into gangster-ridden financial chaos, with tons of dangerous nuclear armoury and chemical weaponry lying about the place and thousands of experts in the field of nefarious activity available to any mad dictator or terrorist leader who cared to buy them a bag of groceries. Nor did the Stasi people simply fade away. Large numbers of them offered themselves to governments and dictators who welcomed the skills and contacts they brought with them. Freedom from the controlled environment of the old Soviet Union had unleashed all kinds of new dangers, added to which there was the instability of previously battened-down nations such as the former Yugoslavia.

Secondly, the astonishing pace of the demise of Communism ran, quite coincidentally, parallel to the great revolution in communications, centred around 'new breed' satellites, mobile telephones, the Internet and computer technology that promised a PC on everyone's desk within a decade – and, unknown then, within easy reach of prying eyes and ears. Within five years the intelligence community was hiring again, but this time a different kind of agent. The cloak and dagger days were well and truly over. What changed in those years of cuts was the age profile of surveillance and intelligence operatives (now much younger), the methodology, the technology and the focus – changes which were, by the late 1990s, as dramatic as those in the international political arena.

The emphasis was rapidly upgraded from a netherworld populated by old-time spies, subversives and agents of influence maintained by virtually every major nation for ideological purposes, or to counter them. In their place came a state and private intelligence community facing a much wider brief with specialist activity that flourished with the new technology: state-aided economic and industrial espionage, the war against terrorism, the tracking of weapons of mass destruction, organised crime (with particular emphasis on drugs and illegal immigrant rackets), electronic money laundering, and a range of other assorted phenomena ranging from computer hackers to school shootings.

New aims and directions led the law enforcers and the watchers towards a quite parochial level of surveillance, ultimately down to that guy taking an illegal pee in a shop doorway or tossing a beer can into a park flower bed. Privacy issues were no longer to revolve around state surveillance or the phone-tapping powers of the police. With the IT age came a whole range of additional technologies that together constituted an assault on the privacy of the individual on a scale previously unimagined.

This book is not intended as a publicity exercise for the campaigners against these intrusions – those organisations are already demonstrating their capabilities in that regard. Instead it may perhaps be seen as a kind of balance sheet, setting out the global erosion of privacy and human rights against a backdrop of law enforcers worldwide seeking greater legal powers of interception, while industry and commerce are grabbing the opportunities for surveillance virtually without regulation or controls.

Part I looks at how surveillance is directly affecting you today – from overt forms such as CCTVs to more clandestine operations. Part II explores the state agencies behind modern surveillance including the National Security Agency and MI5. It also takes a look at the most powerful surveillance system available to these agencies – the Echelon system. Part III explores in greater depth the gadgets and technology used by today's spies, security agencies and private organisations.

What is the armoury of today's spies? Who are they targeting? How widespread is surveillance by commercially orientated groups against the unsuspecting populus? *What information do they hold on you?* . . .

PART I

■

WATCHING YOU –
HOW SURVEILLANCE
AFFECTS
US ALL

CHAPTER 1
THE NAKED INDIVIDUAL

A **CURSORY GLANCE AROUND YOUR** home town these days gives you a rough idea of general surveillance. Antennae, communication units, roadside and CCTV cameras are often in evidence to provide physical observation of you or to track your car. Cameras with sound are also proliferating in public places, while the motorway system in Britain is the most intensely monitored road network anywhere in the world. Most surveillance, however, is covert and often unsuspected. From information available to the public we can discover many clues about the probabilities and sources, but the state agencies and private intelligence specialists are not fond of authors rummaging around in *their* trade secrets. This is especially true if they are located in the United Kingdom, where freedom of information is still a far-off dream.

The USA, and lately the Republic of Ireland, have laws which demand greater openness. In researching the whys and wherefores, the arguments on both sides of the security fence, I travelled to Las Vegas in the autumn of 1999 for a convention in which these topics were to be fully discussed. It seemed an unlikely setting, this garish city where anything goes. In fact it turned out to be quite the reverse, and there was none better to explain why than ex-US secret serviceman Jack Albright, one of those who left the service after the fall of Communism, when the tough got going.

He had selected our meeting place and the elevator zoomed to the 108th floor of what is the tallest free-standing observation platform in the United States – the magnificent Stratosphere Tower, part of a new hotel of the same name. The location was apt for two reasons. Sin City, as Las Vegas is still affectionately called by the locals in spite of the supposed departure of the Mafia, has enlisted an army of security specialists to run an operation that is comparable to the guarding of Fort Knox and is bigger in its manpower and more sophisticated in its technology than a good many small nations.

Secondly, across the town in the Las Vegas Convention Centre, some of the electronics giants (such as Sony, Motorola, Honeywell, Mitsubishi and Polaroid), which are among the thousands of companies engaged in the manufacture and supply of aids to state and private intelligence agencies and security companies around the world, were displaying the latest hardware and software for every conceivable aspect of the business on forty acres of floor space. Admission was by electronically tagged badges only: no recording devices, cameras or video equipment were allowed.

The exhibition, coupled with the annual convention of ASIS International – the globally orientated American Society for Industrial Security – was why we were both there. Allied to the main event were informal gatherings of former FBI and US secret service agents, along with ex-intelligence people and Special Forces operatives from the rest of the world. They included a large contingent from Britain, who are among the 32,000-strong membership of this organisation.

Albright, in his early fifties, had retired from the service three years earlier and taken a private contract, partly because he had come to the end of his career progression and partly because the rewards were better. Like most of the delegates, he retained close links with the intelligence forces in state employ on both sides of the Atlantic. Slender, fit and showing his age only by the greying temples and lined forehead, he had moved into the forefront of the internationally burgeoning private intelligence and security sector 'alongside a bunch of kids who know all about cyber-technology and use words with which I am not familiar, but not so much about the tricks of the intelligence game'.

He wanted to explain his choice of meeting place and waved his arms towards the windows of the elegant lounge of the Stratosphere Tower. It was nearly dusk and a great mass of neon creations all the way down the Las Vegas Strip would soon surge into spectacular activity.

'What d'ya see?' Albright enquired.

The panoramic vista of the Las Vegas valley, surrounded by the orange and pink mountains, was visible from every angle and he answered his own question: 'Everything . . . everything as far as the eye can see,' he said, lighting a Cuban cigar and blowing a smoke ring towards the ceiling. 'What you have here, at the top of this tower, is total surveillance of Las Vegas and that is repeated down there, on the ground. This place is, in reality, like a fortress, well lit and being watched from every conceivable angle. Below us in this hotel, for example, there is a casino hall covering 97,000 square feet. Here and in every other casino, every slot machine, every crap table, every wheel of fortune, every card dealer and every roulette spinner, all the gamblers – in fact everybody, period – is under unremitting observation. The whole of the Strip is on candid camera twenty-four hours a day – thousands of computer-controlled cameras, most of them unnoticed by the average punter, are churning out pictures for the watchers on a huge bank of television screens. They have special built-in alerts for anything untoward. They can zoom in close to a particular table, even look at a player who might be trying to beat the system or a dealer giving a good hand to an accomplice. Many areas are wired for sound. Most have the very latest gear, which includes infra-red, night-sight units and heat-seeking motion detectors originally developed for the military, which can take a look at dark zones. Virtually all electronic communications are monitored. If there was a hint of anything coming down, by way of card sharping, cheating, a heist or, perhaps, a terrorist attack, the likelihood is that it wouldn't get past first base. *Ocean's Eleven* just isn't possible.'

Albright's point was not lost. Las Vegas was a mirror – if slightly distorted – of the electronic revolution that is taking society towards total surveillance. The 'New Spies' have vastly more effective technology and are focusing increasingly on techniques of mass observation. The situation is one in which the state-employed surveillance operators have been joined by an equally well-equipped and mushrooming private security industry, guarding everything from dictators to oilfields, cybersecrets to abortion clinics. This development has advanced with such speed that laws controlling surveillance and interception have been simply outpaced.

The privacy lobby and the human rights movements had long ago drawn their battle lines for gross intrusions of privacy and abuse of laws governing electronic interception. They had every cause for concern. Within the likes of the National Security Agency, CIA, FBI, MI5, MI6, Mossad and the organisation formerly known as the KGB, nothing had changed with regard to their perception of spying: their belief that society still needed to be watched for its own protection. What seriously worries the privacy campaigners now, however, is the ever-expanding monitoring of the public without any real measure of accountability. The legal constraints that do exist are being pushed to the limit.

Across the board, new communications and surveillance systems are causing alarm among those who campaign for the right of the individual to go about his daily life without the fear of being clandestinely observed. High among their concerns are the vast new databases of photographic imagery and DNA profiles being built up as part of the war on crime. One of the areas causing most anxiety, however, remains the ability of state-sponsored or private organisations to intercept, watch and photograph on a scale unimagined a few years ago – an ability which has permitted a considerable invasion into what were previously safe, private areas of life, often involving very personal data and family secrets. The advent of digital communication technology has been combined with existing wireless and wireline equipment so that voice, documents and images can be merged into a single on-line folder and whizzed to another place in an instant.

Wireless equipment, originally a method of voice transmission, has been developed for the mass market of the mobile telephone. With this development has come the ability to transfer the whole range of data and imagery through modems, faxes, private branch exchanges and local area networks, linking computers and hand-held Dick Tracy-style mini-screens for the networking of material that may include proprietary information, medical records and confidential financial reports. Whether wireless or wireline connected, the whole package can be stored, copied, accessed, networked, published, sold and, for those with the wherewithal, be made available for inspection by third parties – thus exposing very private and secret material to the risks of intrusion, interception, theft and misuse.

Every hour of the day, private and business communications and confidential personal histories flow through computer networks. Even those who do not use the Internet, or do not even possess a computer, would be astonished at the amount of information about them as individuals that is available through the system: financial transactions, credit cards, medical records, insurance details and now, most insidious of all, personal habits and the basic stuff of life, all stored on globally interconnected databases.

The personal information being networked covers every corner of private life, virtually from cradle to grave, to provide accumulations of records that amount to complete and composite on-line databases of human existence. They include:

- potted biographies of the occupants of up to 98 per cent of households in the industrialised world, allied to extensive credit records;

- personal profiling in taste, shopping habits and consumer details gleaned from form filling, surveys, magazine subscriptions, credit card usage and Internet use;

- personal financial details emerging from the purchase of insurance policies, financial products, credit databases and bank references;

- movement tracked by change of address and house purchase details;

- current address and location of an individual, partners or others living at the same address, and financial data concerning all occupants of that address;

- car registration tracking, change of car and vehicle location systems;

- landline and mobile phone records, who you phoned, who phoned you, where you were when you made the call;

- very private details ranging from tax records to medical history;

- pre-employment screening using techniques which are often carried out secretly and border on the illegal;

- observation in the workplace where Northern Ireland-style covert bugging and videoing of employees, forensic examination of their personal computer files, e-mails and voice-mails and clandestine testing of urine or other samples for drug use are becoming increasingly commonplace; and

- identifying imagery, through photographs, video film, digital storage systems with copies of fingerprints, eyeprints or DNA profiles.

These are but a few of the growing areas of personal surveillance which are often not covered by data protection laws and which must represent some sort of challenge to Article 12 of the Universal Declaration of Human Rights, which reads: 'No one shall be subjected to arbitrary interference with his privacy, family, home or correspondence, nor to attacks upon his honour and reputation. Everyone has the right to the protection of the law against such interference or attacks.'

Across the world, more and more lists containing millions of names, personal histories and assets are being accumulated and can be accessed by high-speed search engines for instant on-line reference. According to the calculations of Simon Davies, the British director of human rights watchdog Privacy International, by 1999 every citizen of the industrialised nations appeared in about two hundred of these databases; that is now an underestimate.

The sheer volume of information stored electronically and floating around in the ether, courtesy of the Internet and wireless communication systems, has emerged along with another phenomenon – the advent of a virtually constant state of on-line existence for businesses and individuals. This in turn has spawned a change in the whole concept of the communications industry. The benefits have been reaped by those on both sides of the legal divide, but at what cost? 'On-line' equals 'at risk' – an assessment contained on the official website of the Department of Trade and Industry of Her Majesty's Government. It begins its preamble to advice to business with the words: 'The Internet is inherently insecure . . .'

Crime on the Internet will be the growth area of the twenty-first century. A substantial document on the subject drawn up by the United Nations paints a nightmarish scenario:

> The burgeoning of the world of information technologies . . . has opened the door to antisocial and criminal behaviour in ways that would never have previously been possible. Computer systems offer some new and highly sophisticated opportunities for lawbreaking and they create the potential to commit traditional types of crimes in non-traditional ways. In addition to suffering the economic consequences of computer crime, society relies on computerised systems for almost everything in life, from air, train and bus traffic control to medical services and national security. Even a small glitch in the operation of these systems can put human lives in danger. Society's dependence on computer systems, therefore, has a profound human dimension. The rapid transnational expansion of large-scale computer networks and the ability to access many systems through regular telephone lines increases the vulnerability of these systems and the opportunity for criminal activity. The consequences of computer crime may have serious economic costs as well as serious costs in terms of human security.

The herd mentality surrounding the stock flotation of companies connected with e-commerce created a kind of euphoria that over-shadowed this darker side of the new media and communications business – that of the ability of law enforcement, private businesses and criminals alike to intercept and analyse communications and track individuals across the networks, using databases crammed with personal information. Laws drawn up in the 1980s were quickly overtaken and the protection of privacy became lost in the pigeon post.

Britain's Home Secretary Jack Straw, in words reminiscent of similar statements by Louis Freeh, director of the FBI, said in a consultative paper on the future of authorised telephone interception published in June 1999, 'Those who drafted the current legislation fifteen years ago could not and did not foresee the extraordinary pace of change in the communications industry. Faced with dated legislation on interception, sophisticated criminals and terrorists have been quick to put the new technology to use. The law must be revised if we are to preserve the ability of the law enforcement and intelligence agencies to detect serious crime and threats to our national security.'

It is that last phrase, 'national security', which provides the legal loophole for all kinds of state-sponsored surveillance techniques that sail close to the wind, and Jack Straw's words masked the irony of that particular can of worms: that Britain houses the world's largest communications interception station, a facility that unlocks the door to global surveillance on a scale which is beyond the comprehension of ordinary mortals. The station is the multi-billion-dollar set-up operated, financed and controlled by the Americans that, in a report presented to the European Parliament in 1998, was branded as being used to monitor 'routinely and indiscriminately' millions of communications, faxes and e-mail messages across Europe every day. In fact, that is only a fraction of its capability.

The increasing use of electronic spying by state intelligence and law enforcement agencies will be fully examined in the course of this book, but initially let us look at some of the surveillance technologies that are directed at non-criminals, in other words members of the general public, as they go about their lives.

SURVEILLANCE TECHNOLOGIES

A fair indication of the most recent developments was on show in the display halls of the ASIS convention in Las Vegas which, in 1999, was larger than ever before: 640 companies with products on show in 1700 booths. All the latest gear that goes to make up the needs and requirements of the modern security department on university campuses, in hospitals, schools, workplaces and public areas was there. Most will be put into the appropriate setting as each aspect is examined in later chapters. For the moment it is sufficient just to mention a few of the very latest techniques.

Perhaps the most significant development in most recent times is the worldwide growth in the sensitive issue of PIV – Personal Identification Verification systems. Identity confirmation is all the rage, and will become more so in the future. That was also apparent at the ASIS show, with fifty-five companies displaying ID products of various kinds. Another thirty-one companies were introducing the latest technology in biometric identification using body parts, such as scanned images of faceprint, eye retina, hand geometry and thumbprint, and voice recognition. Several systems are capable of instantly rejecting anyone carrying an unauthorised or stolen ID, even if the bearer is in disguise. The hair colour may have been changed, a beard may have been grown or spectacles added to conform with the false ID, but the new software will identify individuals by mapping bone structure and the uniqueness of the position of the eyes, nose, mouth and ears.

High on the list of recommended goodies was a 32-bit software suite for the design and manufacture of identity cards with a difference. This particular product was produced as a smart card with built-in features that could be used to access a mini-biography of the holder from an on-line database. The card is carried in the purse or pocket and acts as a hands-free entry and exit tool, i.e. it is not necessary to swipe. It can be read by a machine from a distance of up to two metres. It also allows the card controllers rapidly to integrate additional checkable images including signatures, fingerprints and biometric features. This, says the sales pitch, 'brings image functionality into applications such as access control, time and attendance, point of sale, human resources management and inventory control'. Translation: the card can be issued to employees, for example, to enable management to control entry to any building or part of the building, check time of arrival and departure, track movements while at work, call up personal information from a database, check credit status, and discover personal habits, drug use, previous employment history and any convictions for theft.

France and Germany are already experimenting with a similar

invention, putting some of these characteristics on to credit cards to prevent fraud. The logical next step is an all-embracing national ID card that will provide access to all known information about the holder. Many nations have introduced photo-ID cards for the entire population, although similar attempts have been met with fierce opposition in the UK, Australia and the USA. Even so, backdoor attempts are being made in most countries that do not have them, such as in the UK where all new driving licences must carry the holder's photograph. Most American states also have photo-driving licences and, indeed, few financial transactions or credit card purchases by individuals are completed without a request for photographic identification.

In 1999, one New Hampshire company put forward a proposal to create a database of the nation's entire stock of driving licence photographs which could be checked instantly on-line. The company, Image Data LLC, received the support of several members of the US Congress, which was used in promotional material about the system. 'True ID technology has widespread potential to reduce crime in the credit and checking fields, in airports to reduce the chances of terrorism, and in immigration and naturalisation to verify proper identity.'

Several states had already agreed to cooperate and had sold 22 million driving licence photographs to Image Data when the whole scheme suddenly went pear-shaped. Privacy groups were in uproar when it was discovered that the company had received $1.5 million in federal funds and technical assistance from the American secret service. Some of the states asked for their photographs back. One test case ended up in court, where a state judge rejected the attempts to have the material returned, saying the company's True ID system is 'no more intrusive on the privacy of an individual than showing the driver's license itself'. The scheme may well have been temporarily shelved, but it signalled a potential development in the future.

Industry and commerce long ago introduced their own ID systems which were soon to be upgraded to interface with computer-held data. What is known in the trade as 'badging' arrived in the 1990s, with a profusion of identity-confirming add-ons about the employees wearing them. Today, most major companies insist on identity badges or smart cards being worn or carried by all employees or visitors. Many of them will be 'active badges', which are in effect electronic tags emitting a signal that can be read and identified by receivers located in various parts of a commercial complex and can be used to track the movements of workers. The people locators can be upgraded to be linked into telecommunication systems to ensure that the employee is never out of sight, even when travelling.

Other 'active badges' can be customised for specific people-tracking functions. In 1999, workers at the Tropicana Casino in Atlantic City were confronted by a system known as Hygiene Guard. Based on the smart card transmitter principle, it had an interactive network of sensors to monitor whether a worker had washed his hands after visiting the toilet. Unless an employee operated the soap dispenser and stood for at least thirty seconds at a running tap, an infraction would be recorded on a computer in the human resources office.

Equally, the science of biometrics is earmarked for a major role in identification verification in the future, using digitally stored photographs along with retina scans, hand geometry, fingerprints and voice recognition. The police forces in numerous countries have adopted the methods of DNA profiling pioneered in Britain, through which databases of samples taken from scenes of crimes, suspects or convicted criminals may be submitted for comparison with existing database samples and modern software will find any existing match in minutes. No comparable investigative procedure existed prior to 1995, and the human rights and civil liberties campaigners jointly warned of the risk of inaccuracies, particularly as the databases increased in size.

In February 2000, civil rights' groups fears were realised when police in Bolton, Lancashire, ran a test on a sample taken from the scene of a burglary and discovered that it matched a man in the West Country who had a previous history of domestic violence. The Bolton police arrested him, but then discovered he had a cast-iron alibi. When they sent the DNA sample back for a retest the results sent shockwaves through police forces around the world, including the FBI whose own system was built on the British model. British scientists admitted it was a mismatch, but said it was a 37 million to one chance. Liberty and other civil rights campaigners said it was nothing to do with chance, but was due to the fallibility of a system which had sent many thousands of people to prison and whose accuracy could no longer be guaranteed. At the time of writing, the implications were immense – that thousands of those whose convictions relied solely on DNA evidence would be launching appeals against conviction. If DNA matching is indeed suspect, the possibilities are enormous; in Britain by May 2000, 63,000 convictions have relied either in part or wholly on DNA identification.

The procedures for DNA testing vary throughout Europe and although in the mid-1990s only four member states of the European Union possessed any legislation on the taking and storing of DNA profiles, by the turn of the century, eight had followed Britain's lead in creating DNA databases. The UK also introduced the most stringent rules concerning the taking of samples, including testing by force if necessary. This is not the case in most other European countries. The February 2000 bulletin of Statewatch, the British-based privacy and human rights information centre, reported the case of a Dutch woman who was arrested in London during a non-violent demonstration against an international arms conference. After being charged with a breach of the peace and damaging a pavement by painting slogans on it, she was subsequently asked to provide a DNA sample. She refused, believing it to be her right and claimed she was then physically restrained by five police officers while swabs were taken from the inside of her mouth.

In Britain, DNA testing of suspects is conducted in the same way as taking fingerprints. Samples from anyone found guilty of a recordable offence are stored on the national database. Samples given voluntarily during an investigation or from a suspect who is subsequently acquitted are destroyed when the investigation has concluded. There are, however, moves towards a considerable expansion of Britain's own DNA database. Statewatch pointed out that Britain's Police Superintendent's Association has already called for every child to be profiled at birth and entered into the database. As of January 2000 the UK database alone contained around 700,000 samples. Of these half a million were of personal DNA profiles and the remainder retained from scene-of-crime investigations. Further, discussions were well advanced among European Justice and Home Affairs ministers for greater cooperation to set up pan-European DNA databases.

Similar scientific applications, which use elements of the human body for other forms of surveillance, are becoming commonplace. Another product on display in Las Vegas can be used for hair testing to determine whether the owner is a drug user. The Psychemedics

Corporation of America, for example, is marketing a product for human resources investigators which 'uses hair analysis to screen potential employees for drug abuse'. It is difficult to assess the extent of drug testing in the workplace because much of it is carried out secretly and illegally; pulling out a strand of someone's hair might be sufficient grounds for a major lawsuit in the USA. Many different kits are available to determine the presence of a number of illicit drugs. Psychemedics provides some statistics: it boasts that it has completed more than 2 million hair tests and that the proprietary process was, by September 1999, being used by more than 1600 companies in the United States and overseas 'for pre-employment and random drug screening'.

Another interesting toy for the bosses is a voice-analysing telephone, one of a family of revolutionary 'truth verification' tools developed to interface with a desktop PC. It can be used without the person on the other end being aware of the monitoring and, according to the publicity material:

> It is an ingenious method of detecting vocal stress, a simple yet powerful software tool for identifying deception in your home or office. It samples the voice and every spoken word while the software is running and enables you to verify the truth during a one-to-one conversation. When vocal stress is detected, System Decision messages appear on the PC screen during the conversation suggesting possible causes for the change in vocal pattern. Depending on the analysis, the following messages may appear on screen: Telling the Truth; High Level of Excitement; Confused; Subject is Not Sure; Exaggerating; Being Sarcastic; Inaccurate or False Statement; High Stress; Extreme Excitement.

Once the conversation has ended, the machine produces a special profile report for a closer look at the results. While the manufacturers are confident of their claims about accuracy, others are not so sure. The prospect of employers and managers using such a machine is naturally viewed with deep anxiety by employees rights' observers, who complain that the extensive use of telephone analysis technology is in itself causing distress among employees. According to a recent report into workplace monitoring by the Ontario Information and Privacy Commissioner, the invasion of an individual's privacy has a far-reaching impact on the quality of work life.

Many major corporations have installed telephone management systems that automatically record every form of telephonic activity. British Telecom call centre workers are constantly monitored by computer-based analysers and get regular charts comparing their performance with that of other workers. In the USA, airline reservation and sales staff wear headsets that monitor the length and content of every single telephone call, as well as toilet and lunch breaks. A 1999 Privacy International report records one instance where telephone calls received by airline reservation agents were electronically monitored on a second-by-second basis: agents were allowed only eleven seconds between each call and twelve minutes of break time each day. One clerk observed: 'It's like being connected by an umbilical cord to the computer.'

The technology now being used to monitor employees ostensibly for health, safety or security reasons, Privacy International records, is extremely powerful and extends to every aspect of a worker's life. In addition to all forms of electronic surveillance, there are both open and covert psychological analyses, aptitude and performance surveillance, vocational interest tests, and personality and honesty monitoring – all of which raise issues of privacy, control and fairness. 'Surveillance and monitoring have become design components of information systems and the modern work environment,' says the Privacy International report. 'The use of this technology is often justified on the grounds of health and safety, customer relations or legal obligation. The real purpose of most surveillance, however, is for performing monitoring, personnel surveillance, or outright discrimination. Even in workplaces staffed by highly skilled information technology specialists, bosses demand the right to spy on every detail of a worker's performance.'

Workplace surveillance is destined to become one of the major issues of the coming decade and is more fully investigated in Chapter 4. Nor can it be viewed in isolation. Like the networks and interfacing that link the in-vogue systems of ID controls, performance monitoring and checks on personal habits and interests, it is simply part of the 'big picture' of surveillance which emanated originally from intelligence and military creations, and now has the Internet at its heart.

CHAPTER 2
DATAVEILLANCE AND THE LAW ENFORCEMENT AGENCIES

IN THE MID-1990s, databases became the prime tool in the on-line progression of law enforcement. They also became the life blood of private businesses and corporations. Every conceivable kind of list has been loaded on to the local computer networks of companies or government offices and even more on the Internet. Millions of man hours were utilised as the database revolution took off, and suddenly we possessed a new word for the twenty-first century: dataveillance. Databases are the real beating heart of modern surveillance techniques as they affect the public at large, whether criminally inclined or not; and, as we shall see, much of this surveillance capability is in private hands, run by companies which are trusted to self-regulate.

Private enterprise is a major player in pioneering many of the advances in this arena, with the creation of profiling techniques and mind-boggling software whose full capabilities are known and understood only by true computer buffs. They share the honours with the state-run organisations which are where this modern phenomenon began – inside the international intelligence and law enforcement agencies. Put together, their powers of observation represent a watching brief on us, the public, on a scale that is barely possible to comprehend. Private sector surveillance will be looked at more closely in Chapter 3. This chapter explores what we know about the state security systems currently in use.

The FBI, unsurprisingly, is at the forefront of the technology. On 15 July 1999, the world's largest crime-fighting agency introduced a new data accessing system which will be seen as a pace-setter by police forces around the globe. They will eventually follow the on-line delivery of criminal intelligence from a computer network which can be accessed instantly by officers out on the streets of US cities in their patrol cars. In terms of bringing its investigations right to the heart of the scene of the crime, the FBI has invented the system that beats all.

On that day, FBI director Louis Freeh launched a $180 million National Crime Information Centre, a massive computer network which among other things also hosts the national 'Instant Criminal Background Check'. The system will serve more than eighty thousand criminal justice agencies throughout the USA and link to the Canadian police networks. Features include single fingerprint matching and mugshots available on-line, with a searchable database producing results within seconds, compared with the existing system which might take hours or even days to achieve the same results. The sheer power of modern computers enables the centre to handle 2.4 million transactions a day, with storage of and access to over 39 million individual records. These records include those of stolen vehicles, articles, securities, wanted persons, missing persons, gangs and suspected terrorists.

The information is organised into seventeen databases which provide instant information on everything from stolen guns to the possible identity of a man with a scar over his left eye. They also include the names of every person held in federal prisons and every person out on parole, and offer extensive cross-checking analysis to supply details of possible offences committed in different states by the same person.

The FBI will make the newly developed software accessible to all law enforcement agencies free of charge; they simply have to provide the hardware. It will be available across the country, and down to the level of police patrolmen in the form of scaled-down hardware, such as a laptop computer, hand-held fingerprint scanner, printer and digital camera mounted in a police patrol car. Using this equipment, information can be captured and sent via a police car radio for immediate checking in the crime information centre. This, of course, is in addition to the FBI's world-beating database of names – its central register, which contains roughly 78 million entries. It is the big daddy of name-dropping; but elsewhere others are doing a good catch-up job in establishing people-monitoring systems.

On 3 January 2000, a computer in Strasbourg, which has the specific function of keeping track of the movement of individuals, edged to within an ace of 9 million records on its database. All those named within it have one thing in common. They are on a pan-European watch-list compiled in recent times that is constantly updated and reserved for 'persons wanted for arrest, extradition, criminal proceedings, or under discreet surveillance, or to be refused entry at external borders, or aliens, asylum seekers or illegal immigrants. ...'

Descriptions, aliases, last known addresses, passport numbers, car registrations, identifying marks (such as a scarred face), skin (colour of), age, place of birth, tendency towards violence, the possibility of being armed and all other known facts and cross-checkable detail are also logged into the computer for instant retrieval at any one of fifty thousand networked computer terminals positioned across the European Union. It is a throw-back to Northern Ireland, where a similar system was invented in the early 1970s for the first computerised databases in the Province. The man who invented the system was a British military officer, fed up with having to make endless lists of names of suspects and potential terrorists gathered from traffic checks and routine searches in the Province at the time of the Troubles.

The Strasbourg system runs on much the same lines, but with the advantage of advances in technology, and provides the last word in analytical data covering the movement of individuals and property across continental Europe – and, since April 1999, the UK and the whole of Ireland. The Strasbourg computer is the central control of what is described as 'the rapid IT transfer of detailed intelligence'. It is used following alerts through the SIS, which is the name of this operation. The initials in this instance stand not for Secret Intelligence Service but for the little-known (or more likely, virtually unknown) Schengen Information System.

THE SCHENGEN INFORMATION SYSTEM

Schengen is, in fact, a small town in Luxembourg where in 1985 delegates from France, Germany and the three Benelux countries met to discuss the thorny issue of border controls which would disappear under European Union proposals. Britain, under Margaret Thatcher, and Ireland were refusing to have anything to do with such a scheme, but the five nations meeting at Schengen actually came to an agreement to abolish national border controls between their countries while at the same time strengthening policing of their common external borders. The agreement effectively threw a ring around the five nations, but allowed free movement of their citizens within it. In the early months of 2000, those same five nations had second thoughts about this decision because of the rapid movement across Europe of asylum seekers, but by then the creation of their people-watching machine was well established.

In 1990, after a suitable trial period, the Schengen Convention was agreed upon. It set in stone outstanding issues of law enforcement and intelligence gathering and established a chain of contact to be used by the police of one nation in cooperation with their counterparts across the border in pursuit of criminal activity. As part of that scheme, a multi-national, cross-border database was set up to include the registration of people and their assets or stolen property, such as cars, boats and lorries, and opened the way for general surveillance of anyone involved in criminal, or even suspicious, activity within the overall borders of the five nations. Proven wrongdoing is not a prerequisite for registration. By 2000, the Schengen Information System was one of the largest registers of its kind in the world. Although restrictions were placed on any kind of 'hot pursuit' activity, an alert system through SIS would launch an immediate cooperative effort from the police forces involved and, if necessary, the assistance of the intelligence services of those countries could be enlisted. Thus they were able to call upon all the facilities available at a national level – including interception and bugging – in a joint attack against whatever piece of wrongdoing, or suspected wrongdoing, was under investigation at the time.

The system worked so well that Italy, Spain, Portugal, Greece and Austria all signed up to the Convention, which further opened the way for various types of covert intelligence activity and cross-border police collaboration in the surveillance of 'persons presumed to have taken part in a criminal offence to which extradition may apply'. The scope of operations was broad and deliberately vague. Cases under investigation within the Schengen territory trebled in the first five years of the Convention's existence, even though it remained an inter-government agreement outside the EU. Other states became more interested in the project, however, after the establishment of a second tier of cooperative investigation – one that took the whole process into the realms of deeper secrecy. It came with the creation of what is known as the Sirene manual, the title being an abbreviation for Supplément d'Information Requis a l'Entrée Nationale. The Sirene system is, in essence, a complex network linking national police and security services in each of the Schengen countries through a second sophisticated computer-based information system aimed at providing 'supplementary' details on people or property registered on the SIS exchange.

Through the Sirene system, police authorities in one country who have arrested or are tracking a person who has been entered on the SIS by another country may request secret and perhaps unconfirmed intelligence reports on that suspect which have not been stored on the SIS database. The Sirene system was not mentioned in the public documents relating to the Schengen Convention, although all member states were required to set up a permanently staffed Sirene office with responsibility for the exchange of information with other nations. It remained secret until in March 1997, when the director of the Portuguese Sirene office let slip some highly confidential details of the operation. He boasted that it was a far more efficient system than the traditional Interpol methods, and revealed also that those engaged on the project had access to material gleaned from telephone interception and bugging procedures. 'It follows that they have access to masses of information all the time,' said the director.

Sirene offices have established close connections with the offices of public prosecutors, immigration services, police, ministries of justice and internal affairs, and technicians engaged in the collection and dissemination of information, which is transmitted exclusively over its own electronic mail system. The Sirene offices are also required to answer requests from other police forces within the group as quickly as possible; the time in any event 'should not exceed twelve hours' whereas contacts between, for example, Interpol offices – many of which are not computerised – may take several days.

The Sirene set-up was in fact among the one thousand pages of binding decisions and declarations made by the signatories of the Schengen agreement. One other clause which went largely unnoticed was that all matters that came within the scope of Schengen should remain secret, regardless of national legislation or government requirements.

This remained the case when in June 1997 the European Union, having studied the results and completed long, secret and delicate negotiations with member states, decided to launch a takeover bid for the Schengen Information System and integrate it in its entirety into the European Union structure. The Schengen Executive Committee, which had run the operation so far, was to be replaced by a European Union-appointed group, the Justice and Home Affairs Council. This move was incorporated into the Amsterdam Treaty, signed by EU foreign ministers on 2 October 1997, although it did not become effective until May 1999 when all governments concerned ratified their membership.

In 1997 – the last year for which figures were available for research – just over fifteen thousand aliens were identified in the then seven countries who had access to the Schengen Information System databases. These numbers rose dramatically in more recent times as the system was expanded to cover the whole of continental Europe and with the influx of asylum seekers and refugees fleeing the troubles in and around the former Yugoslavia. Britain has had its own particular problems in that regard with increasing numbers of immigrants entering the country by both legal and illegal means, many of whom had actually travelled through – or had been ejected from – other European Union countries.

As the whole issue became a political hot potato, Britain applied formally to the European Union in May 1999 to adopt what was described as a 'pick and mix' participation in the SIS – avoiding the open borders policy but giving access to databases and for the National Criminal Intelligence Service to link up with the Sirene Bureaux across Europe. The British application was treated with some apprehension by other states. Members of the European Union Schengen Working Group meeting in July 1999 recorded their concern that the UK application was 'very security-orientated and would to a large extent not cover freedom and justice-related aspects'. Even so, it was agreed that Britain would be able to access SIS data relating to criminals, suspected criminals, missing persons or stolen vehicles and limited access to data covering 'aliens to be refused entry'.

Thus, the entire European Union now has the benefit of the Schengen system along with its ready-made databases provided by the Strasbourg centre and the Sirene network of 'second level' checks. The move has been generally welcomed by law enforcement agencies, including the FBI, which saw the possibility of extending its own contacts with Europe. To many, however, the development held worrying connotations which once again highlighted the difficulties in striking a correct and workable balance between the needs of surveillance and the rights of the individual. Thomas Mathiesen, professor of sociology of law at Oslo University, foresaw inherent dangers in his paper 'On Globalisation of Control: Towards an Integrated Surveillance System in Europe' published by Statewatch in November 1999.

> Bureaucratic registers have been used for both individual and aggregate registration, surveillance and 'treatment' before in European history. On the individual as well as the aggregate level, the fate of the Jews and other population groups in the 1930s and 1940s is a case in point, and there are many other examples. An excellent – and tragic – concrete example, is the way in which the German occupational forces in Norway during World War II used various existing registers established for other purposes in persecuting Norwegian Jews. Over 50 per cent of 1400 Jews in Norway in 1942 were exterminated while the figure for Denmark [where there were no registers] was under 1 per cent of 5600.

The professor pointed out that the Norwegian authorities had stated on a number of occasions that Schengen's purpose was to fight serious international crime, a statement frequently repeated by the partners in the Schengen cooperative. Early statistics, however, painted a rather different picture. They showed that the nations on mainland Europe, and especially Germany and France, were utilising the Schengen system of cooperation to identify unwanted aliens, immigrants and asylum seekers who had been refused entry elsewhere and might have gone underground. The object was to move them on, probably towards Britain. The numbers were alarming. Professor Mathiesen established that by the end of 1995 the German Ministry of the Interior, for example, had entered 2.3 million records in the SIS, of which 70 per cent related to unwanted aliens.

Professor Mathiesen also identified that the system was used against Greenpeace during demonstrations over French nuclear tests in the same year. Peaceful demonstrations in Amsterdam during the European Union summit in 1997 were also met by heavy-handed police action in which 609 people were arrested; among them were a number who were supposedly on the Schengen lists. They included a group of Italians who were arrested and deported, and twenty-nine Danish nationals who were taken back to Denmark by military transport plane escorted by a fighter. Victims of police brutality in Amsterdam were later awarded damages. Professor Mathiesen noted in his paper: 'Observers viewed the police actions which took place – and which involved helicopters, armed vehicles and so on – as a large-scale training manoeuvre for the protection of the European Union's powerful institutions.'

Britain's hopes of a partial opt-in to the Schengen Information System, while retaining control over its borders, was announced by Home Secretary Jack Straw in April 1999. John Abbott, Director General of the National Criminal Intelligence Service, immediately pushed his plate forward to represent the UK in the SIS and in the provision of the Sirene office for second-level information. Abbott reckoned UK law enforcement would feel the benefits in the area of technical cooperation and, since the NCIS already houses the UK's National Central Bureaux for Interpol and Europol, its status as a 'one-stop shop' for handling incoming and outgoing national and international data exchange is highly envied by the rest of Europe.

THE EUROPOL DATABASE

Europol, the European Union's response to organised crime, is essentially another organisation which fosters police cooperation across

Europe. It was officially launched on 1 October 1998 following the ratification of the Europol Convention by all fifteen member states. Britain's NCIS was appointed by Jack Straw to be the UK's sole representative for Europol, and John Abbott became the UK representative on the Europol management board. Europol is another kind of computerised database, linked to every police force in the European Union and aimed at securing a rapid and secure exchange of intelligence between all member states.

The system was first agreed under the Maastricht Treaty in February 1994 and was given priority targeting in the areas of drug trafficking, illegal immigration, sex slavery, stolen vehicles, money laundering and the trade in radioactive materials. The UK was the first member state to ratify the Europol Convention, in December 1996. A key aim of the UK presidency of the European Union was to complete the process of ratifying the treaty, which it achieved two years later.

During 1999, Europol's remit was expanded to include terrorism and other serious organised criminal activity. Expansion has already been planned for the early part of the twenty-first century, with additional analytical functions being added to enable Europol to undertake strategic intelligence projects in areas of organised crime affecting groups of member states. John Abbott said: 'Whether it is drugs or trafficking in people, organised crime is big international business. Just as top-level criminals operate across borders, so law enforcement must be totally capable of cooperating across borders. With our NCIS officers based at Europol headquarters in The Hague, we are able to exchange intelligence on these criminals quickly and securely. This brings us one step closer to ensuring that there is no hiding place for those who bring misery into our communities.'

Europol was already established as a joint police unit concerned with drugs investigations within the European Union even before ratification and formal acceptance by all member governments. As such, it provided an additional interlinked computer database set up to operate with rapid access by law enforcement and intelligence operatives throughout Europe. It is undoubtedly the largest and most extensive of them all, and as such has attracted the attention of privacy campaigners. They have good cause for their concerns.

The Europol computers have three principal subsystems. The first is a central database recording the details of criminals and others suspected of having committed or taken part in criminal offences, or who it is believed will commit an offence. The brief is wide enough to mop up past, present and future suspected criminals. As much personal detail as is known must be entered into the registry, even 'suspected crimes or possible membership of criminal groups', along with 'other characteristics likely to assist in identification, including any specific objective physical characteristics not subject to change'. The second level of information is derived from actual work files for specific analysis and may include details of possible witnesses, victims or persons whom there is reason to believe could become victims, contacts, associates and informants relevant to the suspect under suspicion or surveillance. Thirdly, an index system has been created in such a way that it is possible for widespread cross-checks to be performed relating to criminal connections, but at the same time strictly prohibits the recording of information on the grounds of 'racial origin, religious or other beliefs, sexual life, political opinions or membership of movements or organisations that are not prohibited by law'. Finally, Europol is able to link up with other nations outside the European Union, such as the United States, Canada, Australia and elsewhere, and thus its now massive databases are available for the global interchange of information and technical facilities.

As we enter the twenty-first century, Europol, linked to the Schengen Information System and the Sirene secondary system, represents one of the largest information storage, retrieval and exchange systems outside the USA, with some seventy thousand computer terminals in permanent on-line mode and with the names of millions of people registered for instant research. Although Europol is not a police force as such – merely an adjunct to the national police forces across Europe – there are undoubted signs that ambitious police and intelligence officers would like the European Union to have a fully fledged crime and intelligence service, with its own serving officers at the helm of what is already established as a vast, increasingly integrated multinational registration and surveillance operation. Those in favour point to the resources of emerging crime syndicates based in Europe, and to demonstrate the usefulness of the project, draw upon the early experiences of cooperation set up through Europol in the fight against drugs. A number of case histories are already available.

Operation Carl

This started in Sweden in May 1997. A Swedish criminal organisation was suspected of being responsible for importing large quantities of drugs into Sweden. The main target of the investigations was living in Belgium, from where the trafficking of drugs was being conducted. Links with criminals in other member states were soon ascertained. The case was transferred to the Swedish desk at Europol in August 1997, and contacts were established with other countries that resulted in investigations and operations in several member states. The case showed that Danish nationals had an important role in the organisation and that drugs were also being transported to Denmark, so a Danish operational team started an investigation in the autumn of 1997. In addition, the Spanish authorities supplied support and assistance with surveillance during the operation, mainly in the Malaga area. In September 1997, the German authorities seized 21 kg of amphetamines near the border with the Netherlands and two Danish nationals were arrested. Information also revealed that the supplier of the amphetamines was staying in the Netherlands, which led to a request for assistance in that country. Surveillance was conducted on several occasions by different Dutch teams.

During the course of the operation several cross-border surveillance operations were conducted, involving a number of member states. Two successful controlled deliveries were also carried out, one of 30 kg of amphetamines from the Netherlands to Denmark in November 1997 and one of 25 kg of cannabis in January 1998 from Spain to Denmark. The operation ended on 15 April 1998 when the main target was arrested at Las Palmas airport following a request from the Dutch authorities. Altogether 62 kg of amphetamines and 160 kg of cannabis were seized in the operation, and about twenty-five suspects were arrested in Denmark, Sweden, Germany and Spain. The role of the Europol liaison officers in this pan-European operation enabled an information exchange to take place between the national teams involved, which would not have been possible using the traditional channels of communication.

Operation Pristina

This is a large-scale operation being carried out by the Italian authorities against a criminal organisation of drug traffickers operating in nine European Union member states and six other non-European Union countries. The group of criminals, mainly originating from the Kosovan city of Pristina, are spread out all over Europe. Europol became deeply involved in the operation in two ways: firstly it provided analytical support at the request of Italy, with the support of seven other member states. The request was essentially aimed at establishing links among targets in different countries and finding the main reference telephone numbers, from more than five thousand, so as to discover the local heads of the organisation in order to dismantle it. Secondly, Europol was requested to suggest new fields of investigation. By hosting operational meetings Europol brought together officers from ten countries, including three non-European Union countries, and three magistrates. The operation, which was still ongoing at the time of writing, had already led to the arrest of more than forty people and the seizure of about 170 kg of heroin in various European countries.

Operation Primo

This started in June 1997 when the Italian authorities identified a 'safe house' for the storage of cocaine and synthetic drugs smuggled from the Netherlands. An Italian target was put under observation in September, together with a German national and a Yugoslav national, and a considerable amount of intelligence was collated. The Italian Europol liaison officers joined forces with their counterparts on the Europol German desk and eventually the investigation brought in officers from Austria, Belgium, the Netherlands and the UK. The exchange of information showed, in particular, that police forces in many European Union countries were conducting investigations into members of the same organisation without coordinating among themselves. New connections were also discovered in Sweden and Denmark, and eventually the key figures under investigation were identified as being part of a major international drugs cartel whose operations were linked to Thailand, Hong Kong, Brazil, Argentina and Bolivia. The volume and complexity of available information entailed regular reviews and conferences to process the intelligence collected so far. These were run by Europol's Analytical Department so that the information could be processed on a pan-European basis. This in turn led to the identification of a criminal network across the European Union, pivoting around a German national born in Poland but by then living in Amsterdam. The network was dealing with trafficking in cocaine, Ecstasy and cannabis, as well as associated money laundering. All in all, twenty criminals of various nationalities were arrested, important amounts of illicit drugs and cash were seized and a secret laboratory discovered.

Operation Bellomo

This was initiated by the Drugs Department of the Portuguese Judicial Police in March 1998. It had information that several individuals had rented a luxurious villa near Lisbon. Surveillance showed that the suspects used three cars with Italian plates. The Portuguese desk at Europol was immediately contacted and, in less than one hour, the Italian desk informed them that the vehicles had recently been stolen in the Milan area. As a result of that information, the individuals were followed and seven more luxury cars were discovered. Again, following a quick response from the Italian desk, it was established that all had been stolen in Italy. The organisation was dismantled, and two Italians and two Belgians were arrested. The cars had all been stolen in Italy by the Italian and then delivered to one of the Belgians. The latter forged vehicle documents, and it is believed that the cars were to be sold to several garages in Portugal. The leader of the organisation, also an Italian national, never left his own country and is now on the run, an international arrest warrant having been issued against him.

Operation Calabaza

This began in November 1998 when British liaison officers informed the Spanish desk at Europol that a consignment of shirts and trousers from a company in Panama had arrived at a container port in the UK, and that 200 kg of cocaine was hidden among it. The container had been sent by a company registered in Spain, listed as dealing in electronics parts. It turned out that the Spanish authorities were already investigating the company for suspected drug trafficking. A controlled delivery was authorised, with the container being followed across Europe, using the Europol liaison desks to keep it under observation. It was duly loaded into a vessel bound for the port of Bilbao, and then transported by train to Valencia. Finally, the criminals picked it up in Valencia on 17 December. At its eventual resting place, the Spanish police moved in and discovered 207 kg of cocaine packed in parcels of 1 kg hidden inside. Eight people were arrested, and four vehicles, one gun and a number of documents were seized. The papers demonstrated the manner in which the group had used several companies as fronts for drug-running operations from South America. The entire organisation was dismantled as a result of the joint operation between UK and Spanish police, linked through Europol.

It must be said that law enforcement agencies across Europe, and especially Britain, are anxious to promote these successes as examples of the benefits of cross-border cooperation. Many privacy and human rights campaigners believe, however, that their agenda goes well beyond stated aims of Schengen and Europol and that the whole concept could well serve as a prelude to the formation of a far greater strategy for law enforcement, leading towards the creation of the European Union's own all-embracing police and intelligence units. As will be seen, the PR machine is a vital tool in the armoury of international agencies, softening up public opinion with horror stories prior to the introduction of new and often unpopular measures that intrude further into the rights and privacy of the public at large.

Examples will abound in the ensuing pages, prompting time and time again the question: Just how much protection do we need ... and what is the cost in terms of liberty surrendered? As we will see in Chapter 3, public opinion is at the moment running with the law enforcers but all that may well change as they begin to encroach even further into the realms of personal privacy.

There is no doubt that these developments in Europe form one more substantial inroad in the overall levels of global surveillance that the agencies are keen to achieve, using the argument of combating organised crime and terrorism as their platform for public acceptance, and there are many hands at work behind the scenes pushing towards certain goals and ambitions. There was much unseen liaison, for instance, between the FBI and the European Union over invasive new measures to prevent the use of encryption techniques on the latest telecommunications equipment that had the potential to beat interception. The secrecy was vital in the attempt to keep from public view exactly what the proposals entailed before the politicians were swayed and decisions made.

In May 1999, the European Parliament approved laws which will provide a major gateway to intelligence-gathering requirements. They will force all telecommunications companies in Europe to make their equipment wiretap-friendly. In doing so, the Parliament laid the foundations for an eavesdropping system capable of intercepting all mobile phones, Internet communications, fax messages and pagers throughout Europe – a system which is similar to the American National Security Agency's Echelon System.

Codenamed Enfopol, it will be capable of tracking targets wherever they travel. Officially known as the 'International User Requirements for Interception', it will create a data processing and transmission network which involves not only the names, addresses and phone numbers of targets and associates, but also e-mail addresses, credit card details, PINs and passwords. Mobile phone records can be merged to create a comprehensive location tracking system against suspects, although, as Louis Freeh pointed out on one of his tours of Europe to get international cooperation for mass telephone-tapping powers, the crooks are already one jump ahead. 'They buy up lots of phones, and just switch them around or throw them away when the trail gets hot,' he moaned.

And so at the start of the new century, systems of search and cross-checking that were virtually unheard of in police practice only half a decade earlier are widespread. The advances in storage systems allow not only a vastly increased base of records on individuals and criminal activity, but also photographic and video images of criminals and property.

BRITISH POLICE SYSTEMS

At the heart of the British system is the Police National Computer and around it, throughout the 1990s, has been strung a substantial array of interlinked databases with searchable records and images which cover all criminal activity from major incidents of drug running down to a parochial level of community crime, such as stolen bicycles.

The London Metropolitan Police, for example, has its own bureau, formed in 1992, to manage its links to the PNC. In 1995 the bureau took over management of the Phoenix Project, introduced to provide police forces with immediate access to information about active and serious offenders. The database now contains practically everything there is to know about anyone who has fallen foul of the law, from arrest details to criminal history. It also keeps subsidiary specialist lists of, for example, all known prostitutes in the London Metropolitan Police area, current disqualified drivers, or missing persons. The Metropolitan force, like most police forces throughout the United Kingdom, has formed separate specialist computer-based divisions of activity.

Its most recent addition is Systems for Intelligence and Detection, otherwise known as the SID project, which targets the most active criminals and is used to build a database of intelligence about their activities. SID is managed by the Directorate of Intelligence and central to its operations is CRIMINT, a criminal intelligence database which holds all relevant logs. Rapid searching and researching of this data make it possible to track even partial numbers and names. Among its operational software is the 'i2' Analyst's Notebook, used to extract subsets of data which allow crime analysts, for instance, to chart connections between known criminals.

There is also computer mapping software, which gathers information from all crimes that have taken place within the Metropolitan police jurisdiction and plots the locations of incidents on to maps of the area. These are used to identify patterns and concentrations of crime. It also includes high specification hardware and software to scan, produce and cross-check photographic images and produce quality colour prints. CRIMINT has been delivered as one of a portfolio of products which include powerful PC workstations, colour scanners and printers, still-frame video capture and mapping software. It is available to all Divisional and Area Intelligence Units and, by mid-1999, was accessible through any workstation linked to the divisional local area network.

Another of the Metropolitan Police Force's databased units is the specialist Public Sector Fraud Unit, known as SO6. It was formed to set up surveillance and investigation of public officials including councillors, corrupt doctors and tax officers on the take. The financially trained team of detectives has around forty cases on its hands at any one time. Their work involves everything from catching evidence of corruption on hidden cameras to delving into bank accounts to track decades of theft. One of its recent successes was to trap a senior Inland Revenue official who was kept under surveillance for four years. The official, Michael Allcock, was tasked by the Revenue to investigate 'ghosts' – wealthy individuals living in Britain who were not paying proper taxes. Allcock carried out this task up to a point, but then came to an arrangement with each ghost which would see them left alone by the Revenue in exchange for 'gifts'. Allcock's gifts included expensive holidays, cruises, free flights, £160,000 cash and the use of a prostitute. Using court orders or surveillance to track his accounts, SO6 eventually acquired enough evidence to bring him to trial; he was sentenced to five years in prison. The databases and cross-checks of the unit have been expanding every month since its foundation in order to deal with corruption at all levels of public sector life.

The Metropolitan Police's own computer network is known as Metnet, and is linked to each Operational Command Unit. All the databases of the OCUs are automatically duplicated at a central site under the auspices of the Crime Report Information System. This enables officers to carry out complex searches that would have been impractical under a paper-based system. Using the central site, a police officer at a CRIS terminal in one divisional OCU can make searches of any range of other divisional databases, which include two years of crime reports for each division.

The archive will eventually hold 6 million crime reports between two and six years old. Response times are four seconds for logging on, two seconds for viewing a local crime report and twenty-five seconds for a crime report from another division, a search capability unheard of at the start of the 1990s. According to Metropolitan Police sources it has had a dramatic impact on crime investigation, especially at local community level.

The Metropolitan Police now lists many successes attributed to CRIS. Examples indicate the use of the network to mop up local crime. In 1999 they included a car crime wave in Surbiton, Surrey, which was wiped out by a computer-generated discovery of a certain pattern of time, location, method and type of car stolen. Further searches produced composite descriptions of possible offenders. Armed with this information, the officers set up Operation Rat Trap, using secondhand cars as bait. It turned out that the crime wave was a one-man phenomenon, and the thief admitted to fifty similar crimes.

Another task, that of solving a crime wave in Battersea, south-west London, which in pre-CRIS days would have needed months of manual sifting and searching, took less than an hour. It culminated in officers visiting a recently sentenced offender in prison. They took him out of prison for three days for a tour of their area, during which he admitted ninety-two unsolved offences, including six burglaries, ten instances of making off without payment from petrol stations, and seventy-six thefts of high-value motorcycles. Officers were able to focus on specific items of property and match the prisoner's claims with reported crimes. CRIS also produced a list of victims, who were then told that their cases had been solved.

Another CRIS-based investigation started in Peckham, south-east London, where two officers stopped a suspect who was wearing a very distinctive brooch. Peckham was not yet CRIS-live, but the officers knew that some of their neighbouring divisions were. They asked a colleague from the Burglary Squad at Brixton to conduct a search on CRIS. After some narrowing down, the system came up with a perfect match. The brooch was a valued family heirloom stolen during a burglary in Brixton. That burglary, together with a detailed description of the brooch, had been reported fully on CRIS by a Brixton PC. The result was that a prolific criminal, on bail at the time, was sent to prison and the victim had her brooch returned.

Databases used by police forces across the UK are increasingly being interlinked for search procedures. Many forces are also setting up their own websites. In December 1999, the Metropolitan Police had 2500 pages on-line featuring current activity and photographs of suspected criminals caught on camera. There was also a search facility to view images of property recovered by the police.

ABUSES OF DATABASES

A darker side to the technology of creating databases was revealed in two reports on the rise of mass surveillance techniques presented to the

Scientific and Technological Options Assessment Unit of the European Parliament in 1998–9. Both reports pointed up the use of dataveillance for political and police targeting. Instead of being used just for investigating crime, the reports suggested, they were also being used by some state forces as a pre-emptive measure. The fastest growing trend in surveillance technology, according to research conducted by Steve Wright of the Manchester-based study group, the Omega Foundation, is towards tracking certain strata, social classes and races of people living in particularly high-risk areas before any crime is committed. In his report to the European Parliament, titled 'An Appraisal of the Technology of Political Control', Wright concluded:

> Such a form of proactive policing is based on military models of gathering huge amounts of low-grade intelligence. With new systems, such as Memex, it is possible to quickly build up a comprehensive picture of virtually anyone by gaining electronic access to all their records, cash transactions, cars held, etc. Such pre-emptive policing means the majority are ignored and policing resources are more tightly focused on certain groups. Such powerful forms of artificial intelligence need continuous assessment. They have an important role to play in tracking criminals. The danger is that their infrastructure is essentially a massive machinery of supervision that can be re-targeted fairly quickly should the political context change.

Wright went on to describe systems which allow the automatic production of maps of social areas combined with databases that allow entire life profiles to be created for virtually anyone in a state who has an official existence. 'Photographs and video material can be included in the record and typically up to 700 other databases can be hoovered at any one time, to extend the data profile in real time. Significant changes in the capacity of new surveillance systems can be anticipated with the advent of new materials ... which will lead to miniaturisation of systems by several orders of magnitude.'

In 1993, the US Defense Department and the Justice Department signed memoranda of understanding for 'Operations Other than War and Law Enforcement' to begin trials which allowed the development of combining surveillance technology with government-held databases. Fingerprints, ID cards, employment records, benefit applications and other data-matching techniques were linked in a trial operation secretly conducted on sections of the population from which there would be little risk of complaint, such as welfare recipients, immigrants, criminals and members of the military. These techniques were then applied up the socio-economic ladder. Once established, however, the system became a model that could be applied to larger groups if and when the occasion arose. David Banisar, of Privacy International, had no doubts about the future possibilities of such trials: 'They facilitate mass and routine surveillance of large segments of the population without the need for warrants and formal investigations, bringing surveillance into a new era in which information about almost anybody is available to almost anybody.'

Nor did law enforcement and intelligence agencies hold the monopoly on this ability ...

CHAPTER 3
THE DATABASE ECONOMY

S TATE-RUN ORGANISATIONS, whose total capacity in the year 2000 for keeping watch on society in the democratised nations which employ them would do the Stasi proud, are not the only perpetrators of mass observation. Like the multi-headed Hydra of Greek mythology, the widespread explosion of communications and the trend towards the globalisation of information networks has produced a substantial contingent of watchers and listeners who are in many ways more active – and certainly more personal – than their counterparts in 'the agencies'.

The storage capacity of today's computers is such that they are self-fulfilling; there's room for everybody and everything, all to be accessed in seconds instead of days or weeks under the old paper systems. File upon file, database upon database, interlinked by some means or other, provide an instantaneous record of public life and the lives of the public. More and more of those public records are being accessed by business and private enterprise for security checks and commercial reasons, especially so in the USA where virtually every known fact about any living person or business is available on-line if you search long enough for it. Now, this trend is rapidly being copied across the globe.

Opinion polls over the past few years have shown a marked rise in worries over personal privacy issues, yet latterly there has been a notice-able, if grudging, appreciation that surveillance in its various forms is becoming increasingly necessary – provided those who run these operations do not go over the top, and that the targets really are the stealers of state secrets, the criminals, the drug barons, the terror groups and the paedophiles. There is even a measure of acceptance in society of the argument put forward by those in authority that law-abiding people who have no intention of engaging in any kind of illegal activity have little to worry about surveillance, but much to gain by way of protection.

The possibility that this great capacity might be used to listen into the telephone conversations and to read the e-mails of Mr and Mrs Joe Smith and family at 56 Acacia Avenue is, on the face of it, not very likely. Sure enough, their communications may well be caught up in the general sweep of the listening-in facilities run by America's National Security Agency from Menwith Hill near Harrogate or by Britain's Government Communications Headquarters at Cheltenham, both of which will be examined in later chapters. But unless members of that typical ordinary family are searching for bomb-making instructions on the Internet, the possibility of their being tapped and bugged by the state is so remote that it is not a great worry – yet.

At the same time, acceptance of that argument misses the point and to some extent disguises serious inroads into personal privacy that are often overlooked. At least we know that the FBI and MI5 are there, going about their business in a manner familiar to us all. The activities of other concerns are far more secretive and unseen and their targets are not criminals or foreign agents but the general public – your average man (or woman) in the street such as Mr and Mrs Joe Smith from Acacia Avenue, who have two kids, own their own home, take holidays abroad, run a car, have a computer, are connected to the Internet, pay tax and insurance, and do all the things that moderately middle-class people indulge in. They are subjected to far greater surveillance, in so many different ways, than even the political police have at their disposal.

The perpetrators of this modern scrutiny came upon the world with such speed in the 1990s that the immediate future now holds great potential for the trend towards total, global surveillance of society to continue. This is especially so when – as is already happening – private and state databases, information networks, imagery and records covering virtually every aspect of an individual's life become mixed and matched in the inter-connectivity offered by existing technology, let alone the developments which will be created by the next generation of communication tools.

The starting point for these developments predates the IT revolution and the Internet by a couple of decades. First there was the creation of credit reference agencies, which took off with the boom in hire purchase transactions following the rise of the consumer society in the 1950s. The second stage came with the junk mail explosion of the 1970s. Over time, the marketing became more sophisticated and consumer targeted as the value of direct mail, then telemarketing and finally the Internet became apparent.

Undoubtedly the most significant development was a gradual compilation of files on anyone who had ever taken out a loan or hire purchase agreement, acquired credit cards, bought a house or had any other form of financial transaction registered against their name. It expanded into an all-embracing consumer-targeting industry, a tremendous and largely unseen activity that affected the material world of millions.

CREDIT REFERENCE AGENCIES

Credit reference agencies, once almost a cottage industry allied to sales of cars and washing machines, built up the most complete and often invasive databases which could be compared in scale to government computer records. In Britain, they equal if not exceed the Police National Computer in size. One of the world's largest such companies, Experian, employs twelve thousand people in the UK, USA, continental Europe, Africa, Latin America and the Asia Pacific region. The company's headquarters are in Orange, California, and Nottingham in the UK. It is a subsidiary of Great Universal Stores, a UK-based holding company that includes home shopping, retailing, the Argos catalogue stores, property investment, and finance and information services.

By the mid-1990s it had computer-based records on 48 million people and 22 million households in the UK. Experian's numbers in the USA are proportionally even greater as a result of credit referencing, consumer targeting and the advent of personal identification confirmation techniques becoming one of the world's growth industries. In

January 2000, Experian boasted a database of consumer marketing information which contains information on the residents of 98 per cent of US households. The company has also built up a similarly huge commercial and industrial database with, for example, 13 million business entries in the USA alone. It is, of course, just one of many such organisations. Experian's own on-line promotional material tells the story.

> In little more than a decade, the world of commerce has changed forever. Mass marketing has given way to target marketing. Products and services have to be tailored to the needs of individual customers. Communications have to be precise and relevant. Front-line staff have to be informed and empowered. Decisions have to be almost instantaneous. ....
> Our information resources and analysis techniques enable marketers to identify the ideal prospects for their products and services. We help them understand the lifestyles and motivations of these potential customers and develop communications that are timely and relevant. .... Information including specialised lists and targeted information – both business and consumer – radically increases the conversion of prospects to customers. Our customised production and mailing capabilities support creative, efficient and cost-effective delivery of these communications. Our knowledge lies in the great wealth of information that we maintain about consumers and how they behave, about businesses and how they perform, and about markets and how they are changing.

An additional line in the Experian promotion highlights what privacy campaigners fear most: 'We are an invisible interface, maintaining the vital link between customer and client, keeping information about the relationships constantly updated and accessible.'

The Experian 'knowledge' forms part of computer software and on-line search facilities that lie at the heart of the daily operations of some of the world's leading companies, as demonstrated by plaudits from some of its customers: 'Experian's information helps proactivity in our relationships with commercial customers. It may be an early warning that the customer is in financial difficulty or a signal that the relationship is ready to be expanded,' says the Citibank Diners Club, which operates charge card products in more than 175 countries. Bang and Olufsen, the home entertainment manufacturer, says that for years it thought its typical buyer was a single professional male between the ages of twenty-five and thirty, with an average income of about $50,000 a year. Experian data systems showed it that 'he is more likely to be a married professional male, aged 50 to 55, with a home, grown children and an average household income of $100,000 and up'.

Eagle Star Direct, which specialises in motor and property insurance in thirty countries worldwide and was the first insurer to provide on-line cover, placed Experian's vehicle information service at the centre of its sales quotation process: 'It provides us with the information we need about a vehicle in a matter of minutes, saving time for the customer and ensuring that we base our quotes on accurate information.' Northern Rock Bank and Building Society, with more than a million customers, first used Experian to develop its marketing database in the late 1980s and the company has continued to manage it ever since. Northern Rock says the databases provide 'a comprehensive and up-to-date view of every customer and is at the heart of a highly successful direct marketing strategy'. Meanwhile, credit card companies utilise Experian as an input and output vehicle – for credit status checking and collections of payments: Barclaycard has 'outsourced' its accounts collection to Experian, which takes in one hundred thousand payments from Barclaycard customers every day.

In the space of little more than a decade, what began as credit databases developed into a mini-history of each and every consumer recorded, so that apart from credit information, specific advice on sales and product targeting could be achieved. Standard credit checks on both individuals and businesses are now available instantly and, in the USA, on-line. Reports may contain exceedingly detailed histories of credit transactions, payment history, 'past due' situations, balances on credit cards and store cards, defaults and county court summonses. Experian, and similar organisations such as Equifax, insist that their security systems make it impossible for unauthorised people to access these details. They are, however, available to all companies which subscribe to the resources of the databases in order to confirm and expand upon the status and standing of potential customers. Many credit reference agencies also offer such services as well as an 'instant snapshot' of a company with which another company is intending to do business; invariably the snapshot will include the names and possible recent credit history of company principals, its tax affairs, bank position, borrowings, debts and creditors.

A sample credit report for a small US business undertaken for this research provided the following information:

> There is a total of 10 supplier relationships reported within the last 18 months. The total recent high credit for these 10 trade relationships is $4,264,700, with the highest single credit being for $1,569,000. The total current balance owed on the 10 trade relationships is $1,803,400, with the highest single balance due of $458,500. The account status for the total $1,803,400 balance due is: 24% current and 76% 1-to-30 days past due. The average days past the invoice due date that it takes the company to pay its balances is 17 days.

In November 1999, Experian brought an additional dimension to its operations by forming a link with Listing Services Solutions Inc., based in California. The two companies merged their national directory assistance businesses. LSSI is a world leader in the development and operation of advanced directory databases, updated daily through electronic feeds that capture all service order additions, deletions and changes made the previous day by the data suppliers. The information is, of course, invaluable to companies whose operations are largely based upon telemarketing and on-line positions.

The globalisation of information technology by consumer database companies has led to the creation of systems for cross-checking that provide a complete history and information on the present whereabouts of virtually everyone. In the USA in particular there can be no hiding place for personal information, as is demonstrated by the searchable databases which come with a subscription that any company or professional person can take out with the National Credit Information Network. This organisation is one of the world's largest suppliers of consumer and commercial credit information, public record data and other background information.

NCI is linked electronically through various computer networks to a thousand credit reporting bureaux across the USA as well as various other state, commercial and information sources. It was the first agency to develop the technology for accessing all the credit bureaux instantaneously, allowing clients to receive consumer information through one nationwide network, much of it in real time. Subscribers do not have to be in any way connected with the finance industry. NCI clients include lawyers, doctors, insurance investigators, private investigators, company security and human resources departments, property companies and major corporations. While many credit reference agencies concentrated on supplying credit information to the large-volume users, such as banking and financial institutions, department stores, mail order chains and automobile manufacturers, NCI extended its service into virtually every corner of human existence. In fact, virtually no one in the USA can keep secrets from NCI, as this list of on-line inquiry options (for US residents and businesses only) demonstrates:

- Credit Reports on Consumers: verifies creditworthiness, addresses of an applicant or subject, employment information, spousal information and age; determines background information on an individual, or can be used for pursuing collection of money owed. Three nationwide databases are searched, containing over 500 million individual files.

- Address Identifier Update: verifies current and previous addresses of an applicant or subject. With just a name and address, this national database will search for the individual and report current and previous addresses as well as any reported social security numbers.

- Credit Reports on Businesses and Corporations: provides a full financial appraisal, as well as information on judgments, liens and assets.

- Criminal History Reports: can be used to determine criminal history records of applicants, employees or subjects before you hire, promote or do business with them.

- Driving History Search: provides driving history for your subject, applicant or employee. This search is a valuable investigative tool in determining driving history and address information. A driving record can be a great indicator of an individual's character (find out about reckless or drunken behaviour, speeding, or excessively accident-prone individuals).

- Licence Plate Lookup: provides the name and address of the owner of a vehicle from a licence plate.

- National Change of Address: provides a forwarding address search; a sophisticated conglomerate of databases. With just a name and address this national database will search for the latest change of address.

- Pre-employment Screening: screens prospective and existing employees before they are hired or promoted; complete on-line background check ... 'as the employer you are responsible for your employees' action and statistics reveal that 33% of job applications contain fraudulent information'.

- Social Security Number Trace: verifies current and previous addresses of an applicant, potential employee, lost friend, lost relative or any subject you are trying to find, by accessing three national databases which each contain more than 250 million individual records.

- Worker Compensation Claims History: can be used to determine worker compensation claims records of applicants, employees or subjects before you hire, promote or do business with them.

- Name/Address/Phone Verification Search: with just a name and/or address and/or phone number this national database will search for the individual and addresses as well as phone numbers, neighbours and demographic area.

- Date of Birth Search: address and phone numbers returned when searched by name and date of birth only. Useful for location and identification purposes. This search queries a database of over 50 million records by date of birth.

In addition, consumer-targeting databases provide detailed information on the personal habits and shopping preferences of the millions of people who have ever bought anything on-line, responded to direct mail offers, bought insurance, financial products or virtually any other purchase which has involved the release of personal information into the database system. Asset histories on items such as cars, boats and property are similarly recorded.

THE JUNK MAIL PHENOMENON

These databases evolved with the second significant development in the creation of consumer lists – the junk mail phenomenon. They originated in the USA and quickly spread throughout the Western world. In the beginning, they consisted of fairly generalised and unfocused lists of names more or less compiled from telephone directories. In the 1990s, direct mail – as readers may have noticed – became incredibly focused; you may have been preselected for a new platinum credit card or found that the unsolicited new product from an insurance company even has your birth date already printed on the quotation. Every time a telesales person makes his unsolicited sales pitch, he already knows as much about you as he needs for his purpose. The days of random selection of telephone numbers are long gone; they produced too many wasted calls. The sellers now are geared to a far greater asset – information about the person to whom they are attempting to sell, categorised and pigeonholed into age, place, job type, socio-economic standing, financial reliability, risk factor and so on. Such stores of information are goldmines – centralised, compartmentalised, sifted, correlated and cross-linked through direct and electronic communications to produce very detailed profiles of the spending capacity of millions of households.

THE INTERNET

These developments seamlessly link to the third part of the modern database jigsaw, perhaps the most unobtrusively invasive medium of all: the Internet. Ironically, it was founded on the principles of free expression, lack of censorship and individual rights and has become one of the most dangerous places for releasing personal information. After a period of uncertainty as to whether it would ever become a commercially viable part of the global economy, the Internet suddenly shot off the graph. Although few people were even beginning to make money from e-commerce ventures by the end of the twentieth century (other than by selling shares in their companies) it provided instant access to millions, cutting across borders, language and prohibitions and launching businesses small and large into the new Wild West, otherwise known as the cybersociety, a wide open place where a buccaneering spirit prevailed under conditions which lacked any real controls.

Here for the taking were so many potential consumers that database creators were falling over themselves both to get on the Web and to raid its riches. America, far more than any other country, went Web wacky and piled everything on to it. Databases proliferated from state and local government organisations, and were copied eventually worldwide, providing information previously only accessible after time-consuming hard-copy searches. The US government even invented a system for putting its social security numbers for the entire nation on-line, but the site was so overwhelmed by visitors and attacked by hackers that it had to be closed within a matter of days.

The powering-up of computers, combined with the Internet, allowed large volumes of data to be reduced to high-density, compact storage, almost inconceivable to the human senses. It enabled the most complex calculations to be completed in milliseconds and searches of massive databases to be achieved almost as quickly. The miniaturisation of processors permitted worldwide connectivity and the rapid transfer of information. So, from an IT tool created by and for a library public, the Internet transformed itself into a largely commercial enterprise with a user population which in 1998 reached 61.4 million in the USA alone and which was forecast to grow to 200 million by the end of 2000. In 1999 the number of websites doubled every thirty-seven days. More than half of all US households are forecast to have access by 2003. While the rest of the world to some extent looked on, temporarily stunned by the sheer speed of the Internet's development, herein lay the mother lode for the commercial database creators and consumer profiling specialists. Soon the rest of the world was chasing the American grandiosity.

The mass of government and local authority websites provided, little did they know it, huge reservoirs of knowledge for commercial organisations. Coupled to that, because of their inexperience and lack of knowledge, few surfers really knew that they were contributing to the biggest intake of data the world had ever seen. And it was so easily achieved. As Internet users began their surfing across the World Wide Web, most were unaware that they were being tracked. Surfers moved from site to site believing that they were anonymous visitors, leaving no trace of their movement through cyberspace. In fact, they were invariably leaving some very large footprints and on the way dropping into those sites data that revealed more about them than they might wish even their closest friends to know.

The direct route to information is the form-filling and registration required by many websites and which may include requests for personal details; it is the first thing that happens when you sign up for an Internet account. The same request will appear on first visits to literally thousands of sites across the Web, including, first and foremost, your e-mail address through which much data will soon be transmitted. The US Federal Trade Commission found that 85 per cent of 1400 commercial sites which it looked at in March 1999 gathered personal information in this way. A surprising number of people actually give it, wrongly assuming that because a website states it has a privacy policy no one else will become aware of the information, or perhaps because they are promised benefits for doing so. That is their first mistake.

That information is gathered up and stored away, and the surfer may have missed the little box in small print somewhere on screen which says: 'Tick here if you do not wish your personal details to be passed on to other companies'; or an even smaller piece of print that says: 'Contact us if you do not want your details to be utilised for commercial purposes.' Either way, it often requires the physical act of doing something to *prevent* your details being passed on and used for other purposes. Like the databases created and stored by specialist consumer groups the world over, your details are analysed and assessed and very likely sold on for consumer-targeting operations.

A 1999 survey of one hundred top Internet sites by the US-based Electronic Privacy Information Centre discovered that only twenty-three sites offered an 'opt-in' policy which required the site operators to gain consumer permission before any collection or use of personal information was made. 'Opt-out' policies, on the other hand, allow companies to make use of information as they wish *unless* a consumer notifies the firm that they do not want their personal information collected or used, which usually means writing, telephoning or e-mailing the company concerned and having your name recorded for privacy purposes. EPIC quotes several examples of 'small-print' notices on pages which state: 'We occasionally make our customer list available for other carefully screened firms – should you prefer not to get their mailings, please let us know.' Those who either missed the notice, or never actually got around to telling the firm they did not want their personal details bandied about, would soon find themselves on more databases.

The information was given voluntarily in exchange perhaps for a service, an offer of travel bargains, an e-mail updating product information or any of a thousand and one other so-called Net freebies. Or it was obtained along with credit card details whenever a purchase was made over the Internet. As the concept of e-trading and surfing caught on, the ways of capturing information about customers and surfers increased accordingly, some using an extraordinary range of methods invented to tap into the secret lives of Internet users. Thousands of competitions appeared with the come-on of winning $1000 or a holiday in the Bahamas – all you had to do was fill in the form, and at once private details were swirling around the system. Others were ingeniously thought out. There was a medical clinic that offered, for a limited period, free advice on specific problems, and all the surfers had to do was fill in their names, postal and e-mail addresses. The hypochondriacs among us replied in their thousands, and the clinic created a very valuable database.

Some lists are dangerous. A US banker in Maryland acquired a list of cancer patients, matched them with his customers and then automatically reviewed the outstanding loans from those who were ill. The US Federal Trade Commission is also concerned about the activities of commercial websites aimed at children: nine out of ten such sites were found to be extracting information from young people about themselves and their parents, with fewer than a quarter of the sites carrying a suggestion that parental consent should be obtained before replying. Even for grown-ups, there are some discussion groups and newsgroups which require joiners to submit a profile of themselves along with their e-mail address. This information is available to all who join in, and to those who don't!

A great deal of other information about the surfer is given away without his knowledge or understanding. This is achieved through 'cookies' – the name given to localised spying devices which some companies attach like limpet mines to your hard drive the second you log on. Cookies were invented to 'enhance on-line shopping' by tracking a series of purchases by the customer during a single visit to a website. Without cookies it would be difficult, but not impossible, to store several purchases in an electronic shopping cart and enable payment to be made. They are also used for sites to build into their system a record of the customer's spending habits and tastes. When you make a return visit to Amazon.com, for example, the welcome sign will have your name imprinted upon it with a selection of book or CD recommendations for your consideration, because by now the company knows your tastes in reading and music. Unless surfers can be bothered to read the privacy notices – often long and tedious – on every website they visit, they have on way of knowing if cookies are being used. But the practice is now widespread.

Of the top hundred sites surveyed by EPIC in 1999, eighty-six used cookies. Multiplied across the Web, that represents thousands of commercial sites. Nor is the cookie information-gathering ability restricted to shopping at one site. They also provide a technique for merchants and advertisers to track consumer preferences and purchases over many visits to many different websites, literally following the surfers' tracks across the Web. It is this second use of cookies, often referred to as 'profiling', that raises privacy concerns. On-line profiling is a technique that marketers use to collect information about the on-line behaviour of Internet users and to produce tailor-made advertising appealing to their tastes and preferences. According to EPIC, it is nothing less than 'a form of on-line surveillance' of all Internet users. Profile-based advertising relies on cookies to generate banner advertisements which will make their appearance with alarming frequency. Some sites may also despatch a program like Java Applets to a user's hard drive so that a site can be configured to your taste when next you drop in, with advertising geared to your interests.

On 21 October 1999 Experian launched what might be seen as the most highly significant and contentious on-line information interface ever invented – one which collates the site visitor's registration information and matches it to Experian's own extensive databases so that an instant portrait of the e-customer may be created. Called Visitor Insight, it is described as 'the first in a suite of e-commerce solutions that will revolutionise on-line marketing'. The sales pitch to potential clients announces that Visitor Insight will allow on-line businesses to increase their understanding of Web registrants in real time. The translation for this is that businesses will be able to obtain an instant customer profile while they are on-line and, says Experian, will allow marketers to:

> customise individual consumer experiences, increase the
> amount of time consumers spend at their websites, improve
> customer service and boost sales. The Visitor Insight Process
> runs seamlessly in the background of an online business
> website. While a consumer registers on the site, Visitor Insight
> supplements information provided by the individual with
> demographic information from Experian's INSOURCES
> database of consumer marketing information, which contains
> data on 98 percent of US households. Using this enhanced
> data, online businesses can tailor product and service offerings
> immediately to the needs of individual consumers. Visitor
> Insight thus provides all the information and verification the
> marketer requires in real time. . . .

The implications of this latest invention are obvious, particularly in the burgeoning field of Internet banking and other financial services. At least Experian provides a 'tick me' box for an opt-out if the consumer does not wish to join in this real-time experience. It must be said, however, that many surfers, even experienced people, do not always understand why such opt-outs are necessary. Many sites do not even offer such an option on registration, and it is not surprising that advocates of Internet privacy increasingly complain at the sheer number of devices used by marketing firms to collect data on consumers. The use of a credit card over the Internet may be safer than presenting it at a city restaurant, but the fact that the e-consumer has been stripped naked in the process is perhaps overlooked by most. Even the inventor of the World Wide Web himself, Tim Berners-Lee, is on record as being worried about the consequences for private life of use of the Internet.

Most worrying of all is the loss of control consumers experience once they enter cyberspace and e-commerce. This is especially true in the case of certain sites which have begun to appear and which could lead unsuspecting surfers into great difficulty and embarrassment. They include some exceedingly dubious porn sites, many of which originate in countries where there is no chance of recourse for wrongdoing – that is, if the victim feels inclined to suffer the embarrassment of reporting the case in the first place. Thousands of surfers are known to have been ripped off by releasing credit card details or, more likely, actually sending cash or money orders to post office boxes run by sites which provide little or nothing in return, apart from access to lurid images on screen. Worse, perhaps, than the fraud is that some sites use all of the tricks the trade has ever invented for the capture of personal details; once in the ring, those details become available on the porn consumer networks and initiate a bombardment of contacts from other groups.

ATTEMPTS TO REGULATE THE INTERNET

Simon Davies, of Privacy International, described the emerging trends in e-commerce as the arrival of a 'surveillance economy' which urgently requires some form of regulation. For once, the USA has been rather offhand about such moves. Although the FBI has set up special units to police the Internet, US officials have accused European campaigners of using privacy protection laws in an attempt to put up trade barriers against the USA as it attempts to reach a potential market of 350 million across the European Union. In this instance America – which had attempted to keep open the channels of international wire tapping – is against controls of e-commerce other than those which will be placed in the hands of the FBI for trapping perpetrators of on-line crime.

There is, of course, a huge US lobby of consumer surveillance and direct marketing companies, along with financial and commercial lobbyists who strongly oppose anything other than self-regulation through codes of conduct set by professional bodies. They are suggesting methods of encryption that will satisfy the FBI and provide customer reassurance, along with ways of erasing individual footprints left in cyberspace. Europe, on the other hand, is leaning more towards regulation by law, a course supported by a survey conducted by the US-based Electronic Privacy Information Centre which looked at the operations of members of the Direct Marketing Association, who oppose any legislative interference. It concluded that 'the DMA's effort to promote privacy practices is having little impact on its new members, even after repeated assurances from the DMA that this approach is effective'.

Pressure from the European Union and consumers themselves may well force some form of legal responsibility on to the consumer database industry, although it will not be hurried into place. As anyone dealing with Internet customers and private PC users well knows, a large proportion of them, while able to surf their way around the world with little difficulty, simply do not understand or cannot comprehend the intricacies of hidden programs and limpets on their hard drives. Even less do they understand that there are now nasty implements that will enable interlopers to enter a personal computer via an e-mailed missive, take a look in the computer files and report back. Even a major US government survey published in June 1998 had to admit that the consumer tracking industry's attempt to set up a voluntary code of the 'most basic fair information practice' fell far short of what was needed to protect consumers.

That theme was examined by Nikos Bogonikolos and his team for the European human rights' study group, the Zeus Foundation, in its 1999 report commissioned by the European Parliament on 'The Development of Surveillance Technology and Risk of Abuse of Economic Information'. He pointed out that dataveillance was significantly less expensive than physical and electronic surveillance, resulting in far larger groups being monitored for specific purposes. One of the techniques singled out for concern in the Zeus report was that known in the trade as 'front-end verification' (FEV), where data supplied by an applicant can be checked, compared or included in the databases kept by a variety of additional sources. Indeed, five months after the European Parliament received the Zeus report, as we have seen, Experian announced its own new FEV system, linked in real time to the company's databases. Although in this case, the company provided the opt-out for customers, others may not be so open. It provided, however, a current example of a specifically designed dataveillance tool used on this occasion in a responsible manner, but elsewhere, as Zeus pointed out, such techniques 'may be of particular value in mass surveillance, capable of trawling through large volumes of data collected for different purposes, searching for discrepancies and drawing influences from them'.

The integration of data stored in various locations would, in the very near future, make it possible for systems to be introduced that would be comparable with credit card swipe machines and provide immediate screening of any individual. The inherent dangers, as Zeus notes, with cross-system checks against individuals is the fallibility of such systems; mistakes often occur where an individual has been black-listed by a third party, leading to: 'discrimination and guilt prediction, inversion of the onus of proof and unknown accusations and accusers as a result of misunderstandings about the meaning of data on the file, or because the file contains inaccurate data which the individual does not understand and has little or no chance of arguing on the spot'.

Both Steve Wright of the Omega Foundation and the Zeus team canvassed dozens of experts for their views and were virtually at one in recommending to the European Parliament that all surveillance technologies linked to databases should be subject to procedures ensuring accountability; firmly established codes of practice should be established consistent with data protection legislation to prevent malpractice or abuse; and clearly stated criteria should be drawn up on how such surveillance data should be stored, processed and shared. 'These controls', wrote Steve Wright in his Omega report, 'should be more effectively targeted at malpractice or illegal tapping by private companies and regulation further tightened to include safeguards against abuse as well as appropriate financial redress.'

Similar views were set out in the report of the Electronic Privacy Information Centre in its third survey on Internet privacy issues, published in December 1999.

> Taken as a whole, we found that more sites are posting privacy policies than did when we conducted the first formal review of website policies in 1997. We have also seen the rise of new associations to promote the development of privacy policies and encourage industry awareness of privacy issues. But when we looked closely at these policies, we found that they typically lacked the necessary elements of Fair Information Practices and were unlikely to provide meaningful privacy protection for consumers. The presence of a privacy policy, unfortunately, does not always ensure privacy protection.
>
> At the same time, marketers are using new and more sophisticated techniques to track consumers on the Internet. Profile-based advertising marks a sharp departure from traditional business practices which allowed companies to advertise products and services and still permit consumers to retain some privacy. In the world of radio, television and print advertising, for example, information flowed freely from businesses to consumers but little personally identifiable information was ever collected. In the online world, every consumer inquiry about a product and every ad viewing may quickly become incorporated into a detailed profile that will remain hidden from the consumer. On balance, we think that consumers are more at risk today [December 1999] than they were in 1997. The profiling is more extensive and the marketing techniques are more intrusive. Anonymity, which remains crucial to privacy on the Internet, is being squeezed out by the rise of electronic commerce. Industry backed self-regulation has done little to protect online privacy. We believe that legally enforceable standards are necessary to ensure compliance with Fair Information Practices. And new techniques for anonymity are necessary to protect online privacy. Until such steps are taken, we have to repeat our advice for the third consecutive year – *Surfer Beware*.

At the time of writing, few countries in Europe had laws which could be effectively used against aggressive or excessive dataveillance techniques, and the USA remained in favour of self-regulation by those involved.

CHAPTER 4
HERE'S LOOKING AT YOU: CCTV

CERTAIN IMAGES OF THE 1990s punctuated public awareness of general surveillance of their lives. It surprised them but did not necessarily appal them, largely because it was visible rather than unseen or secret. A few seconds of closed circuit television (CCTV) footage invariably located at the scene of tragic events – and later broadcast – provides a stark image quite different from the professionalism of television cameras. On screen there is often a slightly blurred image, erratic in movement but with a curious and compelling reality that impacts on the memory in a far greater way than many television shots. Four events spring immediately to mind, brief flashes rescued from CCTV videotapes that were viewed by millions around the world: the footage of Diana, Princess of Wales leaving the Ritz Hotel in Paris with Dodi Fayed and the driver of the car in which she was killed; the innocence of two-year-old James Bulger as he was led from a Liverpool shopping centre to his death by his two young killers; the poignant footage of television presenter Jill Dando out shopping only hours before being mysteriously shot on the front doorstep of her home and the one brief view of a partially hooded man caught on CCTV in London close to the scene of the ferocious nail bomb attack that killed and maimed at the Admiral Duncan pub in Soho.

Such images aided public perception of the capabilities of widespread surveillance of themselves, quite probably affected attitudes, and encouraged the belief that surveillance of this sort is no bad thing. In reality, the technology goes to the heart of concerns about privacy and the rights of the individual. The various surveys conducted by universities and study groups into the proliferation of CCTV cameras show that a running average of around 72 per cent of people do not object to them. But almost the same number are worried that the cameras could easily be abused in the hands of the wrong people, and many fear that those in control of these systems could not be 'completely trusted to use them only for the public good'. One other interesting fact to emerge from the surveys was that less than a third of the people questioned were actually aware when they were being watched.

CCTV IN THE UK

The United Kingdom, which has the largest CCTV network anywhere in the world, is a prime example of the way visual surveillance has changed dramatically since about 1990. The fact that so many admitted they never actually knew when or where they were under surveillance has something of an echo of a famous book on the subject.

It becomes impossible not to mention at this point George Orwell's *1984,* his disturbing portrait of a society that destroys privacy and distorts truth. Words that Orwell created like Newspeak, doublethink and Thought Police have long since entered our vocabulary along with spin doctors and all the other accoutrements of modern politics. Now his other major prediction is also falling into place: the all-seeing eye was already in place as we entered the year 2000, and unfortunately cannot be dismissed with a comforting 'Don't worry – they're not interested in you.'

As has already been demonstrated, it is not a single eye, nor a single system. Even so, Orwell's Big Brother, appearing on the telescreens in buildings public and private and claiming to be watching everything, is not so wide of the mark when all the other existing systems of surveillance are factored in. Orwell's words, written in the 1940s long before such technology was even envisaged, were chillingly accurate as he described the attempts of Winston Smith to think for himself. Eventually he is crushed into conformity by the unrelenting propaganda pumped out by the electronic media and the ability of the Thought Police to maintain a constant vigil over the intimate lives of ordinary citizens: 'The telescreen received and transmitted simultaneously. Any sound that Winston made above the level of a very low whisper could be picked up by it; moreover so long as he remained within the field of vision ... he could be seen as well as heard. There was of course *no way of knowing whether you were being watched* at any given moment.' (Author's emphasis)

In Britain in January 2000, Prime Minister Tony Blair announced further government funding of £150 million for the expansion of the nation's CCTV network. This is over and above the spending on systems installed by local authorities and private and corporate organisations, which is going on at a considerable pace. Even before the government-funded expansion began, in the UK there were estimated to be 1.3 million CCTV cameras in stations, streets, shopping malls, housing estates, town centres and general public areas and probably as many again in workplaces, industrial compounds, factories and so on. They are increasing at the rate of around 20 per cent a year in Britain, America, Australia and lately Canada, and some European Union countries are catching up.

By the turn of the century, most British towns and cities were covered by some form of CCTV surveillance of public areas. Their use on private property was on the rise, and in large urban areas many residents' associations and neighbourhood watch groups had begun independently running their own surveillance initiatives and video response teams as community policing became virtually invisible.

On an average day, a person moving about any big city anywhere in the United Kingdom will be filmed by more than three hundred cameras from thirty CCTV networks; that is not guesswork but the official statistic issued by Home Secretary Jack Straw – so in reality it may be higher. If that same person drove the length and breadth of Britain's 7500-mile motorway system the car would be captured on camera, on video or by automated vehicle recognition systems about once every four minutes, surveillance unmatched anywhere in the world; if the car ended up in the City of London, its entry within the so-called Ring of Steel that was installed to combat IRA terrorist attacks would be automatically recorded by number plate recognition and the car could be tracked throughout its stay. If that same person stopped off to attend a London football match, the face in a crowd would most likely be captured on film and stored, or, if there was trouble, might be handed to the police for visual recognition procedures to be matched against databases of photographs of known troublemakers. If the day ended with a visit to the new Bluewater shopping complex outside London, the car would be automatically recorded by vehicle recognition systems as soon as it entered the car park; the driver could be filmed virtually from the moment of leaving the car to the time of return; and the image could be captured by around several hundred cameras located throughout the complex and in the shops themselves, all stored on timed and dated videotapes so that it would be possible, in the event of an investigation, to produce footage showing a complete record of that person's shopping expedition.

Relatively inexpensive facial recognition systems are being developed by a number of manufacturers and will further enhance the capability of spotting a face in the crowd. Search software already in existence can easily match faces, even from large gatherings of people, at a rate of over two hundred faces a second. By 2002, commercially available software will even recognise faces from poor-quality images. Mass surveillance, mass databases of stored photographic images, mass tracking of people and their vehicles: it is the front line of all the surveillance systems that operate today and, curiously from a public point of view, the least controversial. According to Jack Straw, the people subjected to this video imaging are unperturbed. Straw is the former left-wing activist who became Home Secretary in 1997, and was immediately confronted with having to make landmark decisions on issues of privacy, human rights and freedom of information. He undertook them in a manner that would surely have pleased Margaret Thatcher. Straw says that most of us think mass surveillance by CCTV is a price worth paying for security in such troubled times, when street violence, crime, theft, burglary and other horrors are showing no signs of abating.

In support, the Home Office produced a glossy brochure called 'CCTV: Looking Out for You', which makes much of the theory that city-sited cameras may well be a solution for such problems as vandalism, drug use, drunkenness, racial harassment, sexual harassment, loitering and disorderly behaviour. It points out that CCTV has quickly become an integral part of crime control policy. 'Today's opportunist is tomorrow's professional criminal,' trumpets the HO Crime Control Unit. 'If we decrease the number of opportunities for easy crime, we can reduce the number of people becoming professional criminals.'

CRITICS OF CCTV

The presence of CCTV, says Jack Straw, has brought both reassurance and real reductions in crime, although those claims are disputed by at least three major studies which were completed in the late 1990s. They concluded that there was no definite evidence to support claims of any dramatic reduction in crime; many criminologists believe that crime simply moves out of the cameras' field of vision. What CCTV has done is to provide the police with greater power in securing evidence for arrests, confessions and convictions. It has also pushed them towards reactive rather than proactive investigations of city crime. In other words mobile police patrols, the bobby on the beat and the community police schemes that come and go with the wind are increasingly being replaced by staff sitting in front of a bank of monitors waiting for crime to happen.

Overall, closed circuit television camera systems in town and city centres have failed to match their anti-crime expectations, according to Professor James Ditton of the Scottish Centre for Criminology. After a four-year study for the Scottish Office, the professor called for an independent watchdog to oversee the use of this technology. He told BBC Scotland:

> It has been overhyped and I think that is one of the problems. It was allegedly going to give us these magnificent benefits of reducing crime and making the fear of crime diminish to almost nothing. Although it probably does have some utility for the police it does not have these wonderful great societal benefits, so we really question whether the benefits it does bring us justify photographing everybody who goes into the city every day. The cameras were so vastly overhyped as a magic bullet cure for everything when they were introduced

that we were all blinded to the fact that this was a small addition in police terms, but a rather large incursion in civil liberty terms.

Another study was highly critical of the way the surveillance was focused. For their study and eventual report, entitled 'The Unforgiving Eye: CCTV Surveillance in Public Space', Dr Clive Norris and Gary Armstrong of the Centre for Criminology and Criminal Justice at Hull University shadowed camera operators in three major areas covered by a total of 148 cameras. They took details of a sample 888 targeted surveillances which resulted in just twelve arrests.

Norris claimed that the way individuals were selected for observation seemed to have more to do with the personal preferences – or even prejudices – of the CCTV operators than with what was actually occurring:

- 40 per cent of people were targeted for no obvious reason, mainly 'on the basis of belonging to a particular or subcultural group'.

- Black people were more likely to be watched than would be expected from their presence in the population.

- 30 per cent of targeted surveillances on black people were protracted, lasting nine minutes or more, compared with just 10 per cent on white people.

- People were selected primarily on the basis of 'the operator's negative attitudes towards male youth in general and black male youth in particular ... if a youth was categorised as a "scrote" they were subject to prolonged and intensive surveillance'.

- Those deemed to be 'out of time and out of place' with the commercial image of city centre streets were subjected to prolonged surveillance: 'Thus drunks, beggars, the homeless, street traders were all subject to intense surveillance.'

- Anyone who directly challenged, by gesture or deed, the right of the cameras to monitor them was especially subject to targeting.

- Women appeared to be watched for entirely voyeuristic reasons by some male camera operators.

- Only people wearing 'uniforms' were completely exempt from targeting.

The 888 monitored incidents led to forty-five deployments of police and twelve arrests, seven related to fighting and three to theft. The Hull study concluded:

> The gaze of the cameras does not fall equally on all users of the street but on those who are stereotypically predefined as potentially deviant, or through appearance and demeanour, are singled out by operators as unrespectable. In this way youth, particularly those already socially and economically marginal, may be subject to even greater levels of authoritative intervention and official stigmatisation, and rather than contributing to social justice through the reduction of victimisation, CCTV will merely become a tool of injustice through the amplification of differential and discriminatory policing.

The use of CCTV camera networks is not universally acclaimed, either. There is a divergence of opinion within the European Union, with Denmark banning their use. As many people are ready to point out, recent memory offers examples of how the equipment can be used in the control of society, rather than for its benefit. Cameras were used by the Chinese Communist regime in Tiananmen Square, for example, to film the dissidents. The systems were originally supplied by a German company, supposedly for monitoring traffic; another set came from an American manufacturer. After the 1989 massacre of students a huge amount of CCTV footage was collated and searched by police to identify thousands of students who were subsequently arrested, interrogated and tortured. The film was shown over and over again on Chinese television, with rewards being offered for identification of faces shown or for information leading to their arrest. This was a perfect example of how oppressive governments or dictatorships could use cameras for manipulation of the masses. It also demonstrated that some form of control should be invoked for CCTV wherever it is operating in order to safeguard human rights and to guarantee simple privacy.

All the research conducted at universities calls for a monitoring of those doing the monitoring as the UK CCTV system progresses not only in size but also technologically. New digitalised systems and automatic facial recognition, similar to the automated vehicle recognition used in the City of London, will be in common use by 2005. Even Privacy International accepts that there is no major public disquiet over the use of CCTV but believes there ought to be accountability to some authority to prevent abuses. This is especially important as the digital generation, computer-based and miniaturised systems come on stream. CCTV will soon figure even more prominently as a tool in the investigative armoury of all law enforcement agencies, the media, private detectives and anyone else who may wish to capture the passing public or specific situations clandestinely on film.

Elsewhere, in a society where one household in three has use of a video camera, various other abuses have come to light. In 1999, for example, there were two cases where disreputable landlords had wired up rooms for sound and vision to keep watch on their tenants in their most private moments. One of them had placed a video camera inside a television set purely for sexual gratification. He filmed and recorded on video all that was happening, much to the embarrassment of female tenants who viewed the videos when they were eventually discovered by police.

The use of CCTV is completely unlicensed and unregulated in the UK, and indeed in most other countries where it is widely used. There are no rules in the UK to prevent the sale of CCTV footage to TV or video distribution companies, possibly to be broadcast on international television or over the Internet, as frequently happens. Many police forces around the world run a cottage industry in the sale of video footage from police cars. Many other examples of surveillance on film, ranging from crimes of violence to disputes with neighbours, have moved quickly into the public domain as television production companies have discovered a cheap, quick and effective source of revenue. All they need to do is compile sixty minutes of clips from CCTV material, often without consulting those filmed or their relatives – no matter how upsetting this may be to the victims. What Jack Straw has described as a key tool in bringing serious criminals to justice may also be used for hugely commercial 'tabloid TV', regardless of the invasion of privacy.

The security industry, by whom great numbers of these systems are controlled, insist that modern trends demand such surveillance, and of course the 1990s could offer many examples in confirmation. The list is endless: school shootings, attacks on hospital staff, violence in the workplace, no-go areas in housing estates, heightened fears of possible terrorist or criminal attacks, as well as the need to protect valuable assets and hardware in a multitude of places. All have played their part in boosting both the need and the demand for public areas to be kept under observation.

NEW DEVELOPMENTS IN TECHNOLOGY

Surveillance cameras are constantly evolving into new levels of sophistication. In America, the security system set up on the University of Chicago Hospital campus was seen as excessive and futuristic when it was installed in the late 1990s. Now, it has become a model of likely needs in many public buildings. The system was installed because of increasing numbers of 'security incidents' ranging from theft to violence. Security advisers were called in and discovered that at that time the hospital possessed twenty-six forms of identification for authorising entry, that there was no centralised security control and that each department was running its own procedures – a set-up repeated in hospitals, offices and public buildings the world over. It was very easy indeed to get to the most sensitive areas of the hospital.

What transpired in Chicago was the design and installation of a single state-of-the-art system that would encompass the entire needs of the hospital and include access controls, constant CCTV surveillance of all areas, patient tagging, electronic tagging of infants, critical life point monitoring, paging systems, unique alarms for medical teams, security alarms, fire alarms, motion sensors and car park monitoring as well as Internet and Ethernet connections. The size and layout of the hospital presented a major challenge. It had 4700 employees, 31,000 patients admitted annually from around the world and 500,000 outpatient visits.

Priority was given to monitoring everyone who entered the hospital buildings and to the surveillance of people moving through its corridors. At the heart of the system were two key elements: controlled access to over 640 doors, each with card readers which permitted or denied entry and tracked the person using the smart cards, and a comprehensive CCTV network. More than three hundred cameras were linked to forty-eight video monitors in the hospital's five security control stations. Eighteen time-lapse video recording units filmed real-time video twenty-four hours a day, using nine hundred tapes which were kept in rotation at all times. Multiplex cameras allowed the recording of the output of sixteen cameras on one tape and viewing on a single monitor, so that virtually every area of the hospital could be kept under constant surveillance. Motion detectors and night-sight equipment set off alarms directing camera observation to any possible security breach.

The alarm system was interfaced with pagers which automatically notified designated groups of personnel of a particular alert. It also interfaced with the hospital's e-mail system so that alarms could be automatically delivered to workstations. The CCTV network was designed to cover many functions beyond general hospital security. In the hospital's cafeteria, for example, cameras served as a deterrent to theft and food loss. A camera above each cash register recorded every customer transaction. The system monitored 1430 security points throughout the hospital campus. Its computerised alert for medical staff could handle more than 715 unique alarms, store 25,000 personnel records and process approximately 130,000 transactions per day – all of which required thirty miles of computer network cabling.

But even as those miles of cabling were being installed in Chicago, certain elements of the system were already slightly dated. As with every form of electronic communications and surveillance technology exam-ined so far, the users could hardly keep pace with the innovations. The quality of CCTV cameras and recording equipment has matched the IT revolution in recent years. Many camera systems are controlled and interfaced by computer networks, and may be viewed from remote stations as part of integrated surveillance monitoring.

New computer-based systems, for example, now offer the facility for thirty-two cameras to be handled by a PC, with pan, tilt and zoom capability, and stored on hard drive upgradable to 200 gigabytes of on-line storage capacity which can be accessed and searched immediately from a workstation anywhere in the world. The latest digital systems, meanwhile, provide high-quality on-line images, with long-term storage without degradation, and multiple search capability of event-triggered and intrusion detection.

The whole business is advancing rapidly. The advent of miniature cameras that provide excellent pictures can now form part of an overall surveillance system that is virtually impossible to detect. The latest models are exactly one inch square, which means they can be clandestinely inserted into any surveillance operation where secrecy is of the utmost importance. In 1998, in the UK alone 125,000 of these cameras were sold, largely by spy-gear retailers and suppliers to the security industry. What exactly are they used for? It has to be for keeping watch on a situation or on an individual or group to whom those doing the filming do not want to reveal their presence, possibly in the workplace. In most instances that can surely only result in invasion of privacy.

Many systems for workplaces and buildings also have an audio facility. Trials are already taking place in the USA to add sound to the equation of open surveillance. Direction-finding microphones, attached to lamp-posts, are on trial in Redwood City to pinpoint particular sounds such as gunfire. Again, it is similar to sound equipment first used by the British military in Northern Ireland in 1992.

Other developments have brought innovations in the field of mass photography. Numerous trials have been carried out using still and video cameras mounted on pilotless aircraft drones which have huge potential in filming large crowds, such as at demonstrations and marches. The pictures can be fed immediately back to a central control for use with facial recognition systems or people-tracking software.

The ultimate in capturing images of the environment – and possibly people, in the not too distant future – arrived in September 1999 when a Denver-based company, Space Imaging, blasted into the e-business with the launch of the first commercial high-resolution imaging satellite designed solely to picture the Earth's surface. Smaller, less powerful commercial satellites were already operating; this one has the ability to deliver a close-up shot of any spot on the planet, with clarity guaranteed for images less than a metre square. Called the Ikonos (Greek for 'image') satellite, it was launched at a cost of $750 million. The company plans to recoup its investment by selling Earth surface imagery. A one-metre square, black and white photograph will cost $29 per square kilometre, with a minimum purchase of $1000 in the USA and $2000 elsewhere. Although initially the images will be in print form, it is intended to market the products over the Internet.

Cynical commentators in the USA see it as a novelty situation whereby the Joneses can confirm 'Yes, their pool is smaller than ours.' But it could be used for almost the same purpose by local environmental and planning officers to discover the construction of illegal swimming pools and buildings.

It will provide customers who have not previously had access to satellite imagery with the same view of the Earth that the major spy agencies have been collecting for thirty years or more. Now, if a mad dictator wanted a clearer idea of a particular spot in the world, perhaps showing movements of opposing military forces, he could conceivably charge it to his MasterCard. To make sure that doesn't occur, Space Imaging has pledged to the US government that it won't sell to any powers suspected of terrorist activities. The US government also reserves the right to limit the distribution of pictures deemed a threat to national security. Few doubt, however, that once this information is available over the Internet it will be more difficult for Space Imaging, and for the US government, to control its use.

Conrad Meuller, vice-president of Space Imaging, explained: 'With this capability, Space Imaging will be at the forefront of the worldwide digital information marketplace. With the addition of Ikonos to our existing constellation of imaging satellites, we are able to broaden our reach. Many countries have an intense need for detailed, accurate satellite imagery for a multitude of important applications. By making high-resolution satellite imagery available, we're able to respond to our customers' needs even better.'

Circling the Earth once every ninety-eight minutes, Ikonos is designed to send back digital images of the Earth from 400 miles (680 kilometres) up while moving at a speed of about four and a half miles (seven kilometres) per second. The imagery products collected by Ikonos will be marketed to a range of customers who will include 'agricultural concerns, state and local governments, mapping services, oil and gas, utilities, emergency response, natural resources, telecommunications, tourism, national security, insurance, news gathering and others'. The company says that at present, the images do not give a picture of individuals. Given the rapid pace of the technology, that aspect will surely come into the frame before long.

The quality of satellite imagery has improved dramatically in recent years and a number of major companies, including Motorola and Boeing, have big plans for the future. They have already invested billions of dollars to create satellites capable of mapping the most minute detail on the face of the Earth. The technology is being used for a vast range of purposes and there is little doubt that, in a few more years, humans on Earth will get snapshots of themselves taken from space. The implications are obvious.

Another form of people tracking has been envisaged using satellites. The idea was put forward in a study document issued by the Strategic Studies Institute of the US Army's War College, many of whose predictions have an uncanny knack of coming to fruition. Outlined in a long dissertation entitled 'Conflict Short of War', it poses the possibility that Americans travelling overseas might in future be equipped with an IPLD or Individual Position Locator Device. It will be a communications tag linked to a satellite which will show the exact location of any citizen wearing it at any time of day or night. The IPLD would be derived from the electronic tagging bracelet used to keep track of early-release prisoners, as worn by the disgraced former British Cabinet minister Jonathan Aitken on his release in January 2000.

The device suggested by the American SSI study would be permanently implanted under the skin of regular travellers abroad, such as businessmen and government and military personnel, with automatic activation on departure from US territory. Wristwatch forms of the device are already being tried, with the possibility of using them for two-way communications. It would be the last word in tracking technology and, once introduced, would undoubtedly be pursued for other more general uses in society. If every person in the world who has a credit card can be located in an on-line database in 2.4 seconds, it would not be too difficult to imagine a system of constant communication with a satellite-linked individual. It may sound a bit too Dick Tracy to be true – but then, so did the Internet not many years ago. And in fact, by February 2000 it became reality when a company in Miami, Florida, produced a prototype for commercial use, to be marketed before the year was out.

CHAPTER 5
WATCHING WHILE YOU WORK

SURVEILLANCE IN THE WORKPLACE is another boom industry that emerged during the 1990s and for which a considerable range of devices is now proliferating in every kind of work environment. Legal protection is lax, and surveillance is often imposed as a condition of employment. Closed circuit television monitoring, often covertly installed, is among the most common forms of surveillance but it is just one of numerous techniques devised with the sole object of keeping a check on the activities of employees. According to a study conducted for Sir Trevor MacDonald's ITN *Tonight* programme in February 2000, at least half of Britain's workforce is being monitored by some sort of electronic recording equipment at work. This is very much in line with figures in the USA. Nearly two-thirds of companies surveyed by the American Management Association utilised at least one of eight workplace surveillance techniques listed in the association's questionnaire; some companies had even installed the whole range.

One-third videotaped all areas of workspace, including rest rooms, restaurants and quiet corners away from the actual workstation, in order 'to counter theft, violence or sabotage or drug abuse'. A similar number used other specifically designed surveillance techniques for particular situations. They included checking and analysing e-mails, voicemail and computer files, taping phone conversations, using covert cameras to monitor employee performance, and unseen desktop surveillance devices to record individual workstation activity. Rest rooms and toilets were often bugged with listening devices.

Many companies are installing software to keep track of employees' use of the Internet. It details sites visited and length of time spent on-line. Similar records are kept of all phone numbers called and the duration of each call. Almost a quarter of the companies surveyed monitored the performance of employees in data-entry positions by keeping a record of computer keystrokes from the time at which employees logged on to their terminals or desktop computers to the point when they signed off. A recent but now common addition is the ability of supervisors to view the screens of any of the computers on the internal network.

Reasons for installing any one of these devices fall into four categories:

- to ensure employee health, safety and protection (from abuse or violence);

- to guard against theft of goods, information and trade secrets;

- to monitor employees' performance, attitudes and demeanour;

- to gather evidence in support of court action arising out of any of the previous three reasons.

The devices are generally multifunctional and gather up for bosses and human resources managers useful information well beyond the area of legitimate investigation. They are also often operated secretly, which is of course one of the most disturbing forms of people watching. Discovery of it usually causes a traumatic reaction from the subject who was previously unaware that someone, somewhere, was watching or listening while they went about their daily business at work and was even observing their most private moments, such as visits to the toilets.

How does it happen? Take a closer look at the clock on the wall, you may not have realised it houses a camera lens pointing directly at you. You might also check out the smoke detector across the room. It probably isn't a smoke detector at all; it may also contain a miniature camera which, like the clock, is sending images, and quite probably sound, to a security base that no one knows about, perhaps not even in the same building but at a remote observation post. Pick up the stapler on the desk – it may well house a tiny concealed microphone which listens into all your conversations at your desk. That e-mail you have just sent to a friend or colleague will most likely be read by the computer forensic spooks before you get home – even if you thought you had deleted it from the system. Some companies are even wiring individual workstations for sound, so that they can have a record of everything that goes on at a person's desk, including private telephone conversations. And you may never know that your computer system contains a software package that tracks all individual computer activity and is capable of sending your manager a message whenever you, the employee, are doing something that is not allowed.

And so the electronic revolution and the IT age have brought with them another unexpected, and largely unwanted, phenomenon which most experts believe is merely in its infancy. Security specialists and computer forensic teams are quietly moving into shops, offices and factories to monitor employees, visitors, shoppers and indeed anyone entering them at any hour of day or night.

It is a progressive kind of infiltration, ranging from basic levels of CCTV monitoring that have become commonplace to combat petty theft by employees all the way up to deep and detailed surveillance of employees run on the lines of a state intelligence agency.

WHY WORKPLACE SURVEILLANCE AROSE

This level of surveillance rose hand in hand with other 1990s' workplace innovations which included company liability for a whole range of health and safety regulations, the protection of employees from violence and the protection of employers from liability, but also, more specifically among larger companies, the arrival of opportunities for theft on a grand scale.

Company information, software and other easily transmittable material began to disappear quickly and efficiently into the ether as crooked employees and industrial espionage agents discovered the ease with which they could move valuable proprietary and intellectual information out of the office via e-mail and the Internet. As more and more enterprises turned their operations towards a global on-line existence, the potential for theft, damage, industrial espionage and hacking attacks escalated beyond all previous comprehension. But even that was only part of the story.

Society itself was also becoming increasingly unpredictable, which merely added to the need for workplace surveillance. There was, for example, an outbreak of babies being stolen from hospitals in Britain which prompted calls for improved security. This was further encouraged by another modern phenomenon: violence in hospitals and schools, which eventually spread into many other workplaces. Incidents of workplace violence have tripled in America and Europe since 1970, and employers are often held liable for not taking adequate preventative measures to ensure the safety of their workforce. Then came the school shootings, a series of individual gun incidents in America and mass killings there and in Scotland. The use of drugs, and especially cocaine, in high-flyer banking and brokerage houses also became an issue. All of these elements played their part in the perceived need for greater surveillance in all workplaces.

THE TOOLS USED

Major electronics companies began producing security equipment packages modelled on devices invented for military use which can be customised to clients' requirements but are designed to offer twenty-four-hour 'total surveillance' of buildings and personnel. CCTV cameras are but one part of the system; the rest is spooky, to say the least, and as miniaturisation progresses and the devices become cheaper they can be expected to make an appearance in most twenty-first-century places of employment.

A typical package will begin with access control – entry to the workplace or specific areas of it by way of photographic imaging or biometric identification. These devices may be installed at all main entrances and exits, where everyone who enters is also videotaped. Movement inside the building may require digital proximity cards –

command keys which need not be taken out of the pocket, briefcase or purse and therefore allow hands-free entry and exit. They have an inbuilt electronic device that replies to a radio signal from a card reader that 'interrogates' it, possibly from several feet away, and are gradually replacing swipe cards.

Proximity cards are increasingly being used both for employee identification and for allowing them progressive access to various parts of the building or equipment. A company proximity smart card may permit or deny access to certain protected areas, can be used for computer network access, such as the Internet, and may have an electronic purse function for use in the company restaurant or at automatic vending machines.

It may also be used as a tracking device. Proximity readers installed along the walls of a building allow the tracking of each card and a central security computer can report exactly where the cardholder is at any time, thus providing a timed database record of which area the employee (or possibly visitor) is in and when he leaves. It can log him off his workstation and into the cafeteria, record how long he spent there, how long he took to get back to his desk and by which route he went through the building. It can set off alarm signals in the control centre if the person enters an area to which access is denied. The computer can record whether he went to the toilet, how long he was there and, in some instances, alert security controllers to run video surveillance.

In many cases, CCTV is becoming an all-embracing tool. With miniaturisation and other sophisticated developments it is possible to install machines that are triggered merely to record 'an event'. Motion detectors in sensitive areas may also order a video camera to begin recording. The latest technology at the time of writing also allows control of all security systems from what are termed 'remote locations'. These can be installed covertly or overtly or a bit of both – so that employees never actually know when they are being watched. Thus the district manager who only ever visits the premises on Wednesdays could dial up at any time and watch and listen on his computer monitor to the activities of employees in the faraway office.

Many other forms of monitoring can be carried out without the employee's knowledge. A British company called Cascom markets a

Computer Keyboard Monitoring System. This transmits every keystroke to a wireless receiver which can be located up to 150 metres away. An optional LCD display for the supervisor can be used to display all characters as they are typed. It is sold as the ideal monitor of a worker's performance profile. Many similar products are now being produced to meet the demand. One is a software package whose title makes no secret of its application: Desktop Surveillance, manufactured by Tech Assist Inc., capable of monitoring all computer activity by an employee and costing just $55 (information from *Technologies of Privacy Invasion*, survey and reports jointly published by Privacy International and Electronic Privacy Information Centre, 1999). A company spokesman described it as a 'sort of truth metre . . . it tells you exactly what's happening at a particular desktop'. It can even alert a manager to any activity that is not allowed.

Most internal company networks can now be supplied with built-in eavesdropping features and software. Some software packages, such as Win Watch Professional and Norton-Lambert's Close-Up/LAN, allow network administrators to keep watch on an employee's screen in real time, scan data files and e-mails, analyse keystroke performance, and even overwrite passwords. The trade advertisement for another package has the strapline: 'Look in on Sue's computer screen. Sue doesn't even know you're there!' As one speaker, describing workplace surveillance, said at the American Society of Industrial Security Convention in Las Vegas in September 1999: 'There's really no turning back. If you want to talk about the mission control centre concept of security departments, it's really here . . . today.'

ATTEMPTS TO CHALLENGE WORKPLACE SURVEILLANCE

Laws governing the tapping of its own telephones by a company are vague and allow indiscriminate use. Many industries now record all calls made from company telephones on the basis of consumer protection, security and training. Specifically targeted telephone tapping of the employees themselves, however, is not uncommon and not necessarily illegal. At best, courts may decide it is a breach of human rights. This was confirmed by the decision of the European Court in Strasbourg in the case of Alison Halford, the former Assistant Chief Constable of Merseyside. Miss Halford insisted that the phone-tap had been autho-rised by her former superior, the Merseyside Chief Constable, Sir James Sharples. She said: 'The issue is that he tapped my phones when I was not a criminal, not a subversive person and not a terrorist. The law of the land demands that you should have proper authority for that. What happened to me was totally unethical.'

Lawyers for the police force at the European Court accepted there was a 'reasonable likelihood' that Miss Halford's office telephones had been bugged following a dispute about her promotion prospects. But they insisted that any such taps were not a breach of human rights because the telephones were government property. The case was brought six and a half years after she was suspended from duty follow-ing allegations that she had frolicked in a swimming pool in her underwear. She later made allegations of sex discrimination by Sir James and others, claiming she had been passed over nine times for promotion to the rank of Deputy Chief Constable. The dispute was resolved when the parties reached an out-of-court settlement in July 1992 and Miss Halford received a six-figure sum.

In their unanimous verdict, the European judges said Miss Halford had a 'reasonable expectation' of privacy in making and receiving tele-phone calls at work and there was no evidence that she had been warned that her telephone might be bugged. As her solicitor Robin Makin said at the time, it was a landmark decision, establishing the principle of privacy in the workplace, although the more serious implications were that the police were spying on one of their own employees while she was fighting a sex discrimination case against them.

Sir James Sharples was not moved to apologise or even to confirm or deny the existence of phone-taps 'because to do so would undermine the effectiveness of the technique'. In other words, he was following the age-old principle of admit nothing, deny nothing when it comes to ques-tions about wire-taps. He said: 'The central issue, it seems, is that Miss Halford accepted that English law does not prohibit intercepts of office telephones. She therefore took HM Government to the European Court to ascertain whether that "omission" was a breach of European law. The European Court has concluded that interceptions to office telephones would be a breach of privacy and that English law does not cover such telephones but ought to.'

In spite of that, the British government took no immediate steps to rectify the situation, although it did eventually include the issue in a 1999 consultative document on the interception of communications. Meanwhile, the practice remains widespread in the general climate of snooping on employees. Carolyn Jones, of the British Institute of Employee Rights, maintains that surveillance in the workplace is gathering momentum at an alarming rate and is being used for many more purposes than might legitimately be expected:

> It is becoming more widespread, more intrusive and more secretive, so that when you arrive at your place of work now, your privacy, your autonomy and your basic rights are left at the door. Today, employees can expect to be monitored and surveyed from the moment they arrive to the moment they leave. Now, whether you are doing something wrong or not, having a camera or recording device intruding into your life in this way is totally aggressive and unnecessary, and a breach of basic human rights. It is in itself causing great stress among many sections of the workforce, especially in the area of performance monitoring. Keyboard operators in particular barely dare stop to take a breath. The methods being used are nothing short of draconian. They are totally intrusive and carry so many other implications. When, for example, a person's face no longer fits in the organisation a dossier of videotape may be used to effect a dismissal on any pretext because somewhere in the small print of employment contracts is a little clause which says employers reserve the rights to electronically record, monitor and observe.

One such case was Roz Johnstone, a cleaning supervisor at Leeds Metropolitan University. One day, without warning, the police arrived and arrested her. She was taken to a local police station and questioned. Then, two officers took her into a room with a television set and a video recorder and played a CCTV tape. One of the policemen told her that she had been filmed while at work, the hidden cameras supposedly having been installed to capture evidence of alleged drug dealing. There was no evidence of that on the videos they showed Roz; they were merely recordings of herself talking to two colleagues in a staff kitchen where they had made themselves mugs of tea. However, the police arrested her because she could be heard talking in uncomplimentary terms about her boss. There was apparently bad feeling between them, and Roz said that her husband would beat him up if she had any more trouble. 'It was just conversation with two workmates,' said Roz. 'It was the sort of thing anyone might say. It meant nothing, but the police and the university were trying to make a big deal out of it.' The police released her on bail and told her she might be charged with conspiracy to cause grievous bodily harm to her boss.

In fact, there were no charges and no court case. But Roz was still suspended from her job with a formal letter which stated she had wasted university time by taking an unauthorised coffee break and had threatened her manager. When the police decided to take no action, she appealed and was reinstated. The university stood by its action and maintained that it felt justified in instituting these procedures in the interests of security of the university as a whole. A spokesperson said this would at times involve specifically targeted surveillance, although what happened to the subject once the issue became a police matter was, of course, beyond the university's control.

Many similar cases have occurred but the laws in most countries are unclear and out of date. In Britain, a new Data Protection Act came into force in March 2000 which offered some safeguards, such as an employee's right to know about any information obtained through surveillance methods by employers. Elsewhere, the situation remains complex, especially in regard to computer-based techniques and access to employees' PCs, e-mails and voicemails, which may yet be considered a form of illegal wire tapping. The fact is that, while information technologies have created vast opportunities for personal expression, electronic commerce and ultra-accessibility, they have also ushered in problems never previously encountered.

ABUSES OF TECHNOLOGY

Although employers have been guilty of abuses, so, too, have employees. Theft of the most valuable commodities of a company – proprietary and intellectual information, software and other electronically controlled assets, including company funds – is a real problem. These are crimes largely committed from within the workplace; external attacks by espionage agents or hackers and other unauthorised entry to computer systems also represent a threat, although far less so than internal crime.

In the beginning, when logging on was still a great novelty to workers who suddenly found themselves sitting in front of desktop monitors, all kinds of abuses and unimagined situations began to occur, with employees taking liberties and employers responding with threats of legal action. It was an arena that was virtually lawless because nothing had been tried and tested in court. Everything about the information technology and on-line communications boom and the use of computers at work was all so new that most bosses possessed neither the knowledge nor the experience to set up guidelines; most of them knew even less about the capabilities and vulnerabilities of their hardware than their employees. Even those supposed computer experts who suddenly proliferated in workplaces to supervise operations were, at best, working on a trial-and-error basis.

All kinds of challenges to established practices in the workplace would present themselves, ranging from the simple basis of computer operations to previously unknown difficulties caused by repetitive strain syndrome. Perhaps the most remarkable and, at that time, least quantifiable aspect of the whole business was the sheer power of the machines now being placed in front of previously unskilled operatives – machines which would be upgraded rapidly, as would the skills of the operatives. It was the beginning of a revolution that by the end of the decade saw, for example, the US Department of Defense established as the world's largest single user of computers, with 2.1 million terminals accessing over ten thousand networks on the average day, 95 per cent of which were linked via public circuits and utilised commercial software.

In the early days, in every office where computer networks were installed, numerous personal aspects arose that at the time did not seem especially important. But in the event they proved to be a major area that required monitoring for one reason or another. Minor irritations could become major problems. It was accepted practice in most workplaces that personal telephone calls could be made, within reason, in work time over the company telephone network. But PCs could not be classed as personal. What could they be used for other than work, apart from playing solo or battleships and writing the occasional personal letter or sending rude messages to colleagues over the internal network? It was a problem that grew out of all expectation as more and more firms connected to the Internet.

The Internet was so fascinating that unsupervised staff began spending far more time than was perhaps reasonable just surfing around the websites: a quick look at that week's on-line issue of *Penthouse*, or catching up with the stock market prices, or sending each other lots of e-mails. Nor did it ever occur to anyone that those messages, which might include some offensive words about the boss or a few other indiscretions, could actually be read by anyone other than the person to whom they were addressed – even after they had been deleted. Most bosses didn't know that either.

Meanwhile, others used company time to compile short articles on the finer points of growing chrysanthemums, or writing ten-thousand-word dissertations on the annihilation of the CIA or why Nazism should rise again – all to be posted, signed or anonymous, on the Web. It was such a novelty, this place where anything went: say what you like, write what you like and, as many employers with lots of expensive software lying around soon found to their cost, steal what you like.

It was a combination of all three that eventually contributed to widespread monitoring of employees' computer usage. Crime mushroomed, and the subject will be dealt with more fully in later chapters. An indication of the perceived need for greater staff surveillance is, however, evident from data published in October 1999 by the American Society for Industrial Security. A survey of the Fortune 1000 companies discovered that theft of proprietary information accounted for $45 billion in losses between January 1997 and June 1998.

Manufacturing organisations were hardest hit, losing on average almost $50 million per incident. High-technology and service organisations reported the largest number of proprietary information losses – respectively 530 and 356 incidents. The survey also revealed that companies perceived on-site contract employees as the greatest threat to their proprietary information. Dan Swartwood, Compaq Computers Information Security Manager and a member of ASIS Proprietary safeguards team, reckoned: 'These reported thefts and billions of lost corporate dollars are really just the tip of the iceberg. Survey respondents reported what many of us in the industry have long suspected. Many incidents go unreported due to lack of means to detect losses, or concern that reporting losses could only adversely impact the reputation of the organisation if it ever became publicly know.'

The Internet, e-mailing and the proliferation of information systems is blamed for the significantly increased risks. By 1996, according to research in the USA by the Gallup Organisation, 90 per cent of all large companies, 64 per cent of mid-size companies and 42 per cent of small businesses were using e-mail either by Internet connection or local or internal company networks. In 1994 it had been reckoned that company employees were sending 508 million messages a month by e-mail; within three years the figure had grown to 3 billion a month. These figures were gradually matched, in proportion, across Europe. Recent calculations show that upwards of 80 million workers in North America and Europe alone were using e-mail on a daily basis by the beginning of 2000, and growth rates were predicted at 20 per cent a year.

Various surveys have been conducted to discover the amount of time employees spend in working hours accessing the Internet, and for what reasons. The result has been a further enhancement of company monitoring of its workforces, because a 1997 scan of five hundred companies in America and Europe discovered that 'at least one-third of those employees with company access spent up to an hour a day on the Internet and nearly 12 per cent at least two hours per day, either surfing websites, joining discussions groups or on e-mail functions'.

Another study, conducted in 1998, went further and suggested that a 'significant number' of employees were connected to the Internet for between 20 and 60 per cent of their working day, the higher figure often reached after a major news event or sporting occasion when media pages were accessed. Nielsen Media, the US television and advertising ratings research group, conducted one of the first wide-ranging studies of Internet use; among the results was confirmation of the time 'wasted' on non-company activities during work time. Researchers discovered, for example, that on-line editions of *Penthouse* were called up thousands of times a month at major corporations such as IBM, Apple Computer and AT & T.

In November 1999, Nielsen published results of the first major study of Internet habits among British adults aged sixteen and over. The research found that, of the 46 million adult residents in the UK, 27 per cent had used the Internet in the past month. Of these, 44 per cent logged on every day; 38 per cent were women; 11 per cent were over fifty years old; 72 per cent used the Web for work, 69 per cent used it to research travel destinations and 60 per cent read sports and entertainment news; 27 per cent had purchased goods on-line and 49 per cent had used the Web to compare the price of goods and services. Although work-related statistics were not available for the UK, clearly the US experience had crossed the Atlantic.

All of this activity, and the great amount of company e-mailing, went on almost from the outset against a backdrop of controversy over two issues: the security of e-mails sent over the Internet; and whether or not the boss could read e-mails sent by employees, and if he could, should he? A decade passed without a satisfactory resolution to either question. Indeed, both issues provided reasons why security, observation and employee surveillance were introduced in many offices, often secretly. Computer forensic teams were employed at night to retrieve deleted records of material that had left the office over the Internet; many employees were not aware that this was even possible.

Most e-mail services on the Internet use what is known as 'packet' technology, by which the message to be transmitted is broken into parts and may travel through various routes before being reassembled for the recipient. The system reduces, but by no means eliminates, the possibility of it being read by a third party and, although the use of encryption and passwords further reduces the risk, the possibility of confidential information being intercepted is real. It would present little difficulty, for example, for those engaged on a dedicated mission of interception, such as hackers, industrial espionage spies, foreign agents or state intelligence services.

It is more likely, however, that incidents where security of specific e-mail operations has been compromised have been the result of human error or attacks by hackers. As an example – and as computer buffs well know – Microsoft's Hotmail system came in for regular hack attacks, and in the summer of 1999 the company was forced to introduce a new security system to stop interception of personal e-mails after a way of identifying individual passwords was discovered. In January 2000 Virgin Net, part of Richard Branson's Virgin Group, was forced temporarily to block access to its e-mail service after becoming aware of a potential security issue that could allow hackers entry to 25 per cent of its accounts. Users had to change their passwords to reactivate their account. Such incidents were not uncommon. Many companies in 2000 would still not use any form of electronic communication to transmit sensitive information, and certainly not to send top secret industrial or financial material.

For many employers, however, the safety of the e-mail system was only one of their worries. Internal security breaches far outweighed external attacks. In 1997, after a major Wall Street bank employing nine thousand people in New York, London and elsewhere had suffered a number of security incidents, it set up a surveillance system to monitor all incoming and outgoing e-mails and internal electronic communications transmitted over its computer network. Privacy campaigners would have had a field day, had they known. (It was a major undertaking at that time, given that the e-mails amounted to around 200 megabytes of material a day. Within three years, software packages were available to streamline such operations.)

The security team set up a fairly simple keyword search system, and the results were said to be 'incredible'. On the first search of the previous day's communications, it was discovered that employee social security numbers and other personal information had been transmitted over an open Internet connection. Thus the key to accessing the financial life of a number of employees was sent out over a system that had no protection. It was merely the beginning. All kinds of abuses and errors were discovered by using keyword spotting and keyword exclusion software; by far the majority were not from the usual 'disgruntled employee' but from people doing their job with a mixture of innocence, ignorance or lack of diligence.

The first security breach of proprietary material was discovered when the night-time investigators found via the e-mail back-up system that an incredible thirty-eight thousand lines of proprietary source code had been sent to a third party working at a firm which had supplied the software. This had been caused by a bug in the product. It was followed by three transmissions which included live passwords sent in clear text over the Internet. Then there was an incoming e-mail from an ex-worker asking one of his former colleagues for some proprietary information he had written during his time at the bank; the current employee sent off five hundred lines of material despite the warning it carried that the material might not be duplicated, disclosed to third parties or used for any unauthorised purpose. Clearly it went astray, for back came an e-mail: 'I've been hoping for these progs but they haven't arrived. Can you check my e-mail address? This will be mega brownie points for me to get it working so fast.'

Some of the illicit transmissions were due to pure human error. One new bank employee sent an e-mail to all her friends, with her new desk address and told them how much she enjoyed her job. Then, at the next stroke, she inadvertently sent the same people a confidential memo with a spreadsheet attachment detailing figures relating to an entire trading desk. There were, however, also numerous cases of system abuse thrown up by the monitoring of e-mail and internal communications. One trader was clearly running another business outside the bank, using the company's systems. His e-mails showed he was very busy directing others who worked for his private enterprise. These communications included some remarkably personal information, relating to his personal credit line, various trading positions, pricing contracts for other companies and so on, and the company spooks found it difficult to comprehend that he would risk using open networks to transmit it.

Another trader had set up his own business on the Web, and from intercepted e-mails it was clear that he was hoping it would expand to provide him with a full-time occupation and escape route from the bank. In the meantime, he filled in his time by disposing of some proprietary information to outside sources. One e-mail to an associate contained the blatant admission: 'I can't believe it: I made illicit entry into BG's office and grabbed a floppy with some graphic images we can use [on] our WWW site.' When he eventually discovered that the bank had set up an e-mail monitoring system, he promptly departed.

Over a six-month period of surveillance of the bank e-mail systems, the investigators discovered transmissions to outbound sources of four hundred thousand lines of proprietary source code material; risk management reports; derivatives sent to an employee working for a competitor; trading desk procedures; various transmissions which included user-name and passwords for internal systems; database passwords; trade confirmations of someone selling porno videos; and, in another glaring error, an Internet document which contained names and personal details of a number of retired bank employees.

The FBI was called in twice to investigate some of the abuses, including that of an employee who was leaving to join another company and had, prior to departure, transferred bank technology to his own computer system. The FBI eventually obtained a warrant to take possession of his computer and to search the systems of his new employer.

Among the security-trawled e-mails looked at by the investigating computer forensic team were many which included personal details but contained nothing illegal – merely private thoughts or accounts, perhaps of some sexual encounter. For instance: 'I met him after work and we drank a couple of bottles of wine, and went to the karaoke bar ... drank lots ... I can't resist him ... the next thing I remember is waking up naked in bed with him!' One manager, clearly under stress, was worried that he might be fired in forthcoming redundancies. His e-mail was monitored because he had once mentioned that he was a 'gun nut'. A security report on him recorded that he seemed quite normal but his e-mail was angry. In one missive to an ex-colleague, he spoke of 'all the obstacles and bullshit I run into every fucking day ... upper management is like a den of vipers. Don't bring up guns again at a party. Most people here in NY are fucking liberals and would throw the rest of us in deep dungeons. Every time I've said I'm pro-gun I'm treated like a criminal even though I legally own one.'

Early in the monitoring process, the bank made it known that all e-mail might be subject to scrutiny and that this might necessarily include transmissions of personal information. Contracts for new employees included a clause pointing out that the company maintained the right to audit e-mail systems which might include personal information. These moves did not stop security incidents.

Elsewhere, employers across the board began to hire specialist companies to keep watch over their e-mail and communications traffic. As new software was developed specially for the purpose, having e-mails, computer files and voicemail checked became one of the most common forms of employee surveillance. The software also included an ability to check Internet activity by employees and to record the sites visited.

LEGAL ACTION

Many employers soon discovered that their staff's use of the Internet and e-mail presented a number of legally fraught issues that in some cases ended up in court because there were no legal precedents, and because legislation varied from state to state and country to country. The issues included the establishment of clear rules – which few companies by then had done – governing employee access to and transmission of confidential company information and employee privacy rights over personal information. Many employers had failed even to consider formulating policy about the use of e-mails or making known the possibility of surveillance; conversely, many employees did not contemplate the idea that their e-mail activity might be subject to scrutiny. The two differing interests were soon to clash head-on, especially in globally trading companies which found themselves subject to the law of the country or state in which their factories or offices were located. For example, in some countries an employee's right to privacy might extend to e-mails on the company system, and scrutiny of them might be held to be an 'unreasonable intrusion upon the seclusion of another'.

The first known case to come to court involving the monitoring of e-mail occurred in 1997 when Michael A. Smyth sued his employers, the Pillsbury Company. Smyth's supervisor had sent him an e-mail on the office system which was received on his home computer. Smyth replied and there was an exchange of further e-mails, in one of which he referred to the company's sales managers and said he would like to 'kill the backstabbing bastards'. All of Smyth's messages on the company e-mail system were subsequently read, and he was sacked for making offensive comments. Smyth claimed wrongful dismissal and invasion of privacy, claiming that his employer had assured staff that e-mails would remain confidential. But the court ruled that this right was lost once the offensive threats had been made, and dismissed the case. A legal precedent was established: that the company's attempts to prevent inappropriate comments or possible illegal activity over its e-mail system outweighed the privacy rights the employee might previously have held.

Thereafter legal opinion and court adjudication swung back and forth, showing that at times the technology which employers use for surveillance of Internet use can be used against them. One woman claimed she had been sacked by her employer for no other reason than her age. Her lawyers did not hold out much hope of proving the case, since the company's personnel department had followed termination procedures to the letter. The employee remained convinced, however, and her lawyer decided to hire computer forensic consultants to examine the company's e-mail system. By using the latest software to retrieve deleted e-mail messages from the hard drive, they unearthed an e-mail headed 'For your eyes only' from the woman's boss to the head of the personnel department, demanding that they 'get rid of the tight-assed bitch'. Confronted with the printout, the company was advised by its own lawyers to settle out of court; it did so at a cost of $250,000.

The degree of variation in e-mail cases was also demonstrated by a case which went all the way to the Californian Court of Appeal, when two employees sued the Nissan Motor Company which had a declared policy of prohibiting the use of e-mail for personal reasons. The case arose when Bonita Bourke and her colleague Rhonda Hall were employed in the customer service department of a Nissan dealer. One of their colleagues was demonstrating the benefits of e-mail to a customer and selected an e-mail message sent by Bonita Bourke as an example. Unfortunately, the message selected was of a personal, sexual nature and not business-related.

Subsequently, their boss ordered a review of all e-mail on the company system and discovered several additional personal e-mail messages, including some with sexual content that had been sent by Bourke and Hall. The two women were given written warnings about the use of company e-mail. Bourke resigned and Hall was later fired. They jointly sued Nissan for invasion of privacy, wire tapping, eavesdropping and wrongful dismissal. Both claims were rejected on the grounds that they had signed an acknowledgement of company policy restricting use of e-mail for business purposes, and that they were aware that their e-mail messages were read by colleagues. The court also rejected the wire tapping claim on the grounds that accessing a computer network did not constitute tapping into a telephone line. Nissan had the right to connect to the system as the system operator, and so Nissan's conduct was not covered by the Penal Code.

Four female employees at Microsoft, on the other hand, were substantially compensated after receiving sexually explicit material via e-mail. They claimed sexual harassment after a number of pornographic images had been scanned into internal e-mail messages and transmitted between employees at the company's information and technology division. Microsoft denied its own involvement, but when lawyers discussed the finer points of company responsibility for communications networks they promptly made a $2.2 million payment to be shared among the four women and covered their legal expenses.

A similar award was made to female employees of a subsidiary of the Chevron Corporation. In that case, it was merely a 'sexually hostile statement' that was the cause of the problem. A document listing reasons why 'beer is better than women' was distributed over the company's e-mail system. The various statements, such as 'Beer does not demand equality' and 'A frigid beer is a good beer', might have been considered fairly innocuous in other circumstances. Although the company had not originated the statements, the court held that it was responsible because it had failed to ensure such material was not distributed over the system that it owned. Conversely, a Californian court had to decide whether an Internet service provider was liable for allegedly libellous statements posted on an employer's home page or bulletin board. In this case, a more standard defence was submitted: that the distributor – that is, the Internet company – may only be held liable if it could be shown that it was negligent in not recognising that the statement was defamatory, and in the absence of proof the case could not stand.

Both actions, however, presented further warnings to employers in all countries where similar laws may be applicable: responsibility for employees' actions can come home to roost. Many company executives had previously given little thought to the fact that the simple nature of e-mailing presented a situation that could cost them millions, certainly in the aggressive atmosphere of the US legal system which is also being picked up in the UK with many law firms now underwriting a variety of actions. More often, though, it is the company's inability to protect its own confidential information and trade secrets that causes most concern and which is, incidentally, the area that is least likely to come to court.

By and large, decisions in American courts do not appear to have come out in favour of regarding e-mail monitoring by employers as an invasion of privacy, mainly because the retrieval of messages from a company's own system has not generally been held to be telephone tapping. Even so, the indiscriminate surveillance of workers, manual or professional, has to some extent already been driven to covert operations, as, for example, in the case of the Wall Street bank which utilised keyword recognition software to scan the e-mails.

The starting point for such techniques really takes us into the realms of the heavy stuff: it takes us into the operations of the intelligence and law enforcement agencies, and, surprisingly enough, to a place in the tranquillity of the English countryside. . . .

PART II

■

THE AGENCIES – TIME FOR GREATER OVERSIGHT

CHAPTER 6
AN EYE ON THE WORLD: MENWITH HILL

THEY LOOM OUT OF THE LANDSCAPE like something from *The X-files*: a couple of dozen massive white domes that look like giant golf balls. Surrounded by grazing sheep, they are scattered across fields close to the A59 road about seven miles west of Harrogate in Yorkshire, in the north of England. At night, an eerie glow lights up the sky. The perimeter fence of razor wire is easily penetrated – and has been often by peace campaigners – but these days there are watchtowers, surveillance units and good old-fashioned guard dog patrols to keep the curious at bay. Those who show too much interest will soon discover a military jeep hurtling towards them, and will face questions about why they have lingered, even though they may be on a public road.

Officially, this place is called RAF Menwith Hill, which is a phoney title. It was given to provide the area with a legal identity as British military property and bring it under the laws governing national security; that is blanket secrecy and strictly no admittance. The only physical association with the British military lies in the fact that the sprawling base is on crown land and the fact that 370 employees of the Government Communication Headquarters and the Ministry of Defence are among the 1,983 who work there. The rest are all Americans, employed by the National Security Agency: mathematicians, linguists, physicists and computer scientists. To the National Security Agency this is Field Station F83, colloquially known as The

Hill. It is the largest spy base in the world and epitomises what spying in the twenty-first century is all about: electronics and interception. The place was described in a report to the European Parliament as a key centre, capable of routinely and indiscriminately monitoring all telephone calls, faxes, telexes, e-mails and the Internet across continental Europe and beyond.

The only official admission as to what goes on inside has come from the British – that it is a communications relay station – though from its very beginning it was geared exclusively to the interception of international signals traffic. It has been the home and often the inventor of core components of the Americans' international intelligence surveillance effort since its first faltering steps half a century ago. Since then, its four original radio masts have increased to the twenty-seven radomes – golfball-like protection covers which fit over the satellite dishes, masts and antennae. It is a totally self-sufficient operational centre with its own mini-town, houses, shops, a sports centre, chapel and electricity supply.

By 2000 it was central to a US-controlled network using a system codenamed Echelon that sprawls across the globe like a giant octopus, an Orwellian symbol of hate and menace to all who campaign on behalf of privacy, freedom and other basic human rights. The Hill is well known to Internet researchers, investigative writers and tight-lipped politicians as the most sensitive of all those strategically positioned installations whose purpose is to eavesdrop on the world's signals and communications traffic. British CND campaigners keep a watching brief at its gates, the Menwith Women's Peace Camp was set up right on its perimeter in the early 1990s and they were joined by the Campaign for the Accountability of American Bases. All have had regular brushes with the law and have been under observation by MI5, anxious to limit damage to Anglo–US relations over this very sensitive issue. For five decades, successive government spokesmen on both sides of the Atlantic have steadfastly refused to confirm the existence of Menwith Hill, let alone its true function. However, it is with Menwith Hill that any proper investigation of state-run security agencies should begin.

THE HISTORY OF MENWITH HILL

The high-level classification of secrecy assigned to The Hill and the extreme measures of security vetting which were applied to all personnel dates back to an agreement signed soon after World War II. It was then that the Americans, with the willing participation of the British and other wartime Allies, took the first steps towards the assembly of a massive global interception network, primarily targeted at the Communist bloc but not necessarily excluding the monitoring of allies, friends, neighbours – and their own citizens.

This formal policy of Sigint (Signals Intelligence) and Comint (Communications Intelligence) cooperation between the British and Americans was first established when signals intelligence experts from the two nations began pooling their intelligence against the Germans and Japanese during World War II. On 8 July 1940, when the USA was still neutral, Winston Churchill despatched the British Ambassador, Lord Lothian, to the White House bearing an offer to hand over Britain's latest developments in radar and other scientific discoveries, in which the USA was known to lag far behind, in exchange for information which Britain badly needed.

The offer was made formal two days later with a letter to President Roosevelt from Lothian:

> Should you approve the exchange of information . . . it is
> suggested that in order to avoid any risk of the information
> reaching our enemy, a small secret mission of three service
> officers and civilian scientists should be despatched to this
> country immediately. . . . His Majesty's Government would
> greatly appreciate it if the United States Government, having
> been given full details of any British equipment or devices,
> would reciprocate by discussing certain secret information
> which our technical experts are anxious to have, urgently.

That deal was done, and limited cooperation began. It was not until April 1943 that Churchill finally agreed to reveal to the USA Britain's most secret and remarkable intelligence achievement: that code-breakers at Bletchley Park – Station X – had captured and unravelled the ingenious Enigma cipher used by the Germans for all high-level communications. The Americans could barely believe it, given that the settings for the Enigma machine were changed every day and that the German operators had 159 million million possibilities.

From that moment, the USA became exceptionally keen to maintain and extend links with Britain and eager to formalise the arrangement. On 17 May 1943, the two countries put cooperation between their communications intelligence agencies on a firm footing with what was known as the BRUSA (Britain/USA) Agreement. The Americans were quite certain they had achieved the better end of the deal which was not necessarily true. But the agreement more or less set in stone what was to prove to be one of the most significant and long-lasting Anglo-American pacts in history, despite occasional fallings-out. From the outset, the agreement would permit an ongoing exchange of technical experts and all highly sensitive material collected by BRUSA interceptions of international signals and communications traffic.

Methods for the collection and distribution of intelligence were also drawn up on a cooperative basis and all those engaged in each stage of intelligence gathering, from interception to final delivery, were bound by a rigid security code. The arrangement was further enhanced by Britain's ability to deliver the cooperation of some of the Commonwealth countries – Canada, Australia and New Zealand. On 13 March 1944 representatives of the code-breaking agencies of those nations, together with the British and Americans, attended a top secret conference at Arlington, Virginia. It proved to be a landmark meeting of minds. From those initial discussions emerged a blueprint, energetically pursued by the Americans, for post-war cooperation whose importance took on ever greater proportions when the Iron Curtain slammed shut.

US post-war intelligence chiefs were pushed hard (although with little true guidance) by the Central Intelligence Agency, newly formed out of the Office of Strategic Services. It was keen and ambitious, desperate for an eye on the other side. By the spring of 1947 the Cold War was in full swing and the USA came up with a master plan for 'global oversight'. It was just one of the grandiose schemes that emerged in that era, ranging from plans to assassinate troublesome world figures to experiments with LSD in order to bend the minds of agents and double-agents.

By the summer of 1947 US security chiefs had agreed a deal with their partners – some of whose negotiators were less than enthusiastic – for what became known as the UKUSA Agreement. The cooperative effort came into being in an atmosphere of mounting hysteria over Reds under every bed which was further aroused by the witch-hunts of Senator Joe McCarthy and the outrageous and illegal wire-taps engineered by FBI chief J. Edgar Hoover – one of the most evil influences in twentieth-century surveillance.

America was referred to as the first party to the agreement, with the UK, Canada, Australia and New Zealand as the second parties, although the UK remained linked to the 'special' relationship that existed during the war. It was aimed largely at cooperation on signals interception and from that standpoint the NSA and GCHQ, along with their Commonwealth counterparts, became what one source described as 'blood brothers' in their pursuit of global Sigint surveillance. The same could not be said for the relationship between the emerging post-war mainstream intelligence agencies of Britain and the USA. The newly founded CIA was regarded as a bunch of cowboys by MI6, while the Americans thought the British Intelligence services were run by puffed up, arrogant snobs and riddled with traitors. Both sides were not entirely wrong.

The signals intelligence people disregarded this side-show of squabbles and carved up the globe between them, each taking a portion in line with their geographical position and interception capabilities. The American government would very largely fund the hardware; it was certainly beyond Britain's ability in such austere times. Coverage was aimed principally against Communist countries. Australia's Sigint department took responsibility for southern China and the Indo-China region and gave extended cover especially at the time of the Vietnam War, in which it became embroiled. New Zealand cast its net over the western Pacific, Canada watched the Soviet Union's polar regions, while Britain was responsible for the Soviet Union west of the Urals, Africa and Europe. America's own stations were capable, even from the early days, of surveillance over northern China, Asia, Asiatic Russia and Latin America.

The intelligence cooperative was later extended to include surveillance sites at US bases in West Germany, Japan and South Korea. In addition, the USA put up a surveillance wall which ran from the bottom of the ocean, where undersea telephone cables could be monitored, through submarines to airborne surveillance using aircraft such as U-2s and, in 1962, satellites whose transmissions came back to Menwith Hill.

The rules demanding utmost secrecy, established with the wartime BRUSA Agreement, were reinforced and covered all members of the cooperative. The existence of the UKUSA Agreement was never to be publicly admitted, nor was it by any of those nations for fifty-two years, until March 1999 when the Australian government confirmed in writing to an Australian television reporter, Ross Coulthart, that its signals intelligence agency, Defence Signals Directorate, cooperated with counterpart signals intelligence organisations overseas under the UKUSA relationship.

Elsewhere, there was a rigid clampdown on any information relating to UKUSA or its later offshoots. That included the detail on a seemingly unimportant website of tittle-tattle run by an organisation called the 13th USASA Field Station Association. This is a group of veterans who at some time in their careers were assigned to the US Army Security Agency and who, specifically, worked at The Hill between 1958 and 1966. Although the US military handed over control of Menwith to civilian personnel from the National Security Agency in 1966, what went on there even in the early days remains as stringently policed as ever. When I approached the association for members' reminiscences, the response was an emphatic no. Nor did it end there. Members were urged to have nothing to do with media enquiries from the UK because: 'it could be directed toward embarrassing the US government, the US Army and creating a lot of mischief. The bottom line is that we are reviewing the content on our [Web] page just so it doesn't lead on to more questions ... there is a larger issue at stake here. We have no desire to contribute to any news or publication to include affirming or denying open source material. We accumulated our knowledge on a need to know basis ... our mission was confidential. It still is.'

It was an interesting turn of phrase: 'no affirmation or denial' about Menwith Hill must be given. It is exactly the phrase that the National Security Agency itself still uses – as indeed have British government spokesmen – when challenged about the establishment. According to the National Security Agency in October 1999, confirmation of either the 'existence or nonexistence' of an intercept station at Menwith was itself classified information, despite detailed leakage of its operational capability published by investigative journalists and authors in the last decade or so. In fact, as far as the 13th Field Station is concerned, the National Security Agency clearly believes that information about members' activities all those years ago still falls within the category of confirmation or denial, and is thus classified. Those servicemen arrived at Menwith Hill when it was just a desolate building site in a sea of mud.

In those early days, the US Army Security Agency provided a core contingent of young men skilled in electronics, signals and communications. They were surrounded by a force of regular troops with the dual role of protecting the installations as they were being built and convincing the locals that Menwith was just an ordinary US base, one of many in the UK such as RAF Molesworth, Alconbury and Mildenhall (although the latter two were also doubling as reconnaissance bases for the CIA).

However, as at most US bases in the UK, many Menwith servicemen were to marry local girls who had been regularly bussed into the base from surrounding towns for dances. 'It was party time,' one writes on the website of the arrival of the girls. 'You could find them in the bathrooms, the cloakroom, in parked cars that were not locked and even in the vestibule of the chapel.' This gave the US Army a few headaches. The security clearance rules governing operatives at the base did not permit marriage to foreigners. It was not until November 1960 that the Counterintelligence Corps granted a waiver for the first of these marriages, and allowed the man in question to retain his security clearance and remain at The Hill. But that did not necessarily mean the clearance would be extended back in the United States. One Morse intercept operative recalled that, having married a girl from Knaresborough in the base chapel in a ceremony conducted by the base chaplain, they returned to the United States. Here, now out of the army, he tried to rejoin the security services in the same line of work. He 'called the secret National Security Agency phone number', with which they were all supplied in case of emergencies, and went for an interview. His application, however, was turned down because his wife was not an American. It was considered that a non-American spouse might pose problems.

From those beginnings to the present day, the security procedures surrounding Menwith, built on British soil and operated partly by GCHQ yet under the control of the National Security Agency from 1966, have merely been strengthened. The base extends to 560 acres with two large operations blocks covering almost five acres and a visually spectacular array of dishes, domes and antennae.

It began its operations by monitoring international cable and microwave communications passing through Britain, but they all had to be laboriously intercepted by manual effort. In the mid-1960s, however, Menwith Hill installed one of the first major IBM computers. This was a breakthrough for National Security Agency operatives, who could now mount the first automated intercepts of unenciphered telex messages. As the technology improved, the National Security Agency acquired the ability, under its own intercept programme codenamed Shamrock, to collect all cable and telex traffic from three US telegraph companies.

Added to this, according to James Bamford in his acclaimed book *The Puzzle Palace*, it could now also 'have access to the miles and miles of traffic flowing in and out of the British commercial telegraph system … once received, the tapes would be processed through National Security Agency watch-list alerted computers. Thus the National Security Agency was able to ransack the entire United Kingdom telex and cable systems to locate a reference to Jane Fonda or Muamma Gaddafi.'

The results were, in those early days, considered astounding and the Americans insisted that the security of all personnel should be 'hammered down', especially in Britain which at the time had a Labour government, a Prime Minister – Harold Wilson – whom certain elements of the CIA believed was a Soviet agent, and an intelligence service that had a recent history of being rather leaky.

Menwith became the premier intercept station in the global system as, from 1962, the Americans put more and more intelligence-linked satellites into orbit. Low Earth-orbiting satellites were launched for the specific purpose of intercepting signals from the Soviets, China and other nations' air defence, nuclear weapons tests and early-warning radar systems. The arrival of commercial satellite communications provided another unmissable opportunity for the UKUSA eavesdroppers when on 6 April 1965 the international telecommunications satellite

Intelsat 1 went into orbit to establish the first satellite television and telephone link between America and Europe.

International calls to and from England, for example, were transmitted via satellite from stations at Madley in Herefordshire and at Goonhilly Down near Falmouth in Cornwall. The National Security Agency naturally encouraged its friends at GCHQ to press for the building of two 100-foot dishes near Bude, little more than fifty miles from the Goonhilly site. When Harold Wilson's Labour government baulked at the cost, National Security Agency director Pat Carter and his deputy Louis Tordella played the security card and insisted that the installations were vital to the UKUSA set-up. As Bamford noted in *The Puzzle Palace* when approval was given, the then director of GCHQ wrote to his friend Pat Carter suggesting that 'the aerials at Bude ought to be christened Pat and Louis'.

The advent of satellite communications opened up incredible new interception opportunities, and additional powers for the National Security Agency. US intelligence chiefs, thrilled with the quality of National Security Agency interceptions, wanted to put the agency 'above the clouds' – by which it meant that it was to become almost untouchable, less accountable even than the CIA. Although initially charged with providing military intelligence, the NSA assumed control over all the signals intelligence activities of the US military services. Already wielding heavy responsibilities and power, the role of the NSA was extended further for what the organisation itself describes as 'centralised co-ordination, direction and performance of highly specialised functions in support of US government information systems and [to] produce foreign intelligence information ... it is also the nation's cryptologic organisation and employs the country's leading code-makers and code-breakers'.

As such, it became the managing director of the collection and dissemination of material intercepted and otherwise obtained by ground stations and other facilities scattered across the globe. In this objective its number one partner was GCHQ, with whom its relationship faltered only once, during Britain's ill-fated invasion of Egypt during the Suez crisis of 1956. It was NSA intercepts that informed President Eisenhower of the combined Anglo-French invasion plans, to which Eisenhower promptly responded with threats to face Britain with a run on the pound if it did not pull out immediately. That incident apart, the NSA and GCHQ were very close, although the Americans had the controlling interest through their financial input.

The NSA – well aware of the economic implications for the USA – demanded that, as the technological advances heightened, local employees of fields stations in other UKUSA countries should be subjected to an even higher level of security vetting. The agency produced a document which it described as an 'oath of indoctrination' – a declaration to be signed, for example, by all British personnel. It stated: 'I fully understand that the information relating to the manner and extent of the interception of communications of foreign powers by HM Government and other co-operating governments and the intelligence produced by such interception known as Communications Intelligence (COMINT) is information covered by Section 2 of the Official Secrets Act 1911 (as amended).' The irony of all this was that the two spies who sold the secrets of America's first Rhyolite satellite communications intercepts of Soviet communications traffic monitored at Menwith Hill were Americans who worked for one of the contractors building the machines in the United States.

In 1967, opposition MPs in Australia attempted to discover the NSA's involvement in the country's intelligence and intercept stations, notably at Pine Gap. Australians also had a very close relationship with Britain's GCHQ – so close that one expert said they were virtually 'as one'. Pine Gap was as important to the UKUSA operations at Menwith Hill as was its Bad Aibling sister base in West Germany. The Australian government followed the standard procedure of refusing to confirm or deny the existence of any such stations or of an alliance with other nations. It also invoked a D-Notice, which prohibited media coverage of the monitoring activities. Thirty years later, a very similar response was churned out by the British government, by then in the hands of New Labour. In opposition during the Thatcher years Labour MPs, like the Australians, had on several occasions tried to bring into the public domain some pertinent facts about Menwith Hill and similar bases in Britain. In 1997, they found themselves protecting them with the same vigour.

Privately, the strength of the relationship between the NSA and GCHQ during the 1960s was evident from a letter sent by Sir Leonard

'Joe' Hooper, director of GCHQ, to General Pat Carter on his retirement as director of the NSA in 1969 and quoted in *The Puzzle Palace*:

> Though the extent of our working partnership was new to you ... you showed an instinctive feeling for its nature and depth which was a great strength to those of us who had worked so long in it ... you have consistently gone out of your way to help us sustain and if possible improve our contribution to it ... for this we are very grateful ... you have given every encouragement and made us feel that GCHQ really mattered to Director NSA. I think you believe, as I do, that the professional relationship between the two Agencies remains of great importance to our two countries ... we at GCHQ will do our best to assist NSA in continuing its great and important mission.

It was a crucial time for the pact. As well as the commercial satellite interceptions, the American Rhyolite signals intelligence collection project began in 1970 and over the next seven years five satellites were put into orbit to read the telemetry signals from Soviet and Chinese missile texts. They were also used for a general interception of communications across VHF, UHF and microwave frequency bands and, by 1974, could monitor with ease microwave radio and long-distance telephone calls from Europe to the Far East. They were capable of capturing the conversation, it has been said, of a Soviet general in Moscow talking to his mistress in Yalta. On 12 July 1977, *Newsweek* (and later the *Washington Post*) reported they picked up walkie-talkie traffic of Russian military exercises and once intercepted the Russian leader, Leonid Brezhnev, talking on his car telephone to his defence chief about slotting new weapons into old cases ahead of the arms limitations talks with the Americans.

In 1985, Menwith was given 'expanded mission' status by the NSA. Considerable extension of its interception capabilities was initiated, with part funding by Margaret Thatcher's government and input from British Telecom and the British Ministry of Defence. The expansion included a 50,000 square foot extension to the Operations Building and massive new generators to cater for a new Earth terminal system to support the classified satellite systems. The improvement to this section of the base reportedly cost almost $160 million. Further work and the building of additional radomes continued throughout the 1990s to bring on-line additional systems for data collection from new and larger satellite systems, together capable of monitoring signals communications and commercial satellite traffic across the world.

The station received an award presented internally by the US military for support to naval operations in the Gulf from 1987 to 1988 and another in 1991 for its work before, during and after the Gulf War. The development of Menwith's capability ran parallel to the new hardware and space technology developed to keep the UKUSA partnership abreast of all new commercial and military reconnaissance hardware. Several existing bases were substantially improved in the last decade of the twentieth century, including the one at Bad Aibling in Germany.

The proliferation of Intelsat and Inmarsat satellites, which carry the vast majority of phone and fax communications between countries and continents, required the upgrading and expansion of the interception sites. Intelsat satellites primarily carry civilian traffic, but they do additionally carry foreign diplomatic and government communications that are apparently of particular interest to the UKUSA parties.

At Morwenstow, Cornwall, England, two thirty-metre antennae built specifically for commercial satellite interceptions supply data from Intelsats over the Indian Ocean and the Atlantic. A third Intelsat interception site is at Yakima in Washington state, positioned to capture communications passing through the Pacific Ocean Intelsat satellite. Other stations for additional satellite communications interception have been sited in the Caribbean, Canada, Western Australia, New Zealand and America. By the end of the century American intelligence had the ability to intercept most of the world's important mobile communications and signals intelligence. The four UKUSA partners, who otherwise, surely, would have pulled out, benefit from sharing the information obtained.

At the heart of this operation was Menwith Hill, a key player in a further development that was to bring uproar in Europe and inspire the marshalling of concerted protests by privacy campaigners in Britain and the USA in the last year of the twentieth century.

CHAPTER 7
THE ECHELON FACTOR

BY ITS OWN ADMISSION the NSA, with a good deal of help from its friends across the water, especially GCHQ, led the world in eavesdropping technology. The system was in place and a huge amount of intercepted intelligence was being scooped out of the ether from the satellite, microwave, cellular and fibre-optic traffic every minute of every day for reading and analysis, a task so onerous that it was, and still is, difficult to quantify. This chapter explores the powerful processing system created to handle this material – Echelon – and the uses to which it has been put.

INFORMATION OVERLOAD

The level of information was wide-ranging in both subject matter and importance, targeted during the Cold War days principally towards the Soviet Union – which was doing the same thing from its own international network of spy stations, the largest of which was in Cuba. The purpose, in theory, was to read military, diplomatic and government signals and communications, ostensibly to reinforce the security and economic wellbeing of the individual nations concerned.

As the scope of interception became more sophisticated and widespread, the amount of material gathered increased to staggering proportions, ranging from the minutiae of inter-embassy communications to signals between intelligence agents positioned around the world, and on through the whole gamut of operations up to the serious business of monitoring high-level, top secret government activity and telemetry.

This activity did not include wire tapping in the accepted sense. The tapping of individual or groups of telephone lines or any form of electronic communication by law enforcement or intelligence agencies, from the police to MI5, the FBI or the CIA, was governed, as we shall see, by a totally different umbrella of legal requirements. In all the countries covered by the UKUSA Agreement, the agencies had to obtain formal warrants from the judiciary or government bodies before proceeding with their interceptions which, at that level, were usually in conjunction with a specific investigation relating to crime, terrorism, subversive activities or a suspected spy.

The Sigint (Signals Intelligence) and Comint (Communications Intelligence) interceptions, on the other hand, were generally carried out under the heading of national security and did not need specific warrants. The reasoning in official terms was the same one that had governed intelligence gathering for decades – that it was necessary to keep watch on the enemy within, as well as on the opposition abroad. Blanket surveillance is beyond precise formalities, although surveillance by whatever means against US citizens within the borders of the USA is supposedly illegal without authorisation from a separate and secret judiciary group. According to Washington academic and human rights campaigner Patrick S. Poole, a fellow of the US Free Congress Organisation, in his essay 'America's Spy in the Sky', this group has never refused an application by the National Security Agency since its formation in 1952.

There were, in any event, always ways and means of getting past legal obstacles. There was no reason why the Americans should not conduct surveillance against a non-American in Canada or the UK – or anywhere else in the world – who happened to be talking to a resident in the USA. Identification of person-to-person situations was regularly pursued, so that the name and location of the recipient of a call in the USA from a person in Europe could be noted and, if necessary, become the subject of closer observation. Overseas intelligence operatives were not governed by the same restrictions. Intelligence whistle-blowers have therefore claimed that, by utilising British or Canadian personnel at the NSA headquarters or any of the field stations, intercepts of American citizens could be achieved legally. The same situation in reverse could be applied elsewhere in the five-nation partnership.

So how was this dissemination of material achieved? Could the wood be seen through the trees? And just what did all this information contain? The piles of often tedious and inconsequential paperwork that occupied the hours of analysts and code-breakers in days past had simply grown larger and larger. Keywords and watch-list search systems had been around for years to search intercepts, a task which was dealt with manually until the late 1960s. Specialists who worked at US signals interception in the 1960s would spend hours gazing at printouts of commercial telexes which had been collected for analysis. Each was given a list of about a hundred words to watch for, and they did not focus merely on activity among the Communist nations or other political or diplomatic situations. Lists included commercial traffic, especially relating to commodities that major conglomerates were selling, like iron and steel and gas. This information would be passed on to US firms to improve their chances of beating the competition. Similarly, a US aerospace worker who was at Menwith Hill in the 1970s and 1980s also witnessed the interception of civilian and commercial communications and listened to 'real-time' interception of voice communications; one of those monitored was a US senator (see below). The incoming material was checked for general content and for matching words from the lists compiled by national intelligence agencies, which included names, organisations, locations and other specifics which US intelligence wanted to keep an eye on.

In time the labour-hungry process of transcription, translation and dissemination became virtually unmanageable. By the 1980s, with the increasing efficiency of the global network, mere computerisation of the procedure could not necessarily provide the solution to overload. The pressure was on to meet the needs of the immediate future, at a time when the end of the Cold War was not even imagined. Indeed, it was in deep freeze as the Reagan administration pursued its 1980s' Star Wars project of space-age weapons which owed much to fiction and spin but had the Soviets worried.

PROJECT P-415 - ECHELON

According to British investigative journalist Duncan Campbell's *Interception Capabilities 2000* report to the Director General for Research of the European Parliament, Scientific and Technological Options Assessment Unit, a specialist team of NSA/GCHQ personnel and outside contractors, codenamed Project P-415, began working round the clock to solve the problem of disseminating acquired intelligence. Out of it came what is today known as the Echelon system, a keyword search and find concept for filtering intercepts. It works on the same principle as an Internet search engine, ferreting out targeted groups and names and, at the same time, substantially increasing the scope of existing monitoring techniques. The creation of Echelon was very much a partnership operation between the NSA, which provided most of the funding, Britain's GCHQ, the Communications Security Establishment (CSE) in Canada, the Defence Signals Directorate (DSD) of Australia and the Government Communications Security Bureau (GCSB) of New Zealand. It transformed the procedures of analysing and assessing intercepted material.

The old watch-lists were replaced by computerised databases of words, phrases, names, organisations, corporations, labour unions, addresses, telephone numbers and other keyword recognition prompts amounting to thousands of samples. Each station had its own 'dictionary' of local names and organisations. The system was originally revealed by the research of Duncan Campbell and New Zealand activist turned author Nicky Hager. Both have written comprehensively on the subject.

Data from the intercepts taken from international telecommunications systems can be collated and stored and run past the dictionaries. Any matches, however insignificant, can be plucked out and fed through two further filtering operations before being forwarded to analysts for human evaluation. An oversimplified analogy might be that of a family of five darting through the local supermarket with their trolleys, emptying the shelves of all that they could carry but then waiting until they got home to sort through it and decide what they actually wanted.

With the global link of interception established under the UKUSA post-war agreement, by the nature of the system the progression into non-military usage became inevitable. Between them, seven specific Echelon stations in the participating countries can monitor communications satellites, land-based networks and radio communications. Intercepted data pours in and millions of stored communication messages can be matched against each local dictionary.

In its most up-to-date form, Echelon can detect matches from interceptions of telexes, faxes, e-mails and Internet documents, in fact all forms of modern communications, virtually without exception. Telephone conversations can be monitored in various ways. According to former Canadian Security Establishment agent Mike Frost, co-author of *Spyworld*, published in 1994, a voice recognition system called Oratory has been used for some years to intercept diplomatic calls. Voice recognition remains one of the most crucial areas for experiment and, as this book is being written, is not far from becoming another general-use tool of the intelligence community.

What Echelon can provide is a database of voiceprints of known personalities which include many names totally unconnected with espionage or organised crime. The voice on the intercepts can be matched and identified against the stored voiceprints.

MONITORING DIANA AND THE ROYAL FAMILY

American sources believe that this and general interception were used, for example, to monitor Diana, Princess of Wales. At the time of her death the NSA held 1056 pages of fairly recent transcripts relating to Princess Diana; it insisted that its records were 'currently and properly classified' and if made public could 'cause exceptionally grave damage to the national security'. It is difficult to accept that explanation.

The files, according to my sources, include material gleaned from NSA interceptions made on both British and American soil, as well as elsewhere in Europe. Their existence was confirmed from applications to view NSA documents under the US Freedom of Information procedures, a request which brought a firm refusal. The 'classified' files are also thought to contain interceptions relating to personal telephone conversations between the Princess and Dodi Fayed, who was killed with her in the Paris car crash. A small selection was made available to French investigators during the inquiry into the crash.

The US intelligence community would say the interceptions were made to protect her from terrorists. Such protection, of course, was necessary and applies to all such prominent international citizens and even showbusiness personalities. Monitoring personal and private conversations is part of the deal, and most people subject to such surveillance know it. The NSA is, according to US intelligence expert John Pike, curator of the Federation of American Scientists' on-line archive, 'insatiably curious and monitors everyone of significance'.

Hundreds of other pages of NSA and CIA documents demonstrate the close observation of Diana's movements and words while in the USA and overseas. The few documents that have been declassified showed once again the level of minutiae to which the collation of material on high-profile personalities falls. There are reports from CIA agents, embassy officials and other American personnel around the world. All contained a long list of names for distribution and analysis within the US intelligence system.

This is not unusual, of course, because all intelligence about well-known international figures is based upon reports which start from the ground up, and which contain information which is no more secret than, for example, the daily list of duties to be performed by members of the Royal Family. Some pages detailing Diana's movements, whether in Paris or Africa, amount to little more than a daily diary of her activities. But then the coverage begins to get more sinister and has little to do with wanting to protect her from terrorists. Numerous pages, for instance, relate to the monitoring of the Princess's stance on landmines and the views she expressed after visiting areas where dozens of children had been mutilated by explosions. She supported campaigners who were highly critical of nations which paid only lip-service to scaling out production – the USA included – and so those organisations too were added to the Echelon dictionaries.

The reports of her speeches and summaries of her movements, running to more than seven hundred declassified pages, were drawn in by several agencies including the CIA; why it was even necessary for US embassies or CIA intelligence people to circulate the Princess's views on that topic to such a long list of intelligence personnel remains one of the more abiding mysteries of this particular situation. The mere confirmation of the existence of these documents is in itself something of an embarrassment to the USA. Undoubtedly, the content of those documents which the NSA refused to declassify is worse. This is not, however, to support the ridiculous theory peddled by Mohammed Al Fayed that the British secret service murdered Diana and Dodi on the orders of Prince Philip, or indeed to support any of the allegations he made on this issue. There were other intercepts involving Diana and Prince Charles that cannot be quite so easily explained. These chapters do not run with conspiracy theories. However, given the facts that have now emerged, it remains an intriguing situation that taped calls involving the most controversial members of the British Royal Family appeared in print in the space of a few days – between Diana and James Gilbey (the Squidgey Tapes), and between Charles and his lover Camilla Parker-Bowles (the Camillagate Tapes), both tapes made in 1989, along with a fairly innocuous recording of a conversation between Sarah, Duchess of York and her husband Prince Andrew, and another between Prince Philip and a female relative.

Given the atmosphere in the Royal household at the time, it was a natural progression for journalists of the day to suggest that it was no accident that these conversations were plucked out of the sky by amateur snoops using cheap scanners. It was suggested after publication of transcripts of the tapes that they were skilful recordings and could have been the product of interception, rebroadcast by the security services. What gave the story credence was that the Diana tapes were picked up by *two* people miles apart, with scanners and tape recorders at the ready – and, when attempting to sell them to newspapers, they both gave different dates upon which they made the recordings.

MI5 was in the frame. The agency itself denied involvement in any interception of the Royal Family. The Diana tapes, especially, gave grounds for sixth senses and gut feelings to come into play; but there was no proof nor has any emerged since, and so, like the events on the Grassy Knoll, the site of the assassination of President Kennedy, the tapes must be consigned to the file marked 'Intriguing Mysteries'. It is possible to accept the word of MI5 that they did not intercept Diana's telephone calls – at least, not on that occasion. But they may well have known someone who did. Diana had enemies in high places for whom any request for the bugging or surveillance of her – or of any member of the Royal Family or government – would not be difficult to arrange, even on a private basis.

PUBLIC ACCOUNTABILITY

As ever, the NSA remains steadfast in retaining control of any matters relating to public divulgence of its activities, and that is doubtless one of the reasons why, under the Echelon system, the NSA made certain it was able to tighten its grip on the material made available to its UKUSA partners. It has become apparent that it is not obliged to show any of those nations material which it would prefer to keep to itself. Specifically, targeted interceptions on behalf of its 'customers' – intelligence and security agencies of all member governments – will be delivered as required by prearranged agreements. The rest, according to the report entitled *An Appraisal of the Technology of Political Control*, presented by the Omega Foundation in Manchester to the Scientific and Technological Options Assessment Unit of the European Parliament in December 1997, is routed directly into the NSA computers at Fort Meade, giving the NSA the bulk of the booty and the mammoth task of sifting the material. By far the greater proportion is filtered out and discarded; much less than 10 per cent of all Sigint and Comint interceptions actually reach the human eye for assessment.

At the British end of the operation, the Echelon dictionaries are controlled and managed by GCHQ in Cheltenham but, according to Duncan Campbell, they were originally operated by security vetted staff employed by British Telecom in the same way that the FBI ran its legal operations in the USA. The BT relationship with the intelligence services stretches way back into the earliest days of manual telephone tapping, when the company was in state ownership. Under privatisation of the telecom network nothing has changed and the skills of BT technicians are still required by virtually every section of the British security and intelligence community. On occasions this involvement has become embarrassingly public, as at York Crown Court in September 1997 when two women peace campaigners were appealing against a conviction for trespass on the Menwith Hill complex. The judge angrily criticised

British Telecom for sending documents and a witness to the court to reveal details of top secret high-capacity cables which ran to and from Menwith Hill. BT admitted that they had connected three digital optical fibre cables which were later assessed to be capable of carrying more than a hundred thousand telephone calls at any one time into the base. Since there was no way the base itself could use such a facility, the implication was that the calls were being intercepted.

Electronics experts do not consider it a coincidence, either, that another British Telecom installation, a microwave transmitter called Hunters Stone Tower, which relays hundreds of thousands of calls, was built just four miles away from Menwith Hill and also has connections to the base. At the trial, the BT input developed into something of a fiasco when it sent a solicitor to court to withdraw the documents and evidence given the previous day. Judge Crabtree, having been briefed privately in his chambers by the solicitor, launched into his broadside against BT who, he said, had no business whatsoever to make the disclosures. Furthermore, he said, it was immaterial whether the Menwith Hill station was spying on British citizens and commercial communications and might have cost British companies billions of dollars in lost sales. Applying curious legal logic, he insisted: 'The national interest of the United Kingdom, even if conducted dishonestly, requires this to be kept secret. The methods of communicating to and from Menwith Hill, whether military intelligence or commercial spying, is clearly secret information. The governments of the United States and United Kingdom do not want this information to be divulged. [Evidence] of BT's secret cables in and out of Menwith cannot be withdrawn. Half the cat is out of the bag ... I just don't know what BT think they were doing.'

The document produced at the trial by BT showed that under the auspices of the Post Office, Menwith Hill had been provided with wide bandwidth circuits in 1975, connected on a coaxial cable to the microwave station at Hunters Stone. This station was part of the microwave network which in the 1970s and 1980s carried almost all of Britain's long-distance telephone calls. Afterwards, BT angered by the judge's words, hinted that other telecom companies were also involved in providing tapping facilities at Menwith Hill. Labour's former Technology Minister Tony Benn was also called to give evidence at the trial. He had been Postmaster General when the cables connecting

Menwith Hill to the British communications system were first installed. He said that, although a member of Prime Minister Harold Wilson's Cabinet and a Privy Councillor, he knew nothing of the secret arrangement between the British government and the Americans.

Members of Parliament in Britain – as in other countries party to the agreement – continued to be kept in the dark. Repeated attempts to force some public disclosure about the Echelon system and the activities of the Menwith Hill base failed at the first hurdle. Responses were usually curt and unrevealing, with ministers ducking for cover under the protection of official secrecy. More detail than usual, however, slipped out in a two-sentence reply to an MP who in July 1997 asked in the House of Commons what steps had been taken to ensure that American personnel at Menwith Hill were not monitoring United Kingdom diplomatic and economic communications. (The inference from that question, incidentally, was that all other communications *were* being monitored.) Dr John Reid, the then Defence Minister, replied: 'Senior UK personnel are integrated into every level at RAF Menwith Hill and we are thus in a position to be entirely confident that British staff are aware of all facets of operations and that no activity considered inimical to British interests is carried out there.' It was an interesting reply which, as usual, confirmed or denied nothing but by implication finally admitted publicly for the first time that the British government was aware of everything that went on at The Hill (legal or otherwise, as pondered by Judge Crabtree at York Crown Court) and that GCHQ personnel were engaged at every level of operations.

Occasionally, Echelon and the increasingly expensive techniques of surveillance attracted the scrutiny of government watchdogs, against whom the NSA's global operations were vociferously defended by senior staff and their supporters in government. Similar situations took place within the other UKUSA nations. For almost forty years the answers were generally along the same well-rehearsed lines, with only slightly less paranoia than in America, as being totally necessary and principally designed to combat the forces of Communism.

That premise was supported by a half-century of intelligence agencies pitted against intelligence agencies and a history of spy scandals, nuclear threat and the race for control of space. There were an abundance of side issues which could also be offered in support, such as the

rise of state-sponsored and random terrorism during the 1970s, instability in the Middle East, the Iranian hostage crisis, Afghanistan, the
Lebanon, the IRA and the unpredictable manoeuvres of such leaders as
Colonel Gaddafi and Saddam Hussein. Even so – and even before the
end of the Cold War – there were fears and speculation among journalists, politicians and human rights campaigners that surveillance was
going beyond the criteria of national security and extending rapidly into
mass observation of industry and individuals, mostly because of their
political affiliations or, as in the case of Princess Diana, because of their
high profile.

Gradually the suspicion was building up that legal processes
authorising the targeting of individuals were being side-stepped by
other means, notably by the Echelon system. There is now little doubt
that Echelon will provide the means of interception of civilian communications well into the twenty-first century. As early as 1975 Senator
Frank Church, chairing congressional hearings on such matters, warned
that the technological powers of the NSA could, at some point in the
future, be turned on the American people (and, by implication, all those
in the UKUSA sphere): '... no American would have any privacy left.
There would be no place to hide ... the technological capacity that the
Intelligence Community has given the government could enable it to
impose total tyranny. There would be no way to fight back, because the
most careful effort to combine together in resistance to the government,
no matter how privately it was done, is within the reach of the government to know. Such is the capacity of this technology.'

SURVEILLANCE AFTER THE COLD WAR

Not many years passed before the NSA/GCHQ had the ability to conduct
surveillance against whomever they wished. The collapse of
Communism and the KGB did nothing to curtail either operations or the
development of new, improved techniques. The much-vaunted 'end of
the spy game' prediction that accompanied the demolition of the Berlin
Wall proved to be thoroughly overstated. The Humint (Human
Intelligence) agencies – the CIA, MI5, MI6, the Stasi and so on – all took
a knock, as we shall see in later chapters. For the NSA, however, it was

pretty much business as usual. As far as they were concerned, the only things that went out of style when Boris Yeltsin came in were espionage novels set in East Germany.

The NSA never seemed in danger of having to reduce its manpower as the agency's directorate led the warnings about the threat of terrorism and organised crime. These became the buzzwords that swept through the intelligence industry, as if they were a life raft. In many respects they were but in addition there were numerous dark clouds on the horizon. After the Cold War, there remained a wide-ranging array of separatist and counter-insurgency wars, border disputes, acts of ethnic and religious violence and counter-revolutionary operations, described by the US military as low-intensity conflicts and now called 'operations other than war'.

Internal terrorism was undoubtedly a threat and so was the surge in organised crime, soon to become even bigger with the emergence of the powerful and hugely well-endowed Russian Mafia and its pacts with other organised crime groups. Nor had the Sicilian Mafia and the US Godfathers shown any sign of decline; quite the reverse. The usefulness of telephone surveillance of crime syndicates had long ago proved its worth. In 1982–3, during a major investigation into drug trafficking in what became known as the Pizza Connection, almost twelve thousand telephone calls between drug dealers in the USA, Spain and Sicily were intercepted prior to the smashing of the biggest Italian/American Mafia heroin racket ever known.

The terrorist threat was also confirmed by a number of major atrocities, such as Lockerbie, the bombing of the World Trade Center in New York, and Saddam Hussein's genocidal experiments with chemical and biological weapons with which he killed or injured twelve thousand of Iraq's Kurdish population. These, together with the collapse of domestic controls within Russia, with nuclear components and scientific knowledge going to the highest bidder, provided all the justification the NSA needed to develop even greater ability to conduct its global surveillance.

Far from being scaled down, by the mid-1990s the UKUSA global communications interception operation, now with new improved Echelon, was very quickly being promoted as an essential item in the armoury of its member nations. In America, the heads of intelligence agencies and federal law enforcement officials began a concerted effort to defend the capabilities of Echelon as one or two troublesome Congressmen, and specifically Representative Bob Barr, a former CIA official, began to challenge the Clinton administration over the mass eavesdropping techniques utilised by the American intelligence community and its overseas partners. As figurehead of the intelligence community, Clinton responded in a manner that merely served to batten down the hatches on its behalf.

> Today, because the Cold War is over, some say that we should and can step back from the world and that we don't need intelligence as much as we used to; that we ought to severely cut the intelligence budget. A few have even urged us to scrap the Central Intelligence Agency. I think these views are profoundly wrong. I believe making deep cuts in intelligence during peacetime is comparable to cancelling your health insurance when you're feeling fine. We face a host of scattered and dangerous challenges. . . . There are ethnic and regional tensions that threaten to flare into full-scale war in more than thirty nations. Two dozen countries are trying to get their hands on nuclear, chemical, and biological weapons. As these terrible tools of destruction spread, so too spreads the potential for terrorism and for criminals to acquire them. And drug trafficking, organised crime, and environmental decay threaten the stability of new and emerging democracies, and threaten our well-being here at home. Our military commanders must have prompt, thorough intelligence to fully inform their decisions and maximise the security of our troops. Second, we have all source information available on major political and economic powers who are potentially hostile to us.

The speech might have been written for him by any one of several heads of Western intelligence groups. So the message was: selectivity in intelligence targets to meet the changing times. Some observers claim that at this point the surveillance agencies began looking around for other things to fill their days. There would be some spare capacity as targets moved from the ideological and military pursuits of the Cold

War days to terrorists and crime lords. The orders supposed to have come down from on high were that the NSA – and the CIA for that matter – should be used for the benefit of the American nation in other ways, that is by indulging in a spot of economic and industrial surveillance. As far as Britain was concerned, it was already a legal requirement that GCHQ should look out for intelligence that bolstered the nation's economic wellbeing as well as its security.

The awesome potential of the Echelon system was ideally suited to any extension of its surveillance activities into what was then the less secure world of business or private communications. It was already swinging that way long before the Cold War ended, coupled with a wider brief on surveillance of 'interesting individuals' caught in the Echelon trap by those who were targeting them without the eavesdroppers having to apply for a warrant to carry out bugging and tapping operations.

By using the facilities of individual nations, it was possible to bypass legal requirements in any one of the participating countries and enable the home agency to plead innocent of putting its citizens under surveillance. There are numerous examples. The movement of money, through the European banking system, from trade unions in the Soviet Union during the British miners' strike was apparently monitored through a joint operation of the NSA and GCHQ. The monitoring was conducted by NSA listening posts, largely through the joint NSA/GCHQ satellite station at Morwenstow, near Bude in Cornwall, although interception of confidential banking transactions was restricted to tracing drug money-laundering operations.

Margaret Newsham, a contract employee from Lockheed, was posted to Menwith Hill to take charge of a dozen systems that powered the Echelon computers. In April 1988, she told congressional investigators looking into NSA abuses that she had heard 'real-time' intercepts of South Carolina Senator Strom Thurmond. The senator, however, was reluctant to press for a thorough investigation, even though he was aware that he had been a target of the NSA for some while. Around the same time, Maryland Congressman Michael Barnes became aware that his phone calls had been regularly intercepted in the 1980s, during the Reagan administration. He told the *Baltimore Sun* in 1995 that he only became aware of it when a Washington journalist passed him transcripts of his conversations, given to him by contacts at the White House. Phone calls had been intercepted and recorded, including a conversation he had had with the Foreign Minister of Nicaragua in which he had protested over the implementation of martial law in that country. CIA Director William Casey, later implicated in the Iran-Contra affair, also showed Barnes an intercepted cable which reported a meeting between Nicaraguan embassy staff and one of Barnes's aides. The aide had been to the embassy on a professional call regarding an international affairs issue, and Casey asked Barnes to fire the aide. Barnes replied that it was perfectly legal and legitimate for his staff to meet foreign diplomats. He added: 'I was aware that NSA monitored international calls, that it was a standard part of intelligence gathering. But to use it for domestic political purposes is absolutely outrageous.'

The Canadian Communications Security Establishment (CSE), meanwhile, assisted in monitoring the activities of two British ministers in the mid-1980s, according to former CSE operative Mike Frost. He claimed that Prime Minister Margaret Thatcher had requested the surveillance, and GCHQ liaison staff in Ottawa made a request to the CSE for them to conduct the three-week-long mission on British soil. Frost said his boss, Frank Bowman, travelled to London to do the job himself. After the mission was over, Bowman gave the tapes to a GCHQ official at their headquarters in Cheltenham. Some years earlier, Frost said, the agency was involved in surveillance of the wife of Canada's own Prime Minister, Pierre Trudeau. Margaret Trudeau had launched on an active social life and the Royal Canadian Mounted Police's Security Service investigated reports that she was using marijuana on a regular basis. It was a big deal then, and scandalous for one in such a position. The CSE, using its alliance in the UKUSA network, began casting an inquisitive eye over her contacts. Frost claimed he and his colleagues were uncertain of the motives for the surveillance; it could have been political, by opponents of Trudeau attempting to stir up trouble, or it might have been Trudeau himself preparing damage limitation.

Frost maintained he conducted eavesdropping operations against both Americans and Britons at the request of both countries' intelligence services, to whom the surveillance data was subsequently passed. It was all part of the service that evolved through the Echelon system. Similar claims were made by Robin Robison, an administrative officer in the Joint Intelligence Unit. He was a Quaker who resigned from his post because of the increasing amount of surveillance he witnessed towards the end of the 1980s. The JIU is the service wing of the Joint Intelligence Committee which collates and analyses intelligence to and from MI5, MI6, GCHQ and Defence Intelligence. Robison claimed that Margaret Thatcher had personally ordered the interception of communications from the parent company of the *Observer*, Lonrho, after the *Observer* had published articles in 1989 concerning money paid to Thatcher's son, Mark, in commission following a multi-billion-dollar British arms deal with Saudi Arabia. Despite facing severe penalties for violating his indoctrination vows, Robison said that he had delivered material relating to Lonrho intercepts to Mrs Thatcher's office.

ROBERT MAXWELL

The phrase 'in the interests of national security' can cover a multitude of sins, never more so than in the case of Robert Maxwell, the Czech-born ex-politician who bought the *Daily Mirror* with its own money by mortgaging its property and pension fund surplus in advance. Later, he bought the *New York Daily News* in his vain bid to outdo Rupert Murdoch in the global media empire stakes. His faxes, telephone calls and Inmarsat calls had been regularly monitored, especially in the late 1980s during his toing-and-froing between London, Moscow and eastern European countries with whose heads of state he was on good terms. Several interceptions were made at the special request of the Bank of England.

Two officials from the Bank of England were seconded to the economic intelligence section of the Joint Intelligence Committee when Maxwell was under observation. Since his empire was already on the edge of the financial precipice, there were people in high places who were well aware that things were not as good as he said they were. But Maxwell's declining business fortunes were not the reason for intelligence surveillance, and never had been.

His increasing contacts with Israel and the arrival of Mossad agents at his eyrie at the top of the *Mirror* offices surely did not go unnoticed by MI5, or by those around him. It was Maxwell himself who alerted Mossad to the presence of Mordechai Vanunu, an Israeli scientist who was about to blow the secrets of Israel's nuclear programme to the *Sunday Times*. He received that information via *Mirror* editorial director Mike Molloy and myself after one of Vanunu's former associates tried to sell the story to the *Sunday Mirror* in advance of the *Sunday Times* article appearing. Maxwell picked up the telephone and called someone at the Israeli Embassy while Molloy was still in his office, having related the details and indicated that the *Sunday Times* had a statement from Vanunu. Within forty-eight hours of Maxwell's tip-off, Mossad had kidnapped Vanunu and smuggled him back to Israel to face an eighteen-year prison term in solitary confinement. Was British intelligence aware the kidnap was about to happen? The answer is very likely yes.

I was in the middle of this sad affair, drawn into it as an editor working for the Mirror Group. I resigned shortly afterwards. Maxwell was a classic example of a businessman whom the state felt obliged to monitor because of his connections, and he was shrewd enough to know it. As is the way of these things, surveillance alone may not produce the kind of material that could be taken to a court of law in a prosecution. Indeed, the surveillance may not even be directed towards that aim, and was not in Maxwell's case. Certain people in the intelligence business, government and banking circles were seriously interested in the move-ments of a man who could be meeting George Bush in Washington one minute and then be flying back to Europe and taking a big kiss on the lips from one of the Eastern Bloc dictators the next. One source told me that MI5 alone had more than thirty-five bulging folders on Maxwell long before his fraudulent activities and theft became public knowledge. By that time he had gone over the side of his opulent yacht, bought with money which, in effect, he had stolen from the Mirror Group pension fund, which was £479 million short at the time of his demise.

Although he was already investing money that wasn't his into Israeli concerns, Mossad was wary of involvement with Maxwell; some would put forward the conspiracy theory that they threw him over the side. All concerned knew his exact location, who he was talking to and about what. Proof of exactly what happened remains elusive and is beyond the scope of this work. In any event the Maxwell story has been thoroughly explored by Tom Bowyer. The point is that Robin

Robison from the Joint Intelligence Unit confirmed that Maxwell, like many others, was an easy target. He said: 'My impression was that GCHQ could intercept anything they liked. Every overseas call, every telex, every fax. They didn't need to put on a phone-tap, they just flicked a few switches.' Maxwell himself proved the ease with which such operations could be mounted. He was doing the same thing against staff in his empire and regularly hired teams of international private detectives and commercial analysts to dig the dirt on opponents and competitors, or simply on people he did not like, such as Arthur Scargill, the British miners' leader. His stable of publications provided him with the opportunity to wage public campaigns through editorial columns and leaders.

MOBILE PHONE TRACKING

Like Maxwell, the UKUSA partnership had no qualms about whose calls and faxes they were intercepting. They included a number of civil liberties and human rights organisations, CND, and a range of organisations with overseas connections such as Christian Aid and Amnesty International. The arrival of the mobile telephone brought added dimensions to this ability. There is perhaps no better example of tracking the signal of a known telephone number than took place on 21 April 1996, when a missile fired from the air scored a direct hit on Chechen rebel leader General Dzokhar Dudayev while he was standing in a field near the village of Gekhi-Chu talking on a satellite telephone. A Russian news agency reported that the missile homed into the target by locking on to the telephone's radio signal. The commander of Russian troops in Chechnya denied, however, that Russian artillery or aircraft were in action in the area.

Kremlin innocence was hard to swallow after the news agency Itar-Tass quoted a highly placed source in the Interior Ministry as saying that Dudayev had been killed in a series of retaliatory raids against seven Chechen command posts. The agency said it was the fifth time in the past three months that the Russians had locked missiles on to General Dudayev's telephone signal, but previously he had always ended his conversation before the weapon reached its target. A correspondent for

Russian independent NTV, who visited the scene of his death, reported that it was clearly a 'special operation' targeted at the rebel.

Dudayev had been seen on television bulletins conducting many of his operations and giving interviews over his mobile telephone. Not long before he was blown up, he had been talking to Yeltsin's staff in Moscow about peace negotiations. The curiosity of this killing, however, was the reluctance of the Russians to admit their role in it. Was it because it was not they but the Americans – via Menwith Hill – who had been providing location references on Dudayev's telephone? Martin Streetly, editor of *Jane's Radar and Electronic Warfare Systems*, was doubtful whether the under-equipped Russian military had the ability at that time to home in on the phone signal. At a conference on information warfare a month later a number of the world's leading Sigint and computer security experts discussed the case, the first known killing by telephone-directed missiles, and came to the conclusion that it was politically and technically likely that the NSA had helped the Russians kill Dudayev. Those with longer memories may recall that it was the NSA who first located Che Guevara in Bolivia through intercepted radio communications; he was killed while trying to organise a revolution.

Yeltsin's precarious position at the time and the need to sustain an oil consortium's pipeline running through Chechnya were reasons enough for the NSA to provide the location of the Chechen leader. The rebels were not unaware of this and it is believed to be one of the reasons why, in the aftermath, they regarded all non-nationals coming into the country with suspicion and as possible spies. Western aid workers and telecoms people sent to the region were always in danger of being kidnapped, tortured and murdered, as some eventually were. The US intelligence community was panicked by the possible repercussions of the Dudayev killing and tried to keep the lid on the story, on the basis that 'we have people on the ground out there'. They were all fairly promptly withdrawn but Menwith Hill, GCHQ and the Bad Aibling field station in Germany are all believed to have contributed to the surveillance effort over the whole region.

GCHQ

The success of Echelon as an intelligence-monitoring tool has been recognised by the British specialists – a fact acknowledged in a cap-doffing way by Sir John Ayde, then director of GCHQ, in a 1994 confidential summary of operations and objectives. The station's job was to provide signals intelligence gathered by the then staff of 6500 people at Cheltenham and another 3143 military specialists overseas, supervised by GCHQ, in the interests of national security and the economic well-being of the UK, and to support the prevention or detection of serious crime. It was – and still is – organised in two groups: the national signals intelligence centre and the Communications Electronics Security Group (CESG). The GCHQ staff, all subject to severe repercussions under the Official Secrets Act, were informed that their objectives were aided by collaboration with other countries and, although the British operation did not want to permit this 'to reach a point of overdependence', they had to 'maximise' those benefits to the full.

The memorandum, to be found in the Statewatch Archive, insisted that the UKUSA intelligence relationship was of 'particular importance … our contribution must be of sufficient scale and of the right kind to make a continuation of the Sigint alliance worthwhile to our partners. This may entail on occasion the applying of UK resources to the need of US requirements.' It went on to record some interesting statistics including that of the deployment of GCHQ staff and budget, 50 per cent of which was applied to the collection of intelligence. It was thus essential to ensure that those resources were efficiently applied against ever 'changing targets'. The document spelled out the fact, however, that the historical and principal reason for the existence of GCHQ was to service its customers at home, that is the intelligence services, the military and the government.

At the time of writing, the cooperation between all the UKUSA nations is as firm as ever with an ongoing interchange of staff. Canada's CSE, for example, continues to maintain liaison staff at both NSA and GCHQ, which remain the lead partners in every sense. The NSA and GCHQ offer courses to staff from the other three nations and some selected members spend time working at NSA and GCHQ as 'integrated members' of specialist groups. The relationship goes from strength to strength.

CHAPTER 8
SOMEBODY IS LISTENING: REVEALING THE TRUTH ABOUT ECHELON

ALTHOUGH IT WAS HOTLY DENIED that it even existed, rumours about Echelon were gradually replaced by hard facts. The security measures which surrounded it had even precluded prime ministers from making a full appraisal of all that went on in the supposed interests of the nations involved. But the detail of America's global interception ambitions began to filter into public view in the summer of 1972 in the context of the USA announcing it was withdrawing its troops from the ground war in Vietnam.

THE TESTIMONY OF PERRY FELLWOCK

In August 1972 a former employee of the National Security Agency, at that time protecting his identity with a pseudonym but later revealed as Perry Fellwock, placed on record his recollections of his work as a senior analyst in what was even then described as the 'largest and most sensitive and far-flung intelligence gathering apparatus in the world's history . . . not a sparrow or a government falls without NSA's instantaneous knowledge . . . gained from over 2,000 agency stations that dot the five continents and the seven seas'. (Its headquarters building covers 1,400,000 square feet and is distinguished from other security headquarters on the US inventory of such places by the fact that it has no windows.) A transcript of Fellwock's testimony is now maintained for posterity on microfilm in the Butler Library at Columbia University. It covers a crucial period in American and Australian history.

At the time, the NSA international network was estimated to provide 80 per cent of all US intelligence of a significant nature, and its personnel were so indoctrinated into the security of the place that it remained virtually unknown to the American public twenty years after its creation. Fellwock, a twenty-five-year-old staff sergeant in the US Air Force Security Service, decided to risk prosecution, as the Vietnam War was hurtling towards ignominy for his country, and tell the truth about his experiences at NSA listening posts in West Germany, Turkey and Vietnam. His taped recollections, running to sixteen pages of close type, brought forth many previously undisclosed facts on the history of the NSA, its global mission and its partnership with the 'WASP' (White Anglo-Saxon Protestant) nations (Canada, Australia and New Zealand) linked politically to the United Kingdom. Fellwock also revealed that the first American killed in the Vietnam War was, in fact, an NSA operative employed at the agency's main base at Phu Bai.

The Fellwock papers dealt not just with the agency's tactical mission across Indo-China and its intelligence support of military commanders pitted against the North Vietnamese and Viet Cong. He also confirmed the electronic interception techniques which, even then, enabled the NSA to log the call signs for Soviet aircraft, the numbers on the sides of each plane, the precise positions of nuclear submarines and the location of every Soviet missile base.

Routinely, he claimed, the NSA network monitored all Soviet military and diplomatic radio and signals traffic. He made the then astounding claim that the USA had violated the Geneva Convention by attempting to enforce a WASP communications intelligence dictatorship over the 'Free World', on the back of its activities against Communism. Given that he was anti-war, some of his claims seemed at the time far-fetched. In retrospect, they were perhaps only a slight exaggeration of American electronic interception capabilities. That was more or less confirmed when the NSA decided not to prosecute its erstwhile operative, its chiefs apparently reasoning that the extent of its operations would be blown wide open by a court case which – in the hyped-up anti-war feeling that existed in the USA at the time –

might have attracted massive media attention, whereas so far the disclosures had not.

DUNCAN CAMPBELL AND NICKY HAGER

Duncan Campbell was not so lucky. The British journalist was instrumental in the next stage of the disclosure process relating to the NSA, its British Commonwealth counterparts and subsequently Echelon. In 1976, he interviewed Fellwock as part of his own investigation into the equally sensitive and largely unknown activities of GCHQ. All anyone knew about this organisation was that it was the signals arm of British intelligence. Even the full story of Bletchley Park had yet to be told. Campbell's subsequent article, written with American Mark Hosenball, was published in *Time Out* magazine in June 1976 under the headline 'The Eavesdroppers' at a time when MI5 and Special Branch were getting exceedingly steamed up about alleged subversive cells operating within the British media and British life in general. 'GCHQ directors were apoplectic,' says Campbell. 'The more so because the combined efforts of the GPO (who tapped my phone from May '76 onwards), Special Branch and MI5 (who followed me around) revealed that we had actually got the article without breaking the Official Secrets Act. I had done my research from open technical sources.'

Even so, Hosenball was promptly deported from Britain, having been declared a threat to national security. Philip Agee, the now famous whistle-blower of CIA activity, was also linked into the inquiry and similarly sent packing, eventually taking up residence in Germany. Campbell himself was arrested some months later along with another *Time Out* journalist, Crispin Aubrey, after it was discovered that in pursuing the story, they had spoken to a former signals intelligence officer, John Berry. All three were charged under the Official Secrets Act. Campbell was also accused of espionage. In what became known as the ABC trial (for Aubrey, Berry and Campbell), the prosecution case fell apart and was thrown out. It was a landmark development for Campbell but did nothing to lessen the diligence of the NSA/GCHQ secrecy campaign. Even a congressional committee in Washington investigating the NSA in 1988 never got round to releasing its report. Campbell managed to retrieve some of the committee's findings, and finally discovered that the communications intelligence agencies of the UKUSA Agreement had developed a computerised system that could intercept and analyse civilian communications into the twenty-first century. Eventually, he became the first to mention the word Echelon in Britain. He followed that up with an important article in Britain's *New Statesman* published under the headline 'Somebody's Listening'. Other work on signals intelligence as it existed then was undertaken by researchers such as James Bamford, who uncovered some of the innermost workings of the NSA for his book *The Puzzle Palace*.

The pursuit of journalists by 'the agencies' continues unabated. Campbell himself remains under surveillance as do most who delve into matters of military and civilian intelligence. I have had numerous exchanges with the Ministry of Defence Home and Special Forces Secretariat and the D-Notices Advisory Committee over previous works and was confronted by requests for deletions from both *Death of a Hero* (1999) and *SBS: The Inside Story of the Special Boat Service* (1997). The latter attracted hand-delivered correspondence from the MoD containing threats of unspecified action if I did not agree to delete forty-two pages of text by a given deadline and not show that material to another living soul.

My colleague Tony Geraghty was raided by the MoD police following the publication of his book *The Irish War* in 1998; they searched his house from top to bottom, took away his computer and much research material, and eventually charged him and former army colonel Nigel Wylde under the Official Secrets Act. He was arraigned before a court where he was bailed pending his trial. In December 1999, he was informed by the Director of Public Prosecutions that the case was being dropped. The MoD subsequently conceded that the book was embarrassing rather than damaging. *The Irish War* describes the growing use of computers by military intelligence in identifying targets, including automatic photographing of vehicle registration plates by a system codenamed Glutton. 'In Northern Ireland, where around 3,000 killers are thought to be at large among a population of 1.5 million, at least 1 million names are now on some security agency's computer,' Geraghty wrote. Two other computer systems, codenamed Vengeful and Crucible, he added, 'provide total cover of a largely innocent population'.

Meanwhile, New Zealand journalist Nicky Hager was also on the trail across the other side of the world. He spent twelve years investigating the ties between his country's Sigint agency, the Government Communications Security Bureau (GCSB), GCHQ and the NSA. With leaked material from former GCSB officers, in 1996 Hager presented an exposé of the previously unknown machinations of the GCSB, giving a detailed description of Echelon which even the Prime Minister of New Zealand admitted was a revelation to him. Hager says that the New Zealand intelligence officers who talked to him did so out of a growing disillusionment with the importance to their own country of access to Echelon information. In some cases, they said, they had been so busy listening in on targets of interest to other countries that they had missed opportunities to gather intelligence in New Zealand's national interest.

THE COPENHAGEN CONFERENCE

Increasing concerns were being voiced among privacy campaigners, human rights watchdogs and politicians in Europe, the USA and Australasia about rumours of the widespread interception of electronic communications. In September 1995, seventy individuals from around the world met in Copenhagen to put a collective voice to those fears at a conference on advanced surveillance technology. The delegates included leading technologists, academics, public interest advocates, government officials, members of the media and industry representatives.

At that time the full power of Echelon and the awesome potential of sites such as Menwith Hill and Bad Aibling was still relatively unknown. The conference programme was wide-ranging and innovative and examined the whole spectrum of privacy issues. Among these was the recently discovered attempt by the FBI to have a 'back door' key installed into international telephone systems. This would make possible a freedom to tap all communications which passed through the systems.

Simon Davies, director general of Privacy International, correctly forecast the imminent arrival of a number of significant technological and political trends, converging to create a society under total surveillance. He foresaw the individual right to privacy being gradually downgraded as an indefinable notion, a selfish concept eventually to be done away with and replaced by the notion of 'data protection' which was much more manageable. It would then become an easy matter to redefine public interest as requiring surveillance. In this, he predicted that some curious partnerships would arise – such as the creation of DNA databases on the grounds of both public health and to identify criminals. Four years later, he was proved to be exactly right – that is precisely what happened. 'Surveillance therefore appears to have a bright future,' he told the conference. 'It is evolving at a rapid pace.'

A similar theme was taken up by Steve Wright, director of the Manchester-based Omega Foundation. Wright told the Copenhagen gathering that his foundation was itself conducting a watching brief on:

> the development of technological fixes to social and political
> problems, a trend taking hold in a growing number of
> countries. This phenomenon has primary and obvious effects,
> but it also has secondary and tertiary consequences, which are
> more important and more powerful than the intended effects.
> That trend is likely to develop in the United Kingdom, for
> instance, where authorities with a long experience in the field
> of surveillance, such as MI5, are increasingly looking for a
> new mission in the area of police activities. There is both a
> demand pull for repression technology and a technological
> push: the technology itself spurs the development of
> surveillance. Unwanted surveillance facilities are often built in
> systems and, once installed, tend to be used.
>
> Other factors are also at play and even the basic
> definition of 'subversion' has evolved in British law: from the
> 'overthrow of government by unlawful means', a fairly
> restricted concept, it has come to include anything which
> 'undermines society'. It is therefore not surprising that the fight
> against subversion has brought about the massive presence of
> cameras wherever a manifestation occurs, with the
> accompanying chilling effect on expression and protests. We
> are moving from the concept of a person as a citizen of a
> community to the notion of a data subject, which makes

exclusion easier. What can be done to counter the
development of repression technologies in a context where any
one big scare may come to justify surveillance, as in the case
where a shopping centre's cameras made possible the
identification of the murderers of a child in Liverpool?
Legislation is a very primitive tool and the economy tends to
take precedence over human rights: the surveillance cameras
installed at Tiananmen Square were built by an American
multinational and sold as advanced traffic monitoring tools. . . .

It was the conflict of the two latter aspects – traffic aides used for
political purposes – that inspired Wright to pursue the theme, spurred
on by new information about international surveillance techniques
which the delegates had brought to the Copenhagen conference table.
They had opened up issues of global importance for both individuals
and business communities, and with the support and encouragement of
Glyn Ford, a Manchester Labour Member of the European Parliament,
the Omega Foundation was commissioned to prepare a consultative
paper for the Scientific and Technological Options Assessment (STOA)
Unit of the European Parliament. Ford, a member of the STOA panel,
declared his hope that the report would be the first step towards greater
openness: 'Some democratically elected body should surely have a right
to know at some level. At the moment that's nowhere.'

THE OMEGA FOUNDATION REPORT

Wright set to work on a comprehensive study, calling upon the views of
international experts in virtually every walk of professional and university life, including intelligence-gathering personnel, the military and
international conglomerates, and drawing upon the original investigations of Campbell and Hager. *An Appraisal of Technologies of Political
Control* dealt with the worrying expansion of many surveillance techniques against society and, in particular, by way of electronic
interception, moved on to detail other depressing elements of modern
society that belong more properly to the Middle Ages, such as implements of torture and methods of state execution.

It was, however, those pages which dealt with surveillance which attracted attention across Europe. An interim report to the STOA Unit was produced at the beginning of 1997 but brought 'no comment' from the British government or its allies in UKUSA. A year later, Wright presented a follow-up which confirmed that what had been rumoured about Echelon was the truth and that:

> within Europe, all e-mail, telephone and fax communications are routinely intercepted by the United States National Security Agency, transferring all target information from the European mainland via the strategic hub of London, then by satellite to Fort Meade in Maryland via the crucial hub at Menwith Hill in the North York Moors of the UK. Unlike many of the electronic spy systems developed during the Cold War, Echelon is designed for primarily non-military targets: governments, organisations and businesses in virtually every country. The Echelon system works by indiscriminately intercepting very large quantities of communications and then siphoning out what is valuable using artificial intelligence aids like Memex to find key words. Whilst there is much information gathered about potential terrorists, there is a lot of economic intelligence, notably intensive monitoring of all the countries participating in the GATT negotiations. With no system of accountability, it is difficult to discover what criteria determine who is *not* a target.

The explosion of developments and the ongoing discoveries and innovations in the world of satellite and telecommunications also came under Omega's scrutiny, and Wright concluded:

> Modern communications systems are virtually transparent to the advanced interceptions equipment which can be used to listen in. Some systems even lend themselves to a dual role as a national interceptions network. For example the message switching system used on digital exchanges like British Telecom's System X in the UK supports an Integrated Services Digital Network (ISDN) Protocol. This allows digital services,

e.g. faxes, to share the system with existing lines. What is not widely known is that built into it . . . is the ability to take phones 'off hook' and listen into conversations occurring near the phone unit, without the user being aware that it is happening. This effectively means that a national dial-up telephone tapping capacity is built into these systems from the start. Similarly, the digital technology required to pinpoint mobile phone users for incoming calls means that all mobile phones . . . when activated are mini-tracking devices, giving their owner's whereabouts at any time and stored in the company's computer for up to two years. Coupled with System X technology, this is a custom-built mobile track, tail and tap system par excellence.

Wright recalled that in February 1996 the UK-based research bulletin and archive Statewatch had reported that the European Union had already secretly agreed to set up an international telephone interception network via a network of committees established under the 'third pillar' of the Maastricht Treaty, covering cooperation on law and order. Key points of the plan were outlined in a memorandum of understanding, signed by EU states in 1995, which remains classified. This action, it was said, reflected concern among European intelligence agencies that modern technology in the development of encryption will eventually prevent them from tapping private communications.

Statewatch reported that the European Union governments agreed to an initiative originating from Washington that they should cooperate closely with the FBI in setting up a system which made the networks conducive to interception, rather than being 'locked out' by privacy and security measures. Under the proposals, network and service providers in the European Union would be obliged to install 'tappable' systems and, when served with an interception order, to place under surveillance any person or group. These plans, Omega pointed out, were not referred to any European government for scrutiny nor to the Civil Liberties Committee of the European Parliament, despite the clear civil liberties issues raised by such an unaccountable system. Wright noted that it was impossible to determine if there 'are not other agendas at work here', and repeated the Statewatch conclusion that 'it is the interface of the Echelon system and its potential development on phone calls combined with the standardisation of tappable communications centres and equipment being sponsored by the European Union and the USA which presents a truly global threat over which there are no legal or democratic controls'.

In other words, the way was clear for uncontrolled wire tapping, bugging and random interceptions of telephone calls, faxes and e-mails whenever and wherever law enforcement wished – and that was in addition to the worldwide operations under the Echelon system. The report recommended the STOA Unit to push for a European Union ruling that all surveillance operations and practices should be subject to real accountability and to ensure that new technologies were brought within data protection legislation.

Statewatch itself also called on the European Parliament to reject proposals from the United States for making the landline, satellite and mobile telephone networks totally accessible to interception by the agencies. Washington wanted to run this system in tandem with Echelon. Steve Wright himself urged the STOA Unit to commission a more detailed report on the constitutional issues raised by the NSA ability to intercept all European communications systems and to examine closely the social and political implications of FBI ambitions to operate a telecommunications surveillance network.

The Omega Foundation concluded with the recommendation that further studies should be undertaken, one of them on the technical data of Echelon. This was given to Duncan Campbell to write. He produced a 25,000-word document bristling with details on the NSA's hardware scattered above and around the globe. It was entitled *Interception Capabilities 2000* and was based largely upon his own original research, which caused further apoplexy among the intelligence communities of the UKUSA nations. The report of the second investigation, *Development of Surveillance Technology and Risk of Abuse of Economic Information*, was based on a survey of the opinions of experts, together with additional research and analytical material by the authors who came from Zeus EEIG. The study was carried out at the request of the Committee on Civil Liberties and Internal Affairs of the European Parliament. Almost fifty experts from universities, the IT sector and government took part, drawn from eleven member states of the European Union, plus Cyprus, Norway and Switzerland.

Fear about the extent of interception of electronic communications was a running theme among the Zeus collection of expert opinions. Two key perceptions emerged immediately: a concern about the threat to privacy, as well as economic and civil rights, posed by clandestine electronic surveillance systems operated by powerful secret government agencies; and anxiety about commercial security posed by the nature of the new electronic business media and its possible vulnerability to interception by government eavesdroppers, competitors and fraudsters.

Since the Omega report the second fear had overtaken the first as the predominant worry among those surveyed, on the grounds that, in the space of a few months, more complex national and international networks had been identified. This massive growth in international networks and the increase in data being processed had made the security and protection of trans-border data flows a matter of extreme urgency.

INDUSTRIAL AND ECONOMIC ESPIONAGE

Even as this new study was being prepared, examples of information theft were coming to light on an almost daily basis. There was clearly a growing worry that the NSA's global interceptions through Echelon had long been directed towards another kind of intelligence war – that of spying on industrial and economic competitors and nations around the globe, largely for the benefit of the United States. One of my own US secret service contacts confirmed: 'Industrial and economic espionage is among the most explosive of all issues. The theft of trade secrets has been widespread, even among nations who are supposedly allies. The ability to counteract these attacks is now 100 per cent essential in the armoury of virtually every major company; it knows no boundaries and, of course, I am not saying that US companies – or state agencies – are not involved. They are, although it must be said that, by and large, America has been the loser rather than the winner in this particular game, and a counterintelligence force was set up to introduce procedures specifically to warn our industries of the methods of capture of scientific and commercial data.'

Other nations would not entirely agree with the 'victim' assessment. Britain, Germany, France and Japan have all complained to the Clinton administration about the overzealous operations of its intelligence agencies in the area of economic and industrial espionage, quite apart from privately run operations. The CIA was caught red-handed in France and Japan, although the French were quite able to launch a counter-attack. 'It is an elementary blunder to think we're allies with countries like America,' said former French intelligence chief Pierre Marion. 'When it comes to business, it's war.' He openly boasts that his service was 'able to obtain' for the French aircraft manufacturer Dassault confidential information from the American competition, which Dassault was then able to undercut. Britain is certainly not whiter than white either. The Intelligence Services Act empowers its intelligence agencies to support the country's economic wellbeing – which, translated, means gleaning commercial intelligence on trade competitors.

In the USA, however, Congress fell totally behind the warning of former CIA director Admiral Stansfield Turner when he wrote: 'The pre-eminent threat to US national security now lies in the economic sphere. We must, then, redefine "national security" by assigning economic strength greater prominence.' At the turn of the 1990s, America began its pursuit of that goal with deeds and words which were in much the same vein as the French: no holds barred.

The fear among Europeans – and among the rest of the world, for that matter – was that Echelon provided the Gang of Five with a competitive edge through its interception of the world's telephony. Duncan Campbell, in his report to the European Union, reiterated the view that:

> within constraints imposed by budgetary limitation and tasking priorities, the United States can if it chooses direct space collection systems to intercept mobile communications signals and microwave city-to-city traffic anywhere on the planet. ... Since the early 1990s, fast and sophisticated Comint systems have been developed to collect, filter and analyse the forms of fast digital communications used by the Internet. Because most of the world's Internet capacity lies within the United States or connects to the United States, many communications in

'cyberspace' will pass through intermediate sites within the United States. Communications between Europe and Asia, Oceania [the Pacific region], Africa or South America normally travel via the United States. US officials acknowledge that the NSA collects economic information, whether intentionally or otherwise.

Colonel Dan Smith, military intelligence attaché to the US Embassy in London until 1993, admitted as much in a BBC interview in 1998, confirming that he had received communications intelligence from Menwith Hill and that: 'In terms of scooping up communications, inevitably since their take is broadband, there will be conversations or communications which are intercepted which have nothing to do with the military, and probably within those there will be some information about commercial dealings ... anything would be possible technically. Technically they can scoop all this information up, sort through it and find out what it is that might be asked for. ... But there is no policy to do this specifically in response to a particular company's interest.'

Campbell's submission to the European Union supports the view of the Zeus report that there is no evidence that companies in any of the UKUSA countries are able to task communications interception from Menwith Hill or elsewhere to suit their private purposes. They do not have to. Each UKUSA country authorises national-level intelligence organisations and relevant individual ministries to task and receive intelligence which includes economic, industrial and even environmental data.

The CIA and MI6, for example, rely upon the monitoring of the international arms trade to track sensitive technology, much of which is available in Britain, America and – to some extent – in other UKUSA countries. All the intelligence agencies, including the CIA, MI5, MI6 and the former KGB, depend on statistics gleaned from interception to assess political stability or economic strength of what MI5 might describe as a 'hostile country' and the CIA as a 'target country'. All the information they might desire is generally available from the Echelon system; where things often go wrong is in the human assessment and handling of that information as it passes up the chain of command, from analyst to prime ministers and presidents.

What happens to sensitive economic and industrial data once it has been scooped up by NSA and Menwith Hill – which, in the hands of private interception agencies, would be described as industrial espionage – is the $64,000 question. British intelligence, by law, must support the interests of the nation's economy, a statement which may be interpreted, as with most things in the world of intelligence-speak, in a variety of ways but may be loosely translated as being given 'carte blanche'.

Similarly, in the 1970s the Americans set up a department, later renamed the Office of Executive Support, which provided a formal route through which NSA data could be diverted in support of economic interests. Tips based on spying regularly flow to US companies to help them win contracts overseas. The Office of Executive Support provides classified weekly briefings to security officials. The *Washington Post* obtained reports demonstrating intelligence support to US companies: 'One such document consists of minutes from an August 1994 Commerce Department meeting [intended] to identify major contracts open for bid in Indonesia in order to help US companies win the work. A CIA employee ... spoke at the meeting; five of the 16 people on the routine distribution list for the minutes were from the CIA.'

In the UK, interception of commercial material is handled by K Division at GCHQ and, according to Campbell, targets may be nominated by the government's Overseas Economic Intelligence Committee, the Economic Staff of the Joint Intelligence Committee, the Treasury or the Bank of England. A former employee in the offices of the JIC confirmed in a Channel 4 documentary that the interceptions trawled from Echelon elsewhere variously included 'company projections, telexes, faxes and transcribed phone calls'.

More than a dozen cases in which commercial organisations have benefited from interceptions have been highlighted in three reports to the European Parliament. Among them was a $1.4 billion contract that the government of Brazil was on the point of awarding to the French companies Thomson and Alcatel for the supply of an environmental surveillance system for the Amazon rain forest. Signatures were about to be exchanged when, reportedly with the personal intervention of Bill Clinton, a competing US company adjusted its prices and won the contract, having been supplied with copies of all the Brazilian faxes and transcriptions of telephone conversations, courtesy of Echelon. The company also provided maintenance and engineering services to one of NSA's Echelon satellite interception stations.

In 1994, French Prime Minister Edouard Balladur went to Saudi Arabia, convinced he would return with a major contract for French industry, for weapons and for the European consortium Airbus Industrie. He came back empty-handed. The contract, worth $6 billion, went to the Airbus rival, McDonnell-Douglas. A French newspaper source claimed that the 'NSA lifted all the faxes and phone calls between the European consortium Airbus, the Saudi national airline and the Saudi government'.

Zeus records dirty tricks, too. On 25 June 1998, in Absheim an A-320 Airbus crashed during a demonstration flight. The accident was reportedly caused by dangerous manoeuvres. One person died and twenty were injured. Very soon afterwards, and before the announcement of the official report, many hostile and curiously well-informed messages were posted on Internet news groups, some predicting future similar accidents. Behind the messages were clear attempts to cover the tracks of those who had posted them. They came from the USA, from computers with misleading identification data, and had been transferred from anonymous servers in Finland.

A similar campaign was directed against the European consortium of Aeritalia and Aerospatiale, following a crash involving an ATR aircraft. The campaign resulted in a two-month ban on ATR flights while test flights in fog conditions were carried out. The manufacturers suffered a tirade of ridicule and hostility from well-informed submissions to Internet news groups (especially to the AVSIG forum, supported by Compuserve). Once again, French intelligence suspected the hidden hand of NSA somewhere in the background.

Companies or individuals in the country which hosted NSA equipment were not excluded from US spying tactics. Ross Coulthart, the investigative reporter with Australia's Nine Network, probed the southern hemisphere connections in the 1990s and concluded that in the UKUSA intelligence community there appeared to be two camps: those who believed that it was best to fall in line behind the NSA because it provided the resources and offered Australia limited participation in a system that its intelligence operations could not normally afford, and those who thought the whole thing was overrated and contrary to national interests.

In 1995, for example, Australian intelligence officials leaked a story to the Australian Broadcasting Company that was, at first sight, damaging to themselves: Australian intelligence had bugged the Chinese Embassy in Canberra. However, the Australians had no access to the actual transmissions; they had merely planted the bugs at the behest of the NSA, which was getting the raw feed. 'Given that both Australian and American companies were bidding for Chinese wheat contracts at the time,' said Coulthart, 'it didn't seem like Australia was getting anything out of this arrangement, so they put the story out there.'

The Australian Defence Signals Directorate (DSD) finally admitted to Coulthart that it worked in cooperation with the NSA, although it could not guarantee that it was always on the same side. Coulthart had hoped for a television interview with the director of DSD, Martin Brady, but instead received a two-page response to the list of questions he had submitted. Since GCHQ and DSD were supposedly very close, and since UK law is similar to that in Australia in regard to secrets, Brady might well be seen as speaking for his British counterparts as well. What is interesting – again – is the double-speak in which the responses are couched. In the end, they allow for all possibilities. For instance:

> The rules prohibit deliberate interception of communications between Australians in Australia; the dissemination of information relating to Australian persons gained accidentally during the course of routine collection of foreign communications or the reporting or recording of Australian persons mentioned in foreign communications.
>
> The rules do provide mechanisms to permit DSD to monitor and report foreign communications involving Australians in some special carefully defined circumstances such as the commission of a serious criminal offence; a threat to life or the safety of an Australian or where an Australian is acting as an agent for a foreign power. Specific approval is required for all such collection and reporting.
>
> DSD does co-operate with counterpart signals intelligence organisations overseas under the UKUSA relationship. Both

DSD and its counterparts operate internal procedures to satisfy themselves that their national interests and policies are respected by the others. ... I make the additional point that a number of your questions seem premised on the proposition that there are intelligence-gathering facilities operated by foreign governments in Australia. All intelligence and surveillance facilities in Australia are operated by Australian agencies or jointly by Australia and US agencies. All activities are conducted with the full knowledge of the Australian government. ...

In the UK, the problems are rather more complex. The Blair government has a different set of criteria to meet. Its UKUSA partnership is now so entrenched as to be virtually unbreakable. Its partnership with Europe is similarly firm, but the two are increasingly pulling in opposite directions, as demonstrated on 29 October 1999 at a meeting of the Council on Law and the Interior in Luxembourg when the three reports to the European Parliament's STOA committee came home to roost. Ministers debated the question of telecommunications monitoring and formally requested the British government to share the interception facilities it gained from the UKUSA partnership. Britain refused on the grounds of its own national security. At the time of writing the issue was still unresolved, and the possibility of Britain being made to conform through legal obligations was being investigated by European Union lawyers.

CHAPTER 9
THE HUMAN TOUCH: AN IN-DEPTH LOOK AT THE INTELLIGENCE AGENCIES

UNTIL RECENTLY, ELECTRONIC SURVEILLANCE remained mostly out of sight. The public image of the spy agencies remained firmly linked to what was known in the trade as Humint – Human Intelligence – the agents and surveillance operatives whose basic tools are bugging, tapping, opening mail, following people around and drawing upon their networks of informers. Three models of traditional intelligence gathering led the world – those of the USA, Britain and the Soviet Union. This chapter takes a closer look at the key agencies in each of these countries.

BRITISH INTELLIGENCE

The UK agencies remain the smallest and oldest in the global arena. Their origins can be traced back to the reign of Queen Elizabeth I and for the most part they have maintained a high level of secrecy concerning their organisation and operations. In comparison to the FBI, CIA and KGB the size of the British agencies is minuscule. Before World War II MI5 comprised just thirty officers, and while at the time of the collapse of Communism it had grown to 2349 people – that is still relatively small.

The occasional disclosure of spy scandals and the fascination of the public with anything to do with spying gave the British Secret Intelligence Service (MI6) and the Security Service (MI5) a much higher profile than they desired. The safety of agents in the field was paramount, especially for MI6 whose operations resemble those of the CIA. They are responsible for gathering overseas intelligence, running foreign agents and organising covert political intervention in faraway places where the British have some kind of interest.

MI5, generally operating on home territory though not confined to it, also attempted to remain behind its wall of secrecy in its quest to protect British secrets from foreign spies, trace and track subversives, terrorists, saboteurs, political activists and anyone else who its agents convinced themselves were potential troublemakers. At one time Peter Mandelson, the future Northern Ireland Secretary, and Jack Straw, the future Home Secretary, were among the latter group.

The British intelligence community's largest and most important group is Government Communications Headquarters at Cheltenham. Its staff are past masters of all forms of electronic surveillance and cryptology on which the Humint people rely for transcripts of coded diplomatic material, signals from agents and all other kinds of spy communications. In 1989 GCHQ employed close on ten thousand people, of whom a third were on overseas or military postings. They included some of the world's most skilled operatives in that field, who have a history linked to some of Britain's finest military hours.

Around the time of the development of Echelon, considered by some as the second most important period in GCHQ's history (the first being its efforts in World War II), Prime Minister Margaret Thatcher decided to ban its staff from being members of any trade union. It was a move which caused uproar but was steamrollered through and remained in force until the New Labour government of 1997 kept its promise and repealed the ban. In all, at the beginning of the 1990s Britain employed around seventeen thousand people in the full-time occupation of espionage, counterespionage and technical surveillance, excluding a substantial number of Military Intelligence people, and contingents in Special Branch and the police.

US INTELLIGENCE AGENCIES

The Americans have at least 340,000 people in their sprawling civilian and military network of eighteen separate intelligence units. The network is so vast that accountability was never at the forefront of its achievements. The whole comes under the collective banner of the American intelligence community although its public face, through years of exposure, lies principally with the CIA and FBI, largely because of some of the more hair-raising misadventures of modern times which were attributed to them.

The CIA's areas of operation fall under three main headings: collection, evaluation and transmission of foreign intelligence; counter-intelligence operations; and covert political intervention on foreign soil, psychological warfare and running overseas paramilitary operations. Most of its employees are in research and analysis, producing weekly bulletins for the supreme commanders of the US intelligence community and the military. They are supposedly able to produce the best intelligence on any person, country or situation anywhere in the world. It is a claim that has often been challenged.

Before the end of the Cold War, the CIA employed twenty-three thousand men and women plus may thousands of others as informers and part-time agents around the world. To this effort was added the Defense Intelligence Agency (DIA), set up to 'improve the intelligence product' to the joint chiefs of staff, plus separate army, navy and air force intelligence units, State Department intelligence, a nuclear intelligence unit, and the National Reconnaissance Office which manages satellite programming for the whole intelligence community. The largest and least accountable of all, the NSA, employed an estimated twenty thousand civilians and supervised thousands of others distributed throughout all of the other US military intelligence services.

The NSA remains the most costly and least public of all American intelligence organisations. It is usually led by a high-ranking military officer and is directly responsible to the US Secretary of Defense, but maintains a level of autonomy that every one of the US agencies would die for. From its headquarters at Fort Meade, near Washington, DC, it has built up, from its creation in 1952, the largest electronic surveillance and espionage machine the world has ever known – overtaking the

Soviet Union's capability in the mid-1980s. Its intelligence is obtained from satellites, aircraft, ships, submarines and ground installations strategically positioned around the world. One of its earliest and briefest public exposures occurred when the spy ship USS *Pueblo* was captured by the North Koreans while conducting surveillance against North Korean and Soviet naval operations in the Sea of Japan in 1968. Its crew was detained for a year.

The US annual spend on intelligence in the early 1990s was estimated at around $23 billion. A decade later this remains the case, in spite of labour cuts. The additional money freed, for example, through the reduction of the CIA by about three thousand staff, has been ploughed largely into new surveillance hardware which itself requires less manpower.

At the fall of Communism, US intelligence had at least three hundred and fifty thousand employees in the United States and overseas, in addition to substantial numbers in the US military engaged in parallel roles. Until 1991–2 their joint forces had been marshalled principally against the Soviet Union and the KGB, and associated intelligence agencies in the Warsaw Pact countries.

SOVIET INTELLIGENCE

The Soviet intelligence set-up was a kind of CIA, FBI and MI6 rolled into one and had an even larger staff than the combined US intelligence services. Created in line with the traditions of the Cheka secret police of the Bolsheviks in 1917, the KGB's foreign intelligence, counter-intelligence and internal security roles provided the model for most other Communist countries and, from 1954, dominated the entire Soviet intelligence system. Its true size and cost was never known but its annual intelligence bill was probably half as much again as the Americans', with at least half a million employees and thousands of other willing helpers across the globe, a number of whom were exposed in the UK in 1999.

ATTEMPTS TO OPEN THE FILES

All the intelligence agencies mentioned relied, for the greater part of their existence, on Humint. Spies and agents remained in place well beyond the end of the Cold War. Those in the UKUSA nations also benefited from an exchange of intelligence on common matters, though by no means to the extent that existed between NSA and GCHQ. The interrelationship between the agencies and the technical intelligence gatherers also permitted a system of denial to emerge, if they so desired. For years, well-known personalities on both sides of the Atlantic had their suspicions of surveillance thrown back in their faces.

Technically, denials by public spokesmen were not necessarily untrue; they were simply repeating assurances from those concerned. As John Ranelagh points out in his devastating *The Agency: The Rise and Decline of the CIA*, that organisation was awash with paperwork recording, in some way or other, most of the events that eventually brought it into deep trouble. MI5 and MI6 offices were similarly stuffed with manually created files. Computerisation in both these British agencies was very late in arriving, partly because of their mistrust of committing anything to electronic storage systems which were prone to interception or damage. By the end of the century, MI5's computer system was being used largely for indexing and cross-referencing while files themselves remained in paper form.

The storage vaults of the NSA, GCHQ and their counterparts in Canada, Australia and New Zealand, meanwhile, housed the real secrets, said Ranelagh, 'locked up on spools and tapes, away from people and paper'. In that way, the Comint people have tended to avoid recent more intrusive investigations once public distrust of the intelligence services had begun to demand more accountability and openness – calls which were answered to some degree in America but have been consistently ignored by successive governments in Britain.

In post-Watergate America, a series of high-level public inquiries and congressional investigations throughout the 1970s and 1980s revealed some of the eccentricities and downright madness behind many CIA operations which have become well known over the years. The Rockefeller Commission was the first to unearth the CIA assassination plots, including those on the lives of Patrice Lumumba in the Congo,

The trend in modern systems is to make the tools of surveillance as inconspicuous as possible. This innocent lamp-style fitting actually houses a powerful Philips G3 EnviroDome™ zoom camera. Many cameras are impossible to detect, fitted behind such standard office equipment as wall clocks, exit signs or even inside the computer terminal, some wired for sound.
(Courtesy Philips Communications and Security Systems, USA)

The uniqueness of each person's fingerprint enables systems like the Fingerscan V20 (above) to ensure that only authorised personnel are granted access to secure areas of the workplace. *(Courtesy Identix Inc)*

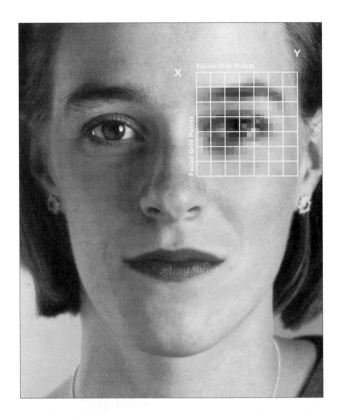

Facial recognition systems create a 'face print' from a photograph based on the unique characteristics of a person's face. They are being widely introduced in the US in efforts to reduce photo identity fraud and the modern phenomenon of 'identity theft'. This system uses a bone-structure template that disregards changes in lighting, skin tones, glasses, facial expressions and hairstyles.
(Courtesy Polaroid Corporation, USA)

Top and middle: They loom out of the landscape, like something from *X-Files:* a couple of dozen massive white domes that look like giant golf balls. This is Menwith Hill, Yorkshire, the most important American intelligence base on foreign soil. *(© John Parker)*

Left: A sister site to the Menwith Hill facility is the National Security Agency base at Bad Aibling in Germany, south east of Munich. This major signals intelligence interception centre is thought to be one of the seven bases across the world in the Echelon system of intelligence gathering. *(Picture from Federation of American Scientists website at www.fas.org)*

FEDERAL BUREAU OF INVESTIGATION

Origin: WASHINGTON, D. C.			File No. 100-1181 MBH	
Made at: SAVANNAH, GEORGIA	Date Made 2-9-42	Period 2-6-9-42	Made by E. H. ADKINS	
Title CHANGED: Mrs. PAUL FEJOS, alias Inga Arvad, Barbara White			Character INTERNAL SECURITY - G	

Synopsis of Facts:

PERSONAL AND CONFIDENTIAL

Surveillance maintained upon subject from
the time of her arrival in Charleston, S.C.
at 8:20 A.M. on 2-6-42 until her departure
therefrom on 2-9-42 at 1:09 A.M. to return
to Washington, D. C. While there, JOHN
KENNEDY, Ensign, U. S. Navy, spent each
night with subject in her hotel room at the
Fort Sumter Hotel, engaging in sexual inter-
course on numerous occasions. Subject was
vexed at KENNEDY'S failure to introduce her
to a Naval officer. Only information gained
by subject of possible espionage value, fact
that KENNEDY proceeding to Norfolk, Va. soon
for training, fire control work, also serious
illness of HARRY HOPKINS, Presidential
Advisor.

-RUC-

REFERENCE: Report of Special Agent W. M. WELCH dated
2-2-42 at Washington, D. C.
Letter from the Washington Field Division to
Bureau dated Feb. 5, 1942.

	SAC			RECORDED
Copies: 5 Bureau (AISD) 2 Norfolk 3 Washington Field (AISD) 2 New York 1 Salt Lake City (Info.) 2 Savannah		65-39058-3/5	FEB 11 1942	

Under the directorship of J Edgar Hoover, the FBI led the world in
the early days of electronic interception of individuals in private
places. Inga Arvad, a Danish journalist and former Miss World was
being monitored because Hoover suspected she was a Nazi spy.
The young naval officer she was entertaining and whose
conversations and love-making were taped for posterity was none
other than John Fitzgerald Kennedy.

CODE   TELETYPE   IMMEDIATE

CONFIDENTIAL (crossed out)

5/24/72

TO   SACS NEW YORK (100-175319)
          HOUSTON   1 - Mr. C.W. Bates
                                                   (C.A. Nuzum)
FROM   ACTING DIRECTOR FBI (100-469910) - 14   1 - Mr. R.L. Shackelford
                                               1 - Mr. R.L. Pence
       JOHN WINSTON LENNON, SM - REVOLUTIONARY ACTIVITIES.

       RENYTEL MAY TWENTY-THREE LAST.

       HOUSTON DISREGARD LEAD SET BY NEW YORK IN REFERENCED TELETYPE

EXCEPT FOR CONTACT WITH ESTABLISHED SOURCES ONLY.

       BUREAU FULLY AWARE PROGRESS OF NEW YORK OFFICE IN DEVELOPING

EXCELLENT COVERAGE SUBJECT'S ACTIVITIES, HOWEVER, ASPECTS INVESTI-

GATION RELATING TO SUBJECT'S APPEARANCE AT INS HEARINGS AND POSSIBLE

PERJURY INVOLVED IN FALSE STATEMENTS MADE BY SUBJECT STRICTLY

RESPONSIBILITY OF INS. INFORMATION DEVELOPED BY NEW YORK SHOULD BE

IMMEDIATELY, IF NOT ALREADY, FURNISHED TO INS. ALL SUBSEQUENT

INFORMATION DEVELOPED REGARDING SUBJECT'S VIOLATIONS OF FEDERAL AND

LOCAL LAWS INCLUDING NARCOTICS OR PERJURY, SHOULD LIKEWISE BE

DISSEMINATED WITHOUT DELAY TO PERTINENT AGENCIES.

RLP:mcm   (8)   CLASS. & EXT. BY
       NOTE: Declas on   REASON-FIM II, 1-2.4.2
                                      DATE OF REVIEW
              Lennon is former member of Beatles singing group in
       England who, despite clear ineligibility for U.S. visa due to
       narcotics conviction in England in 1968, was allowed to reenter
       U.S. during 1971 on visitors visa. Visas of Lennon and wife, Yoko
       Ono, expired 2/72 and since that time Immigration and Naturalization
       Service (INS) has been attempting to deport Lennons.

Tolson
Felt
Campbell
Rosen
Mohr
Bishop
Miller, E.S.
Callahan
Casper
Conrad
Dalbey
Cleveland   COMMUNICATIONS SECTION
Ponder
Bates   MAY 24 1972
Waikart
Walters
Soyars
Tele. Room   70 JUN ... 1972   CONFIDENTIAL   NOTE CONTINUED - OVER
Holmes
Gandy   MAIL ROOM [ ] TELETYPE UNIT [ ]   ALL INFORMATION CONTAINED
                                               HEREIN IS UNCLASSIFIED EXCEPT
                                               WHERE SHOWN OTHERWISE.

John Lennon's interest in various anti-war groups was sufficient for
J Edgar Hoover to keep him under virtual constant surveillance.

Left: The two-faced J Edgar Hoover enthusiastically greets Marilyn Monroe (with his pal Milton Berle) despite keeping her under almost constant surveillance for several years.

Below: Monroe and her former husband Arthur Miller were surrounded by an aura of speculation and gossip and were monitored by all forms of covert FBI surveillance.

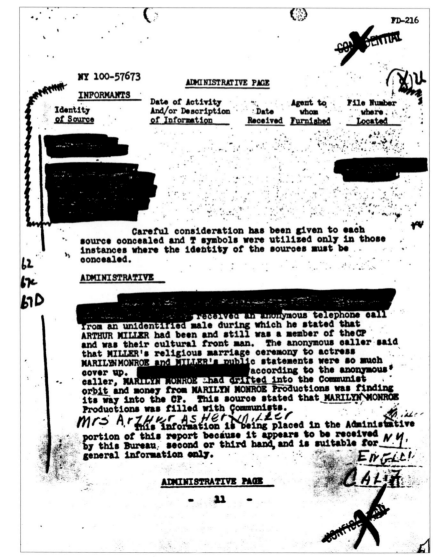

FD-216

CONFIDENTIAL

NY 100-57673

ADMINISTRATIVE PAGE

INFORMANTS

Identity of Source	Date of Activity And/or Description of Information	Date Received	Agent to whom Furnished	File Number where Located

Careful consideration has been given to each source concealed and T symbols were utilized only in those instances where the identity of the sources must be concealed.

62
67c
67D

ADMINISTRATIVE

received an anonymous telephone call from an unidentified male during which he stated that ARTHUR MILLER had been and still was a member of the CP and was their cultural front man. The anonymous caller said that MILLER's religious marriage ceremony to actress MARILYN MONROE and MILLER's public statements were so much cover up. ████████ according to the anonymous caller, MARILYN MONROE had drifted into the Communist orbit and money from MARILYN MONROE Productions was finding its way into the CP. This source stated that MARILYN MONROE Productions was filled with Communists.

Mrs Arthur Asher Miller

This information is being placed in the Administrative portion of this report because it appears to be received by this Bureau, second or third hand, and is suitable for general information only.

N.Y.

ENGLD!
CALIF.

ADMINISTRATIVE PAGE

- 11 -

Left: A vast array of clandestine bugging and tapping devices are now available, although the legality of their use is often questionable depending on the country you are in. They cover every possible situation from bugging offices or private homes to tapping a whole office telephone network. Miniaturisation of equipment, pioneered in the darkest days of violence in Northern Ireland and for American intelligence, produced such trinkets as tiny microphones inserted in walls from the outside. The 'bugs' come in all shapes, sizes and uses. This credit card sized transmitter can be very easily concealed. Slim enough to be slid under a door, it can also be carried in a pocket or left in the back of a book.

Above and left: Other popular bugs include the ball point pen which can be kept in the jacket pocket or left lying on a desk and a simple office calculator. Both fit discreetly into any office situation but are in reality powerful recording and transmitting systems used to bug meetings or simply left lying around in the workplace to monitor employees. Because they are so inconspicuous the manufacturers suggest that these devices can either accompany you into a room or be left behind to transmit conversations to a remote location. *(All courtesy Lorraine Electronics Surveillance)*

Left: The mobile receiver pictured here has been specifically designed for unattended radio controlled monitoring of telephone transmitters.

Middle below: Designed for covert use, this body worn recording system can easily be concealed in a pocket, a bag or about the body. Only a few millimetres larger than the tape, the recorder has a separate extension lead for the microphone and on/off switch to allow discrete control – especially useful in difficult operating conditions.

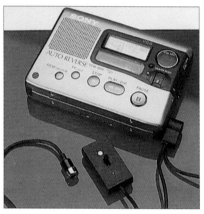

Below: This recording briefcase uses the latest acoustic technology and a system of cleverly concealed microphones and electronics to enable it to record and optionally transmit conversations.

(All courtesy Lorraine Electronics Surveillance)

Fidel Castro and Colonel Abdul Kassem of Iraq. Thereafter, in other public hearings, notably the Senate Inquiry chaired by Senator Frank Church and the Pike Select Committee on intelligence matters, an insistent spotlight was shone on some – but not all – of the CIA's darker corners.

No such wide-ranging investigation has ever been staged in Great Britain, nor indeed among any of its Commonwealth allies. What detail has filtered out has come invariably from occasional spy trials or from a few operatives who were disgusted enough to leave their particular service and risk prosecution and imprisonment by making guarded public statements about why they had become so disillusioned. One, Peter Wright, author of *Spycatcher* which Margaret Thatcher famously tried to ban, did it for the money but his recollections, though fascinating, were unreliable. Others were either prosecuted or ignored by the mandarins, depending on what kind of information might have come into the public domain as a result of a court hearing.

By necessity, some secrets and accounts of intelligence-gathering activities have to remain hidden; but in Britain everything that comes within the sphere of MI5, MI6 or GCHQ is considered so sensitive that it is locked away for years. It was, after all, only in 1999 that Britain released details of the involvement of its intelligence services with Mata Hari, the Dutch dancer executed in Paris for spying for the Germans in 1917.

The ridiculous nature of the secrecy that prevails in Britain at the turn of the millennium will continue for the foreseeable future because the New Labour government and Home Secretary Jack Straw reneged on their pre-election promises to install effective machinery for the release of documents that are well past their sell-by date. The version that Straw came up with in 1999 was regarded by journalists and anti-secrecy campaigners as a joke.

It is also ironical that Jack Straw himself, when a young Labour activist, was a target for MI5 observation during its mass surveillance of suspected 'subversives' during the 1970s and 1980s. His case, along with dozens of others, reveals how unnecessary so much of the time and energy spent monitoring people on the fringes of left-wing movements and trade unions really was. True, there were some who were intent on upsetting the government of the day and were undoubtedly in touch with the Communists, but the extent and coverage of MI5 surveillance was never really justified.

Thousands of MI5 man-hours were spent gathering whatever evidence it could accumulate across the board on the alleged subversive activities of left-wing personalities and politicians, union leaders and heads of campaigning organisations such as CND, Amnesty International, the National Council for Civil Liberties and Greenpeace. MI5 has never had to face the scrutiny of public examination in the style of the Church Committee in the United States, and it was left to the likes of Cathy Massiter to inform the public of a small, and possibly minimally offensive, example of goings-on.

Cathy Massiter and MI5

Massiter worked for MI5 for fourteen years, from 1970 to 1984, when she resigned, disillusioned by what she described as a fundamental change of emphasis. The service, she maintained, had progressively moved away from its post-World War II attack on counterespionage, aimed at the activities of agents of foreign powers, and had begun to concentrate more heavily on domestic surveillance. As the direction of the service changed, she and others became increasingly concerned. Operations of bugging and burgling, which had been acceptable when they were used against a hostile enemy and its agents, were being turned upon the British nationals whom MI5 considered dangerous subversives, an assessment, incidentally, which was left entirely to the officers themselves.

A spectacular raid on the Communist Party of Great Britain when MI5 agents broke into a London flat and copied the files of its fifty thousand members was considered reasonable. So was the monitoring of other Communist front organisations and of true subversives and agents who had infiltrated British life in order to cause mayhem and strife. The same tactics were employed against the IRA in Northern Ireland – although in theory MI5 was not allowed to pursue the paramilitaries of either side on the mainland.

To turn the same surveillance tactics on to domestic targets, whose threat to national security barely registered, was not only against government policy but in contravention of the service's own code of conduct. In other words, some of its operations were illegal. Even so, both Conservative and Labour governments utilised this service to their own benefit. Again this was against the MI5 code of conduct, which states that the organisation shall at no time be used for political ends.

At the time Cathy Massiter was recruited, two branches, KX and KY, were devoted to pursuing the activities of agents of foreign powers on British soil. Eventually, the two were merged and reduced in size. F branch, on the other hand, which was responsible for domestic intelligence, expanded rapidly and created a subsection known as FX. The desk which specifically ran investigations into trade unions increased threefold in five years. Massiter herself became an intelligence officer one year after joining MI5 as a secretary and was soon to witness a quest for more, and better, intelligence on Britain's most powerful union leaders and left-wingers.

The names of these perceived bogeymen are now familiar to all – union leaders like Arthur Scargill and Mick McGaghey and politicians like Tony Benn and Ken Livingstone who, if they had been operating in America, would have been considered raging lefties and subjected to the worst that J. Edgar Hoover could throw at them. True, their views were extreme – sufficient still for Tony Blair to state in the autumn of 1999 that they had brought the Labour Party to the edge of extinction. Whether this merited the surveillance under which they were placed was another matter.

The focus on what was called subversion, but with an exceedingly broad base, began to intensify under the latter stages of Edward Heath's Conservative government, which was brought down in 1974 by the four-week miners' strike which had forced the nation on to a three-day working week. Harold Wilson's incoming Labour government did nothing to halt surveillance operations against the unions and, indeed, demanded more and better intelligence on the powerful union leaders, such as Jack Jones who represented the transport workers, Hugh Scanlon the engineers and Joe Gormley the miners. Apparently the aim was to find ways of getting their unions' backing for the Social Contract that Wilson had promised the electorate would end Britain's industrial strife. It didn't, and the expansion of MI5's domestic surveillance continued.

Harold Wilson: Soviet Spy?

Another irony in the fractious relationship between the intelligence people and politicians of that era arose when Wilson himself claimed he had become a target of MI5. The claim was made after his house was entered without a trace of a break-in in October 1974, soon after winning a second general election, and personal documents were stolen. He was convinced that a right-wing faction of MI5 was plotting against him and wanted him out, a theory which Peter Wright supported in a section of his book. The plot was supposedly anchored to Wilson's regular visits to Moscow, and some acquaintances with Soviet bloc connections.

MI5 denied any knowledge of a plot and continues to do so, although there is no doubt that they, and MI6 and the CIA, took an interest in Wilson's visits behind the Iron Curtain. MI5 certainly had its own 'hotbed of right-wingers' who were not only arrogant and danger-ous but who, as a matter of course, did not consider themselves bound by the strictures of a Labour government. The mystery of the Wilson break-in has never been satisfactorily resolved, though recently I have heard a story that is impossible to substantiate or discount: that Peter Wright himself directed the break-in at arm's length and it was carried out, not by MI5, but by two freelance burglars on the direct instructions of James Jesus Angleton, head of the CIA's counterintelligence unit. He was convinced that Wilson had Soviet links and that the British Prime Minister had surrounded himself with an entourage of like-minded friends and aides; at least two of them did indeed have strong business links on the other side of the Iron Curtain, but then so did many people in public life in Britain at the time.

Drawing on dubious information from recent defectors from Soviet Russia, Angleton became obsessed with the notion that the British Prime Minister had been recruited as the ultimate Soviet asset. It was Angleton, too, who eagerly pushed the theory that the death of the previous Labour leader, Hugh Gaitskell, from a mysterious illness ought to have been investigated more thoroughly, since he had probably been murdered by the KGB to get Wilson into power. Peter Wright recalled that he personally had gone down to Porton Down, the British top secret chemical and biological warfare establishment, to test out the theory –

probably at Angleton's behest; they certainly discussed it between themselves.

The burglary operation against Wilson, so the story goes, was carried out without the knowledge of Angleton's boss William Colby. Two months after the break-in Angleton was fired from the CIA after twenty-eight years' service. His dismissal came after Pulitzer prize-winning journalist Seymour Hersh revealed in the *New York Times* details of Operation Chaos, run by Angleton in response to a directive from President Johnson in the early 1970s. Angleton's team had conducted illegal surveillance, telephone bugging, mail openings and burglaries against anti-Vietnam war protesters and organisations, including a number of British personalities such as John Lennon and George Harrison.

Wilson himself, meanwhile, became as obsessed by the 'MI5 plot' as Angleton was obsessed by Wilson. The rumour mill – undoubtedly propagated by friends of MI5, if not by themselves – never gave up trying to suggest that there was a dark secret in Wilson's past that had lured him into a Soviet trap. As the MP Winston Churchill (grandson of the wartime leader) once pointed out (although not in any way implicated in any such alleged plot): 'The question mark that does arise in many people's minds is the fact that he paid no less than nineteen visits to the Soviet Union. And that does provide the other side with certain opportunities.'

When Wilson surprised the nation by resigning as Prime Minister fourteen months later, the theory that he had been forced out by the discovery of his Soviet connections was widely discussed. That theory was, according to my former *Mirror* colleague and Wilson's press secretary Joe Haines, 'utter nonsense'. Even so, the fact remains that a number of senior people in Wilson's administration were targeted by MI5 and the CIA at the time. They included the deputy leader of the Labour Party, Ted Short (later Lord Glenamara). A number of newspapers were sent photocopies of an alleged Swiss bank account in his name containing a substantial sum. They were forgeries: Short never had a Swiss bank account. Scotland Yard investigators said the forgeries were the work of a professional, and Short pointed the finger at MI5. Tony Benn, in correspondence with me in 1995, recounted some very strange events during that era, the responsibility for which he quite clearly placed upon the security services.

Merlyn Rees, a Home Secretary in the Labour government in which both Short and Benn also served, had earlier cleared MI5 of nefarious activities, apparently accepting the assurances of the department that nothing so terrible had happened. He later changed his mind, and during the Thatcher years, when Labour was in opposition, he called for an inquiry into the activities of the intelligence services and particularly into that period when the rumours of an MI5 right-wing plot were rife.

There had been one other definite attempt to oust Wilson, however, that could be linked indirectly to MI5 through the man who engineered it, Cecil King, then the powerful chairman of Mirror Group Newspapers and its owners IPC. King was an unpaid MI5 agent/informer and in his position as chairman of the *Mirror*, a Labour-supporting paper, entertained many politicians, bosses of industry and union leaders. The guests were drawn from every power stratum of British life. Lunches and dinners at the *Mirror* were always plentifully supplied with fine wines. Loose talk was not uncommon, especially from some like Chancellor of the Exchequer George Brown. King himself was a master of indiscretion and would attempt to force into the *Daily Mirror* rumours about public figures which were often quite unfounded.

In 1968 King turned against Wilson and, as the nation plunged into economic and monetary crisis, became a prime mover in a campaign to oust him. The story, which has become familiar to those who have read Lord Cudlipp's autobiography, began at 4.30 on the afternoon of 8 May 1968 when King and his deputy, then plain Hugh Cudlipp, called upon Lord Mountbatten at his London home in Kinnerton Street, Belgravia. The meeting had been prearranged and Sir Solly Zuckerman, one of Wilson's own friends and advisers, was also present. King proceeded to outline his fears about a situation of national gravity, embarked upon a tirade against Wilson, and said he foresaw widespread public disorder, riots on the streets and the armed forces being called in to deal with their own people. King then made the astounding suggestion that Mountbatten should become titular head of a government of national unity, backed by 'some of the best brains in Britain'. Zuckerman walked out of the meeting, calling King's proposal rank treachery. Mountbatten's extreme vanity was flattered by the idea, but the approach came to nothing. Two days later, King published his famous leader article which was carried on the front page of the *Mirror* under the headline 'Enough Is Enough'. It ran alongside the story of 'Labour's Plunge to Election Disaster' in local council elections. King called for Wilson to be sacked and Labour ousted from office to save the nation from 'the greatest financial crisis in our history'. In fact it was King who was ousted – sacked soon after by the IPC board. Ironically, MI5 director Sir Martin Furnival Jones was given the task of heading an investigation into that and subsequent manoeuvres against Wilson and reported his findings to his own boss, Home Secretary James Callaghan, who replaced Wilson when he resigned in 1976.

Surveillance of Other Public Figures

Cecil King's role as MI5 agent was not uncommon. Cathy Massiter confirmed that there were 'literally hundreds' of agents and paid or unpaid informers throughout British public life, targeting domestic organisations and individuals to what another source described as 'quite an inconsequential level'. Throughout the 1970s, MI5 surveillance of public figures, journalists, teachers, pacifists, lawyers and MPs was carried out through its expanding F Branch. Many well-known names were targeted.

Patricia Hewitt, then general secretary of the National Council for Civil Liberties (later an adviser to Labour leader Neil Kinnock and a member of Tony Blair's government), and one of its legal officers, Harriet Harman (also to become a Labour minister), were placed on record as possible Communist sympathisers and potential subversives. 'They had done nothing wrong,' said Massiter, 'nothing illegal. And yet inquiries were instituted against the NCCL ... police inquiries were sought.'

Labour disputes and strikes aroused the immediate interest of MI5 and, as Max Hastings pointed out in an article in the *Evening Standard* at the time, there was no doubt that there were many Communist and left-wing agitators among the instigators and promoters of industrial strife and unrest. There were few union leaders of the day who were not targeted by MI5, some of them deservedly so. Massiter recalled: 'Whenever a major dispute came up ... immediately it would be a major area for investigation: what were the Communists doing in respect of this particular industrial action, and usually an application for a telephone check would be taken out on the leading comrade in the particular union concerned.'

This obsessive effort in tracking the movements of alleged subversives, which accounted for the time of so many MI5 operatives and the creation of hundreds of paper files, was pursued over a number of years when other areas demanded greater attention and expertise than they were receiving from the British intelligence community. The situation in Northern Ireland, for example, where there was a real job to be done, passed through stages of sheer incompetence, mismanagement, misinterpretation and internecine rivalry between MI5 and competing agencies, including MI6 and Military Intelligence. There were some disgraceful operations including one, led by MI5 and codenamed Clockwork Orange, which was originally aimed at isolating and exposing sectarian killers but ended up being used as a disinformation operation against ministers of the then Labour government. Using tactics which would not have been out of place in East Germany, it was designed to discover skeletons in the closets of politicians in three specific areas: sexual, financial and political misbehaviour. Merlyn Rees (later Lord Rees), who was Home Secretary at the time, said in a BBC interview: 'I discovered that the dirty tricks campaign included a list of politicians of all parties. A psy-ops [psychological operations] was also run against politicians in both the north and south of Ireland ... it was out of control.'

The surveillance of public figures merely expanded under the new Conservative administration of Margaret Thatcher, who occasionally intervened personally. In 1983, a new clandestine department called DS19 had been created at Michael Heseltine's Ministry of Defence to combat the unilateral disarmament campaign by CND and others. MI5 was approached to supply information on the 'subversive' affiliations of members of CND. Massiter herself wrote a report for DS19 containing unclassified material which had, in the main, been obtained through the bugging and surveillance methods employed by MI5 at the time, and were now being used for political purposes. MI5 was also responsible for covert action that was clearly in tandem with Mrs Thatcher's exceedingly overt union-bashing policy – not least in banning the trade unions from GCHQ, and threatening to sack any staff who did not end their membership. She needed that kind of input for the dramatic reforms that she pushed through during her eleven years as Prime Minister, many of which were to be picked up and pursued by New Labour. Tony Blair has made no secret of his distaste for the powerful left-wing factions in the Labour movement which, he said, kept the party out of office for seventeen years.

Increasingly the intelligence services have been criticised for incompetence and bad practice. Many people supported the views expressed by Max Hastings in his piece for the *Evening Standard* on 4 March 1985:

> The tales that emerge from both MI5 and MI6 of demoralised staff and incompetent leadership, of overblown bureaucracies playing with whirlygigs of paper, all suggest a desperate state of affairs in both departments . . . a grim reflection of a staff so poorly directed that they can see neither the purpose nor justice in what they do. On my own occasional encounters with the intelligence services, the same story is always told of high-quality recruits who quickly become disillusioned and leave. As a result far too many low-grade people are tolerated.

The state of affairs outlined by Hastings clearly existed among many departments of the human intelligence units of the world's leading intelligence gatherers. The CIA had, by the mid-1980s, been subjected to searching inquiries into its own appalling record of illegal activities. But more criticism was directed at its failures in the acquisition and assessment of vital intelligence situations around the world, a lot of the information having been completely misread and misjudged by CIA analysts. Society itself was also beginning to turn against the methods of surveillance conducted by the spy agencies – at the very time, ironically, that even greater surveillance of ordinary citizens came on stream with Echelon and the general interception of communications.

The point has been made often enough: what was the benefit derived from mass surveillance of politicians, left-wingers, journalists and public servants during that era? What did it achieve? History has shown it achieved very little during the McCarthy era in the USA.

Similarly, across Europe left-wing agitators were present in every sphere of public life. Everyone knew who they were: people such as Derek 'Red Robbo' Robinson, the man credited with causing numerous strikes in the British motor industry. These people soon became known to the public without help from MI5 or the FBI, largely through their own actions. It was not really the domain of the security agencies to stop them; it was a political and employment issue. Yet much time and energy was expended against them during the 1970s and 1980s on the basis that, because of this surveillance, they were stopped from becoming a more serious threat. That is truly debatable. Even so, according to MI5 sources, minutiae provided the raw material on which to build a profile of a suspect or target group from which further investigations could be developed, and thus cross-linking of records and files became crucial to the MI5 system. Surprisingly, when the world outside had adapted to computers, in 1998 paper files still underpinned MI5 work and remained the main working documents of the service. Extensive computer systems had been installed for the indexing and retrieval of its records which remain the sole preserve of MI5 itself. No government department or other agency has access to its databases, although assessment reports or specific information can be supplied, particularly for a police investigation.

Close on one million files involving millions of names have been opened by MI5 at some time since its establishment in 1909, although the bulk came into existence after World War II. Even so, compared to other accumulations of files and databases around the globe, it was not an especially huge figure. Around one hundred and eighty thousand pre-war files were destroyed in the 1950s and 1960s, and in 1988 just under half a million files were being maintained in the MI5 registry. Of these, thirty-five thousand files involved the service itself: its administration, policy and staff. About seventy-five thousand files related to people or groups of people who have never been investigated but were involved with MI5 in some other way, such as receiving protective security or advice. The majority of files, close on three hundred thousand, relate to individuals who have been the subject of MI5 investigation or scrutiny. Of these, forty thousand are in the highest level of classification and have been placed on microfilm under a restricted code for which officers may only have access for a specific purpose. A further quarter of a million files are considered closed, but may be used by staff in the course of their current work. In other words, the lives of thousands of people who may have come under investigation in the past are still available for scrutiny, regardless of the relevance of their involvements twenty or thirty years ago.

In 1998, the number of files considered active and under current investigation numbered around twenty thousand, of which about a third concerned foreign nationals, leaving approximately thirteen thousand active files on citizens of the United Kingdom. These are likely to remain open indefinitely. A policy of non-destruction of files was adopted in the 1960s when the service experienced difficulties investigating some spy cases because earlier records had been shredded. Even so, since the end of the Cold War a large number of cases have been reviewed and the MI5 directorate has earmarked one hundred and ten thousand files for destruction. These include records of attempts by Soviet and Warsaw Pact intelligence services to recruit spies from within what MI5 considered were subversive groups in Britain. Clearly, thousands of people in Britain during that particular period were being watched and, famously, among them was Bruce Kent, at the time head of CND.

Targeting Bruce Kent

When, in 1999, the spy scandal emerged in which numerous people in British life were named as being 'agents' of Communist governments though never prosecuted, Bruce Kent reflected in the *Guardian* on being 'caught up in yet another time warp CND-equals-Soviet-agents story. My stomach turned over. I remembered it all too well. The sneers, the hatred, the funding allegations and the lies. Some sociologist will one day write a thesis out of my box files. "Dear Bruce, I wouldn't give you the steam off my piss if you were burning alive – you red scum." Nasty and anonymous alongside the nasty and not at all anonymous.'

He recalled past headlines claiming that CND was a tool of Moscow. In 1999, fifteen years after Gorbachev began the process of unfreezing the Cold War, Kent was also discovered to have had a Stasi file: 'They wouldn't have been doing their job if I had not.' *The Times*, which in 1982 reported much of the criticism which Kent made in Moscow that year about Soviet behaviour, now took up the Stasi theme:

'CND, like many peace movements in the west, was manipulated by Moscow.' Kent moaned:

> What a waste of time all this is. In a world which now has at least eight nuclear weapon states, with thousands of nuclear warheads, many not properly maintained, and with nuclear terrorism an active possibility, one would have thought that there were more constructive things to do for the good of the world than to rerun the battles of the Thatcher years. Of course there were – and no doubt are – government agents, paid and unpaid, about. But there were no CND secrets. Was there ever a more open organisation? Anyone could join. Decisions were taken in public and were duly published. We all knew that phones were tapped and the mail interfered with. What we did not know was that MI5 had actually planted an informant in our office posing as a volunteer. A nice old gentleman he was too, even if he subsequently reported to his superiors that I was a 'pseudo-Marxist'. Were there also Soviet supporters within CND feeding information eastwards? Nothing would surprise me. . . . It would only have been significant if such people had managed to change CND policy in a pro-Soviet direction. This they never managed to do. They were heard, politely applauded and regularly voted down. If anything the threats from the various Trotskyite movements were potentially more disruptive.

Even so, MI5 remained convinced that Britain faced a very real threat from subversive organisations and individuals who they believed were openly seeking to undermine parliamentary democracy and had the capability to do so. But suddenly, all that vanished. Subversion went out like a dose of salts, almost overnight, with the fall of Communism. By the end of 1998, MI5 had not a single active investigation against any person or organisation suspected of subversion. In fact, the only resources allocated to this work were a tiny amount earmarked to pay the pensions of retired agents of the anti-subversion group – a task which employed the attentions of just one member of MI5 staff.

CHAPTER 10
TURF WARS: REDEFINING THE ROLE OF THE AGENCIES

READING BETWEEN THE LINES of the few public utterances of those high up in the global intelligence-gathering machine, it was possible to see a pattern of change under way as the twentieth century drew to a close. Soviet leader Mikhail Gorbachev himself predicted an upheaval in the spy trade even before he introduced glasnost and set Communism and the Soviet empire on its irreversible course. His policy of openness also kick-started the decline in the power of the KGB by allowing criticism of it. At the same time he recognised that the Soviet's lumbering intelligence network, stacked with human resources (more than half a million people at its peak), was beyond reform.

Although well versed and equipped in the arts of bugging and tapping and electronic surveillance, the KGB still relied to a greater extent upon Humint (Human Intelligence). Gorbachev had come to the conclusion that classic espionage was on the way out, and he was right. He tells us he was convinced that the future lay in communications interception, satellite imagery and all the new methods of covert surveillance, which would reduce the exposure of KGB agents (and those of the Western opposition) to media attention.

With the demise of the KGB in the offing, the Western powers began unbolting their own intelligence services from the surveillance effort against the Eastern Bloc; such an expense was no longer necessary.

All the major intelligence agencies were soon to be confronted with demands for heavy cuts in their workforce. CIA departures through budgetary cutbacks and the resignation of operatives disillusioned by the sudden reversal of policy were so heavy that some of the agency's most sensitive tasks were threatened.

Its Directorate of Operations, responsible for espionage and covert operations around the world, descended into almost total inactivity. It was also scarred by a number of scandals in the 1990s, including the discovery that one of its case officers, Aldrich Ames, had sold secrets to the KGB. His treachery, exposed in 1994, had led to the execution of a number of American agents in Soviet Russia and had also compromised British intelligence efforts. By the end of 1998 the number of CIA spies had declined to around sixteen thousand, a drop of at least 20 per cent from the end of the Cold War, although the annual budget was still running at around $2 billion. Many opponents of the CIA would have preferred to see a total shut-down, replacing it with an agency untainted by past horrors.

Losses on a similar scale were experienced by Britain's MI5 and MI6. At the time of the collapse of the Soviet empire, MI5 employed 2235, MI6 2303 and GCHQ 6228, plus around three thousand operatives working overseas. By the beginning of 1999, MI5 staff numbers had reduced to 1860, of whom 54 per cent were under forty years old and 47 per cent were women. Its budget was £140 million, about £25 million less than six years earlier. The reductions at MI6 were more or less in the same proportions but they were less drastic at GCHQ, where the budget remained around the £500 million mark. Indeed, GCHQ was earmarked for sparkling new premises and there was to be no undermining of Britain's electronic interception capability. In the meantime there had been some fancy footwork by Stella Rimington, MI5's first woman director, in an attempt to save her organisation from even deeper cuts and perhaps from total annihilation, which many of its opponents would have liked to see.

A NEW ROLE FOR MI5

Rimington said publicly that she was looking to achieve a much wider brief for MI5 now that it was to be freed of such heavy commitments to the anti-subversion cause. With more than 50 per cent of its staff then engaged in counterespionage and investigations into subversive activities, MI5 clearly needed a new role – and fast. As we have seen, subversive activity which had engaged almost a quarter of MI5 people up to the end of the Cold War was by then deemed to be non-existent, and by the end of the decade even counterespionage accounted for a mere 12 per cent of MI5 workload.

Reviews of the role of intelligence services were conducted by the former head of MI6, Sir Christopher Curwen, in 1990 and 1991. They came fresh on the heels of a number of embarrassments including the Michael Bettaney spy case, Peter Wright's disclosures and an awkward setback at the European Court of Human Rights when Patricia Hewitt and Harriet Harman sued the British government. They won their case, brought on the issue of their being investigated by MI5 as possible subversives. Curwen himself came to the conclusion that MI5 should be demoted to a subordinate role but the Home Secretary, Kenneth Clarke, rejected this advice and promptly gave the security service additional powers.

In 1992 it was given lead responsibility for intelligence work against mainland Irish Republican terrorism in addition to primary responsibility for intelligence work in relation to Loyalist terrorism and IRA activity in Europe and elsewhere. The move had been widely anticipated following a number of leaks which may have come from MI5 itself.

In April 1992, the *Irish Times* was sent documents containing confidential minutes of a quarterly meeting held in December 1991 between the Metropolitan Police's policy committee and senior area officers. The minutes apparently disclosed that the police had little intelligence on the IRA's firebombing campaign in the north of England and that the IRA threat remained high. Since 1988, the IRA has mounted over forty attacks in Britain, involving an estimated seventeen deaths. The leaks about MI5's advancement in the fight against the IRA were clearly aimed at demonstrating the need for additional intelligence which, unsurprisingly, MI5 insisted it could provide. Clarke's announcement brought to an end the primacy of the Special Branch in the fight against Republican terrorism after 109 years – the Branch was originally founded to combat Irish Fenian bombings in London.

Nothing, it seemed, would dissuade the Home Secretary from the promotion of MI5 into other areas from which it had previously been excluded. As Clarke made clear in the House of Commons, the ending of the Cold War meant that 'we simply have the opportunity to switch more resources within the security services into this key area of Irish republican terrorism in this country. . . . As a result of political changes, there is greater opportunity for the security service to put more of its resources into that activity.'

Stella Rimington grasped her opportunity. Something of a turf war broke out as she made it known that MI5 would be available to take on high-level investigations across a wide range of domestic issues. This came even as the newly formed National Crime Intelligence Service was pushing to set up its own surveillance unit, with powers for telephone tapping and mail opening, bugging homes and offices, and placing undercover agents in suspect groups. Rimington broke the lifelong tradition of MI5 directors and revealed her identity. She spoke in public to the English Speaking Union in 1995, making her pitch that MI5 should be recognised as *the* 'national intelligence agency' and that it was well placed to act as the intelligence and surveillance arm of the police on serious crimes, drug trafficking and organised crime. Rimington, for once needing some real PR, rolled out a few secrets of her own which had been carefully selected to interest the media. The interest was pretty well assured in the first place with Britain's number one spy chief coming into public view and even hinting about the UKUSA agreements:

When MI5 celebrates its 90th birthday – which it will do in 1999 – we will have been through two World Wars and one Cold War. Those traumatic events have not made the security picture any simpler. In 1909 it was not felt necessary even to define what MI5 was for – it was obvious. During the Cold War, too, national security was a relatively simple concept. It was accepted that clandestine security and intelligence operations were an essential part of the mechanisms for national defence. In the UK even the existence of the agencies involved was only rarely acknowledged officially. Eighty years were to pass from the founding of MI5 before its functions were defined in law and a range of mechanisms set up to provide for our accountability. By 1989, when the Security

Service Act was passed, the threats had become much more varied, but they were still illustrated in what are primarily Cold War terms countering espionage, subversion, and sabotage, as well as terrorism. In 1995 the changing international climate means that everywhere perceptions of the threats to national security are being re-examined. The clarity which the Cold War brought has gone. We must now look through a much more complex prism, which blurs the focus and the depth of the security picture. The former military rivalry between superpowers has given way to greater world economic tensions. *Even political allies may now be prepared to engage in economic espionage against each other* [author's emphasis], in order to advance their national interests. As is all too evident, the collapse of centralised controls in parts of the former Soviet Union, as well as in the Balkans, has provoked regional instability. From that may come new sources of terrorism, and heightened risks from the spread of chemical, nuclear and biological weapons. This new world order has created conditions which also encourage the growth of what is increasingly being called 'organised crime'.

This phenomenon is comparatively new. In many countries – including in the UK – its impact and seriousness are still being assessed. But there seems little doubt that crime of this sort will grow, feeding on those same modern trends that I have described – the increasing ease and speed of communications and travel, and the weakening of controls. If that is true, countering the threat successfully will require those same methods which have been developed to deal with the more familiar threats such as terrorism. This means the same strategic approach, the same investigative techniques. But, above all, it means the same close national and international co-operation between security-intelligence and law enforcement agencies in the context of wider political co-operation between governments.

And so, drawing on that new set of intelligence buzzwords – terrorism, weapons of mass destruction (WMD) and organised crime –

the scene was set for MI5 to hop over the fence and take a look at other projects when the collapse of Communism took away, at a stroke, all the key areas of MI5, MI6 and CIA activity. Rimington had made her pitch to become more involved in the fight against terrorism and organised crime – though it seemed curious of her to place the latter under the heading of a 'comparatively new phenomenon' when it has been around for decades.

Anyhow, it worked, and in 1996 MI5 got its additional powers to 'operate in support of law enforcement agencies in work on organised crime'. It had already expanded its unit for the 'counter-proliferation' of WMD and had recently been awarded wider powers in relation to advising government on 'protective security' and most other aspects of securing the nation's secrets. These developments were much in line with a dedicated agency set up in the United States and copied throughout the UKUSA network. In the process, MI5 gained access to a vast database of information – details on millions of people whose names appeared on government department computer files from the Inland Revenue to the Police National Computer (PNC2).

Thus, MI5 expanded into the protection of the confidentiality and integrity of information and important national assets. It focuses on combating possible acts of terrorism, unauthorised access to buildings, hacker attacks on computer systems, eavesdropping or interception of sensitive communications, and advising on physical security such as ID systems, passwords, locks, building structures, guards, fences, walls and intruder detection systems. It also includes security vetting of all those in state employ who have access to protected assets or sensitive information. Apart from identifying the threat and possible recruitment of spies, MI5's experts also assess the ways in which hostile organisations operate and are likely to attack British interests. The CIA and the FBI – in fact, most international agencies – are doing much the same, creating models and mock-ups of possible terrorist attacks on New York and other major cities.

This expanded role gave MI5 direct access to a network of national and international links which it claims are fundamental to its work in protective security – and which include access to Echelon-acquired material. In addition, virtually all computerised government records on individuals in the UK are available to MI5 because it has to 'advise' all government departments on security aspects and security vetting of staff. Opponents of MI5 were quick to point out that Rimington's campaign smacked of a job creation scheme, a claim supported by some elements of the police force who had no wish to see MI5 moving in on their patch. As a senior figure in the Metropolitan Police pointed out, the MI5 way of doing things, some of which had in the past been shown to be verging on the illegal, and its lack of experience in bringing offenders to court, might even jeopardise successful prosecutions.

Keith Hellawell, at the time Chief Constable of West Yorkshire and chairman of the drugs committee of the Association of Chief Police Officers, said he and other chief constables had been surprised by Mrs Rimington's new moves. 'She had attended the association's spring seminar the previous year and made it fairly clear that MI5 was not interested in encroaching further on police work. It seems that there has now been a change of emphasis. There are obviously going to be changes in the future of policing in Europe and we need to know what is in her mind before we can give any objective comment.'

The police seemed certain that they could meet the organised crime challenge, in spite of the mushrooming of the drugs trade as denoted by a 200 per cent increase in drug seizures in 1994 – 51 tons with an estimated street value of £550 million were seized that year. Was this the future role of the nation's intelligence service? Not according to many of its detractors, who felt that money could be better employed by raising police staffing levels. The point was made forcibly by several staunch opponents of the intelligence service who had suffered from surveillance in the days of the 'anti-subversion police'. They included two enemies, left-winger Ken Livingstone and Chris Mullin, the Labour MP who fought for the reopening of the case against the Birmingham Six who were eventually freed after seventeen years in jail having been wrongly accused of carrying out IRA bomb attacks in the city.

Mullin asked: 'Is not the background to all this the fact that the Security Service is running out of threats, and that new ones are having to be invented to save large public spending cuts that might otherwise have to be introduced to these bloated organisations?' Livingstone, meanwhile, reminded Parliament of MI5's less than laudable history against trade unions, Labour governments and political activists: 'I believe nothing that Stella Rimington has done has changed the culture of treason and anti-Labour bias. I believe the existence of MI5 is a threat to democracy in this country, and has been terribly damaging – fatal in some cases – to those who have been on the receiving end of it.'

Having achieved her aim of drawing attention to the new perils of the world, Mrs Rimington then withdrew into the pristine new riverside headquarters of MI5: a massive new refurbishment job had just been completed on Thames House, Millbank, near the Houses of Parliament. A listed building which retains many attractive original features, at the same time it is now air-conditioned with new workstations and staff facilities that include a restaurant, shop, multi-gym and squash courts. Most MI5 staff are based there, among them linguists, computer experts, communications specialists, scientists and technical staff – the bugging and gadgets department – and generalists. Rimington retired in 1996 and her deputy, Stephen Lander, took over.

With overall staff levels reduced, the annual intake of new recruits – once traditionally sought among Oxford and Cambridge graduates by MI5 spy-spotters – was itself cut, but Lander was determined to top up with 'new young blood'. Those who knew the service well agreed that he needed to continue Rimington's efforts to get rid of starchy formalities and rigid thinking from years past that still hung around like the odour of mothballs.

Recruitment literature produced by MI5 in glossy magazine format in 1998 spoke of a 'first-name culture throughout and a general willing-ness to socialise both inside and outside the office' as if it was the beginning of some startling revolution in office life. MI5 was merely demonstrating how far behind the times it was in some respects by using as a selling point aspects of working relationships that had long been present in most modern workplaces. Even so, some of the chaps from days gone by would have turned in their graves!

The salary levels for new recruits, however, attracted only the most dedicated – as indeed they had for many years. On 1 January 1999 the entry level was just under £17,000 with 'agreed annual increments', whereas elsewhere in London computer graduates could expect upwards of £25,000 and rapid rises. A few jobs within the organisation may involve travel outside London or the UK. All staff must accept a contractual obligation to serve anywhere in the UK or overseas if necessary, although in practice most spend their entire careers in London, and for many it remains tedious work, foot-slogging or pawing over dusty files. Job satisfaction is to be derived from the side of the work which, for those who enjoy spy novels, may (or may not) include the following – a summary of the redefined areas of operation for MI5 at the turn of the century:

- countering of terrorism, espionage by foreign intelligence services against UK interests and the proliferation of weapons of mass destruction;

- work in support of the police services and other law enforcement agencies in the prevention and detection of serious crime; and

- recruiting and running agents, joining specialist teams that carry out surveillance or eavesdropping operations.

The recruitment literature sets up a likely scenario for a new recruit as part of a team engaged in counter-terrorist activities. It does have a touch of oh-gosh! naivety about it:

Against the background of a fast-moving investigation, you would need first to identify the significant information amongst a mass of overt material and secret intelligence. In consultation with the other members of your team, you would then need to decide what to do with it and, for example, draft an authoritative assessment of the group and the threat it poses to be read by officials in Whitehall departments. You might also need to pass intelligence urgently to a police force, or to an allied service abroad in an effort to prevent an attack or intercept a shipment of arms. But how could you do any of this without jeopardising your sensitive sources? The intelligence must be usable, but protecting sources is vital too. If the group is posing a significant threat, you might need to use all the resources available to you to further your investigation. Which would be the most appropriate, proportionate and effective methods of finding out what you need to know? Decisions like these are part of an intelligence officer's daily life. We look to even the most junior of our intelligence staff to identify such problems and suggest solutions. The consequences of getting things wrong may be serious but staff will have the reassurance of senior managers to guide and support them.

Lander's MI5, with its reduced manpower, had an air of very necessary revitalisation and refocusing. The scenario confronting him was changing almost by the month. When the amount of resources devoted to counterespionage was cut from around 50 per cent to 12 per cent of its total budget, the slack was taken up to some extent by increasing MI5's role against the IRA and the increased threat of international terrorism. By the beginning of 1999, work under the 'anti-terrorist' heading accounted for 40.5 per cent of MI5's annual budget, of which Northern Ireland accounted for 25 per cent. MI5's role there may well be scaled down further, although it insists that the new dissidents who make up the IRA splinter groups of Continuity IRA and the Real IRA will require surveillance and scrutiny for some years to come. On the other hand, British Military Intelligence in Northern Ireland and the Royal Ulster Constabulary's Special Branch have between them an unrivalled database that even MI5 cannot match: there are remarkably few residents of Northern Ireland who are not recorded somewhere on those files, whether or not they have committed or been suspected of any crime.

Of MI5's remaining tasks, 17 per cent of resources were allocated to its 'technological department' which includes bugging, burgling and interception of targeted communications; 7.5 per cent was for 'protective security' of government departments, the national computer infrastructure and individuals; 2.5 per cent was for assisting police efforts against organised crime; 2 per cent was for monitoring the creation or trade in weapons of mass destruction and 11 per cent was for oversight, finance and internal security. At any one time, MI5 also has around a hundred officers on secondment to other agencies, including those in the UKUSA Agreement.

Two areas of expansion, in the event of a cutback in MI5's involvement in Northern Ireland, have already been identified. Russia retained a hefty overseas intelligence presence under its KGB replacement, the FSB, and by the mid-1990s operatives were moving back into London and other Western capitals to recruit agents. This time, the emphasis was undoubtedly on economic and industrial intelligence.

As these words were being written, MI5 was already beginning to step up its cover of counterespionage – as indeed were most intelligence services – in the hunt for spies who are providing foreign countries with sensitive information damaging to the UK's national security or economic wellbeing. As Stella Rimington pointed out, these spies are not necessarily working for hostile nations, but for countries who were, and still are, considered allies or friends. (Conversely, as we shall see, Britain is, through other channels, up to the same tricks.) The MI5 role in all this was to 'disrupt the activities of those foreign intelligence officers who talent-spot and recruit as agents individuals who have access to British secrets'. A few of the spies who have been identified in the UK in the past were controlled directly from abroad. By 1999, the majority were run by foreign intelligence officers based in Britain, thus bypassing signals and communications interception.

The second avenue of expansion for MI5 is in monitoring agents from twenty-two countries around the world which actively seek a weapons of mass destruction (WMD) capability, and some of which are hostile to Britain and her allies. MI5 assesses the threat as twofold: that British armed forces will be exposed to such weapons on deployment overseas, and that the UK will itself come within reach of longer-range missiles or be exposed to the more easily transported chemical and biological weapons.

AGENTS, INFORMERS AND WHISTLE-BLOWERS

As MI5 regularly points out to the political hierarchy, much of the material, technology and expertise required for WMD programmes can be found in the UK, although more likely these days it will come from financially stressed areas of the former Soviet bloc.

The one thing that MI5 cannot do without, however, is agents in the field. Unlike the NSA and GCHQ, which collect intelligence through interception, MI5 still relies heavily on agents and informers, especially in its monitoring of terrorist groups. Agents are planted in target groups and report back to their handlers. Every one of the intelligence groups in Northern Ireland has to recruit and run its own agents and MI5 does not have a very good record; in fact it has an appalling catalogue of misinterpretation, overzealous activities such as support for the use of sensory interrogations and sheer arrogance in pushing operations against the IRA when peace deals seemed a possibility. The Dirty Tricks department has left a nasty stain on the 1970s and 1980s. In those years, MI5 was consistently wary of peace talks with the IRA because it believed any relaxation of the military and intelligence onslaught would give the terrorists a breathing space to rearm and re-equip. MI5 has a specialist team of agent handlers, better trained now than in the early days of the Northern Ireland troubles when mistakes could have fatal consequences. Successful agent operations can run for years. MI5 has informers in public organisations, especially those which, though not now considered subversive, may have policies which are considered against the public interest, such as some of the more militant animal rights campaigners. Keeping them active comes down to the training and skills of the MI5 handlers.

Examples of the quality of MI5 staff among those who have been revealed to the public in recent years has not always inspired confidence. Michael Bettaney is a classic case – an intelligence officer who was assigned to duties in Northern Ireland, operating from MI5's operational headquarters at Stormont. He spent much of his time as an agent handler, in spite of his well-known problems with drink. The pressures of the job and the surroundings mounted. His conversion to Catholicism could also have been read as another sign of his mental disquiet. He remained in the employ of MI5 even though he was investigated for dishonesty, had a conviction for being drunk and disorderly and had been overheard making comments about retiring to a dacha. On his return to London, where he gave lectures and training to would-be operatives on counterespionage in Northern Ireland, he made a bungled attempt to pass secrets to the Soviet Embassy. He disclosed to the Russians what MI5 had discovered about the intelligence organisation within their London embassy, thus allowing them to make alternative arrangements. At his trial in 1984, Bettaney received a twenty-three-year prison sentence and was released in 1998.

The blame, however, was not entirely his. He was obviously under significant pressure in Northern Ireland, and had given clear signals of his mental state – all of which reached the ears of his superiors. He suffered a severe punishment for a crime against national security that MI5 ought to have seen coming and should have prevented by placing the man in medical care, rather than allowing him to go staggering about the streets of London. One of the steps MI5 took in the aftermath of the Bettaney case was to try to offset possible disclosures by disillusioned or disturbed employees by setting up a system of staff counselling.

Since 1987, after an internal inquiry into the Bettaney case, MI5, MI6 and GCHQ staff have had access to an external counsellor who is available at all times for 'private consultation by any member of the three services who may have concerns about the nature or propriety of their work'. Under the terms of reference, the counsellor sends a report to the Prime Minister of the day. The number seeking counselling is never revealed, but personal problems are not uncommon. All officers of the secret services are thrown together in relatively small groups, all sworn never to talk about their work to friends or relatives, and when they go home at night they can say nothing about their day. In possession of information which is at times disturbing, often worrying and occasionally bizarre, the officers are driven in upon themselves, seeking only the company of others in the group so that they are able to talk freely. Loyalty to each other is generally paramount. The group mentality is promoted by the MI5 system of compartmentalising the work specialists. Sources have indicated that this alone has, in the past, created conditions where the group made day-to-day decisions on procedure and action, rather than involving superiors. By keeping operations at that level, who is to know exactly what goes on?

The rules to which the Security Service is supposed to adhere have often been ignored and deliberately set aside to allow a 'flexible' approach to investigating the group's theories. Little local plots by officers on an anti-subversion desk, for example, could easily have bypassed the control system. There is sufficient evidence from whistle-blowers past and present that illegal acts were commonplace, that controls were lax and that cover-ups for those suffering from mental strain or other personal problems – like Bettaney – were taken for granted until that person crossed the line. Then, the power of MI5 and the laws of the land came down upon them.

Cathy Massiter was, curiously, never prosecuted. Peter Wright's disclosures in *Spycatcher* initiated one of the most controversial attempts in history to silence a former MI5 employee; Margaret Thatcher personally directed the campaign to stop publication of his book. The ensuing court proceedings turned into a farce and *Spycatcher* became an instant worldwide bestseller, much criticised and challenged though it was. In the event, Wright was later shown to be a rambling, unreliable old man. But at the time the affair developed into an international battle, played out in the courts of Australia where the book was to be published, which aroused great public alarm about the workings of British intelligence. The issue became not so much about the book's content but about whether or not such matters should be publicly discussed. In the end it all went terribly wrong for Thatcher and MI5, who lost their case, and the book was published. Behind the scenes the effects were to rumble on for years, and may yet lead to greater openness.

David Bickford, a lawyer who was parachuted into MI5 in 1987 to help sort out the mess, confirms: 'The Peter Wright affair was the absolute cataclysm which showed that this super-secrecy was no longer apposite in the modern world. The world had changed. The defence against Peter Wright was obviously a great mistake. The agencies learned from that, equally as they learned from the Bettaney case, that you had to have more of a searchlight on to the activities inside the agencies.'

Bickford, whose views will be considered more fully in Chapter 13, brought a breath of fresh air to the workings of MI5. He admits, however, that the changes he would personally like to see regarding the issues of secrecy are, in 2000, still not in place largely because of opposition from Whitehall mandarins rather than from MI5 itself. Blanket secrecy is, he says, no longer necessary and the agencies should be more open about their work and aspirations. On the other hand, it is obviously not good intelligence practice to have ex-members of the service going about disclosing operational techniques which, in the event, may seriously compromise major investigations and even cost the lives of intelligence officers and agents.

Modern whistle-blowers like David Shayler continue to be vigorously pursued to keep the lid on what they may know. The ex-journalist who left MI5 and began filtering his knowledge into the public arena eventually fled to France to escape arrest for breach of the Official Secrets Act. He told his story to the media, and attempts to extradite him from France to face prosecution failed. From his lips came the allegation of British involvement in a plot to assassinate Colonel Gaddafi. He insisted that it was a matter of conscience that drove him to flee the country and make his revelations about MI5, and not the considerable improvements to his bank balance that resulted from newspaper serialisations.

Another whistle-blower, Richard Tomlinson, a former MI6 officer, was prosecuted under the Official Secrets Act for revealing information against national security in his outline for a proposed book. He was jailed for twelve months and has for the most part lived abroad since his release.

Perhaps the most significant outcome of these cases was what they revealed not so much in terms of secrets as in terms of the quality of MI5 staff. As a student at Dundee University, Shayler had achieved some notoriety as editor of a satirical student magazine in which he had published extracts of *Spycatcher*. A brief enquiry at the John Hampden Grammar School in High Wycombe, Buckinghamshire, might also have revealed some character traits that were at variance with a career as a spy. 'He is a born rebel who likes to sail close to the wind,' wrote Roger Addison, then his form master, in Shayler's school report at the end of his lower sixth year. Addison was not surprised that the adult Shayler had caused a national outcry. He said: 'He was an intelligent young man who did well at his A-levels... but he was always the sort of boy who raised questions such as why pupils had to wear uniform and the like. He would push things to the limit.'

After university he won a place as a trainee journalist on the *Sunday Times*, where there are five hundred rejections for each successful applicant, but he left within six months. Even so, he was offered a job by MI5 in November 1991 and remained for nearly six years. After leaving MI5 he was suspected of leaking sensitive information to a national newspaper. In August, 1998 Shayler, whose girlfriend Annie Machon was also a former MI5 officer, alleged that MI5 had bugged

Labour ministers including Peter Mandelson in their youth. The government's response was to obtain a court order preventing the publication of further confidential disclosures and to attempt to extradite Shayler from France.

In August, 2000, after long negotiations between the Home Office and his lawyers, Shayler voluntarily agreed to return to the UK amid intense media interest. He was arrested as he stepped off the ferry from France and taken to a police station in London where he was charged with breaking the Official Secrets Act. He was released on bail to await trial, which at the time of writing, had yet to be fixed.

NEW DIRECTIONS FROM THE TOP

Stephen Lander has undoubtedly tightened recruitment but, as already mentioned, constraints on pay may limit choice. None the less, he has imposed some exacting requirements for recruits, with rigorous vetting procedures to establish the candidate's integrity and reliability. Apart from a series of interviews, candidates have to go through a tough two-day selection programme which includes psychological profiling.

Lander is a very British and tight-lipped intelligence careerist who had had wide-ranging experience in both MI6 and MI5 before being appointed director general of the latter in 1996. Across the Atlantic at about the same time George Tenet, well known among those around him for his very American informality, became head of the CIA. Unlike the correct and smart-suited Lander, Tenet drives a Jeep, takes lunch at McDonald's, plays opera very loudly in his seventh-floor Washington office, sometimes does not even bother to shave and has been known to turn up for White House meetings wearing sunglasses and a leather jacket emblazoned with the logo of the CIA.

The link between the two men when they came to power, however, was the need to confront the lack of confidence and declining morale in their respective agencies, which for a while faced extinction in their existing form. Both had been severely hit by budget cuts which tore into their manpower and by declining targets in the post-Cold War gloom. Tenet adopted a more gung-ho approach to recruitment and was apparently intent on reversing the anti-Humint trend. He set about resurrecting the Directorate of Operations, much criticised in its previous life. CIA agents warmed to his approach and his apparent liking for more traditional methods of spying. This, evidently, stems from the realisation that the NSA and its associates have the avenues of Comint all sewn up.

In a move that surprised CIA critics, who believed the agency's cloak and dagger days were over, Tenet began the reconstruction of CIA espionage and covert operations around the world. This he did largely on the back of increased threats from terrorism, organised crime and the proliferation of WMD, an argument very familiar to intelligence followers in the UK. The failure of US intelligence to predict the attacks, allegedly made by international terrorist Osama Bin Laden's private army, on two American embassies in Africa with considerable loss of life actually worked in Tenet's favour.

It could be said that the downgrading of Humint, and the closure of US bases around the world which doubled as listening posts for the CIA, had undermined the agency's effectiveness. It was a claim that did little to convince CIA critics in Washington, but in 1999 Tenet persuaded the Clinton administration to back the agency's long-running campaign to halt the trend to replace Humint with electronic surveillance and interception methods. Tenet's case – similar to that put forward by Stella Rimington in 1995 – was that new threats made the conventional approach of the CIA more important than ever. And so, like Stephen Lander in Britain, the CIA has been sending its talent-spotters back to the university campuses.

Tenet has promised to hire at least two thousand additional spies by 2005, submitting that otherwise the CIA will 'become a second-rate organisation'. The Clinton administration supported his claim and awarded the CIA an extra £180 million funding. Among the first to receive the benefit was a new counter-terrorism command post, with a wall of video monitors and the latest workstations at the very top end of modern technology. Tenet has made it clear, however, that much of the extra cash will go towards reinventing the Directorate of Operations and re-creating overseas bases from which the CIA can operate. What purpose this reinvigoration of the world's most hated agency will serve, only time will tell.

CHAPTER 11
THE RING OF SECRECY

SECRECY SURROUNDING THE INTELLIGENCE services remains battened down in most countries, although America, Canada and Australia have in recent years increasingly come under the public scrutiny of government committees. There has never been any searching, open inquiry into the working of MI5, MI6 and GCHQ. Unlike America, where regular congressional committees keep intelligence services on their toes, Britain has virtually no government oversight into possible abuses. That is not because the intelligence agencies themselves are necessarily opposed to it, but because of a culture of secrecy that exists among the mandarins of Whitehall. They are fearful that if there is more openness about MI5, for example, it will expose other government departments to similar scrutiny.

MOVES TO GREATER OPENNESS AND ACCOUNTABILITY

What little oversight of intelligence agencies exists in Britain is 'completely ineffective' according to David Bickford, the former legal adviser to MI5, in evidence and a memorandum to the House of Commons Select Committee on Home Affairs, December 1998–March 1999. He delivered a devastating assessment of the toothless nature of the British government's Intelligence and Security Committee, chaired by former Conservative Secretary of State for Defence Tom King. It was, he said, more or less counting 'paper clips and security passes' while international crime ran out of control, terrorists were allowed to go free because of the inadmissibility of MI5 wire-taps in court, and agency work on major issues such as information warfare and the proliferation of weapons of mass destruction was barely considered. In other words, there was no machinery for the British government to examine what goes on behind the closed doors of the agencies or inquire into their work, practices and systems. And it was Whitehall which kept the lid on it.

The nearest Britain had moved towards some form of limited oversight had come in 1989 when Patricia Hewitt and Harriet Harman, then two senior officials of the National Council for Civil Liberties (now known as Liberty), had taken the British government to the European Court of Human Rights. They had complained that MI5 had investigated them as 'subversives' purely because of their association with the civil liberties movement, and had sought to have their files destroyed. The British government had refused point blank and the case had moved to the European Court. David Bickford was among the MI5 advisers in the case and he told his superiors that they would without doubt lose because no legislation existed for oversight of the agencies. Bickford made a startling admission: 'No one, not even the legal advisers, were aware of the European Convention on Human Rights, let alone the delicate balances of rights that existed in relation to national security. They were truly shocked when they learned that they would lose the Hewitt and Harman case.'

The judges did indeed rule in favour of the two women, which proved to be a landmark decision as far as British intelligence was concerned: it was ordered to take account of the European Convention on Human Rights. Harman and Hewitt thus went into the legal history books as having been instrumental in creating a form of oversight of British intelligence which Bickford himself admits had 'been a long time coming'. Even so, it was given grudgingly by the British government and had little real effect.

The 1989 Security Services Act was drawn up only in the face of the certainty of losing the Harman–Hewitt case. It provided for the absolute minimum oversight of the agencies – just sufficient to satisfy the European Court. In fact it was an almost farcical, if not arrogant, response. Under the Act, the oversight Commissioner and Tribunal could only investigate the agency if a successful complaint had been made. But because some 98 per cent of complaints against the security service were – to use their parlance – 'found to be frivolous', only 2 per cent were ever investigated. The agencies would also be given ample time to prepare their responses and the proceedings, according to Bickford, were: 'methodical and bureaucratic ... the complaints system does not lead to a thorough review of the possibilities of abuse within the agencies. It is too narrow in focus and orderly to do this ... very different to the case [in some countries] where an independent third party, with a staff, has indiscriminate access to the agency's work. Everyone, from directors to desk officers to secretaries, is put on the spot. Not only by questions as to possible abuse or ineffectiveness but also as to major policy issues.'

Bickford, a solicitor previously employed by the Foreign Office, was, to use his own description, 'catapulted' into MI5 to help shake up management after the scandals of the 1980s. He was involved in all decision making and discussion of MI5 policies during the following decade and his role gave him access to past events which, he discovered, were not covered by any form of legislation. In 1999, he was called to give evidence to the Commons Home Affairs Committee. His testimony provided wide-ranging and surprisingly frank responses to many of the issues which are covered in this book.

Bickford indicated that by the mid-1990s the agencies themselves were ready for change and did not fear oversight in the slightest. The expansion of MI5 operations into the fight against organised crime, and a general redirection of focus from the narrow confines of Cold War secrecy, had persuaded MI5 director Stephen Lander and other leading figures within the service that the agencies would have to lift the veil from many aspects of their work in order to gain public confidence. It would also be necessary to redefine the approach to evidence resulting from secret operations that could be given in court, which again was hidebound by restrictions from the past.

However, the MI5 bosses were simply blocked from altering their stance. Whitehall went along with the Security Services Act 1989 oversight because it was forced into it, and even then accepted it only for what David Bickford describes as 'presentational reasons'. In other words it was a PR move in the wake of the Harman–Hewitt action, yet the agencies themselves were prepared to accept more openness and agreed that broad parliamentary oversight was a necessary balance. But Whitehall nurtured a culture of 'protective secrecy' towards the agencies. This sprang in part from the mystique the agencies themselves had carefully cultivated during the Cold War era, and in part from Whitehall's failure to understand that Cold War secrecy was no longer appropriate for the new work the agencies were embarking upon. As Bickford explained in his evidence to the Commons Select Committee on Home Affairs:

> I think there is going to be a general push towards the intelligence agencies becoming more open about that sort of work. What are they doing about it? How do they get involved in defeating organised crime? What are the problems of organised crime? What are the problems of terrorism and super-terrorism and what are they doing to defeat that? I see that there will be a demand for more openness in that respect in the future.
>
> Whitehall does not. It has always been my view that Whitehall operates on the basis of secrecy. It is traditional in a sense. If the intelligence agencies reduce their secrecy this has a knock-on effect on to, for instance, the Ministry of Defence or the Foreign Office because if the intelligence agencies can talk about issues that have hitherto been secret within them, then obviously that reduces the scope for secrecy in the other departments. This is one of the major reasons why the intelligence agencies had such a battle to reduce their secrecy in the first place.
>
> One of the problems is that it is within the ring of secrecy. Oversight that is within the ring of secrecy must always be considered suspect. There is too close a relationship that is shrouded in secrecy between the members of the body and the intelligence agencies. That is not a criticism of either. It is just a fact of life.

The lack of more effective accountability that the public could trust was underscored when the government called for internal reforms and the appointment of independent inquiry officers following the publicity over the claims of Shayler and Tomlinson, in which apparently illegal activities by both the security service and the secret intelligence service were uncovered. Any independent investigation would, under existing rules, be totally secret. The investigating officer would report to a body that was also secret, and thus his credibility could be called into question.

Whitehall was unmoved by the fact that the British intelligence agencies wanted to shed the secrecy mystique as far as possible without damaging national security. This attitude was demonstrated to some extent in the 1996 Arms to Iraq inquiry headed by Sir Richard Scott. Scott's eventual report censured government departments for being economical in their disclosures during the trial of executives of Matrix Churchill, accused of illegally exporting arms in the run-up to the Gulf War. The trial eventually collapsed. Scott, however, specifically excluded MI5 and MI6 from that censure and referred to their willingness to refer documents to the defence. Furthermore, Bickford maintained:

> The Whitehall view was that any loss of secrecy relating to the agencies would lead to difficulties in sustaining high levels of secrecy in other areas of government. This was evidenced clearly in the continual battle the Security Service had with the Home Office to be free to use information gathered in sensitive operations to prosecute terrorists. There were constant problems with the Home Office ... the Security Service had a series of successful prosecutions which went to the heart of the terrorists' capabilities. Because of this success they were able to circumvent some of the Home Office obstacles. For instance, there was unwillingness in the Home Office to assist the service develop secure judicial procedures for converting their secret information into evidence. These were finally secured by the service through the Attorney General in a particular case [where] ... fortunately, the police urgently needed such procedures and the Security Service had had them prepared and idling for two years. But the overall battle remained.

On the one hand the Security Service saw the benefits of more openness and of using intelligence for the first time to convict terrorists and to aid the police in the future fight against organised crime. On the other, the Home Office and Whitehall were fearful that the consequent reduction in secrecy surrounding the service would lead to an erosion of long-held principles of secrecy surrounding government business as a whole. These concerns led Whitehall in 1994 to advise Ministers that, whilst some form of parliamentary oversight was politically desirable, it should be within the ring of secrecy and have only very limited access to the operational functions of the agencies. ... There is always the danger that it gets too dark and the way is lost. Equally important, it is always the case that day-to-day tasks in the high pressure of intelligence work may overtake the need to look up and out. Moreover, strategic planning is best prompted by outsiders asking difficult questions.

Bickford made a clear point that Tom King's Intelligence and Security Committee and the oversight Commissioners were not asking such questions. They were not legally empowered to do so, nor was there a real understanding in Whitehall of the radical and immediate changes that will fundamentally affect the way in which the agencies will go about their business in the future. The expanded brief of MI5, and to a lesser extent M16, has taken the work of the agencies into the domains of law enforcement, customs, immigration, finance and commerce. Bickford unflinchingly informed the Intelligence and Security Committee members that they simply did not have the tools to achieve this essential element of oversight. Their mandate did not give them the power to access background information on either intelligence or other 'vital components' in the fight against the new threats.

They were also, he pointed out, within the ring of secrecy and had no direct access into the workings of the intelligence agencies other than through the bureaucratic process. This system prevented them from 'roaming around operational policies and activities of the agencies'. The agencies were as good or as bad as their operational success. The management, administration and financing of the agencies might look immaculate, but this meant little in terms of real effectiveness. Oversight which excludes operational effectiveness is 'like investing in a quoted company without knowing what its bottom line is'.

The committee should deal with operational issues and inquire into possible abuse as well as operational effectiveness. It should also address strategic issues and consider changes in the law. Such changes should, for example, allow informants to give evidence in court, enable gang bosses on whom there may be no direct evidence of crime to be tried (along the lines of US anti-racketeering legislation) and allow transcripts of telephone-taps and GCHQ electronic eavesdropping to be used in criminal trials, which is at present not permitted in British courts.

If change is to come to the British system it is clearly some way off. As the new century began, MI5 was battling with the Home Office over a number of controversial issues that would undoubtedly expose operational activities to a greater public awareness through media reporting of court cases.

THE FIGHT AGAINST CRIME

Not least on the MI5 agenda was the use of informants' evidence which it would like to see run on similar lines to practices in Italy and the USA. Under existing rules in Britain, informants and all those who run informants face prosecution for participating in crimes committed. It is standard practice in intelligence and – increasingly – law enforcement operations to have agents and informants infiltrate criminal or terrorist organisations. It is a painstaking and dangerous task, sometimes lasting years. The intelligence people believe that a good informant has to be deeply involved with the group he has infiltrated, and consequently into the crime they might commit. If, as David Bickford put it, 'a wheel comes off and the informant carries out some sort of criminal act that is outside the actual information he is giving', he faces prosecution.

Because of the risk to their own lives, informants are run by the intelligence agencies under strict guidelines. The American intelligence community overcame the problem of using the evidence gained from informers and agents by obtaining pre-clearance from the US Attorney General or district attorneys for immunity from prosecution. This provided the intelligence and law enforcement agencies with a legal basis for running their operations. In Britain MI5 wants a similar system, but the debate reached impasse when the Home Office ruled against any change. British agents and informers thus run on the premise: 'Let's hope this is going to be all right on the night.'

MI5 officers frequently give evidence in court and can, as we have seen, expect no favours from the judges. Legal advisers work closely with officers running informants because, at the end of the day, they have to decide what evidence is required for the trial. This goes to the defence as well as the prosecution and, because the agent's identity has to be protected, he or she will not participate in the trial itself.

Under the British system all the files, together with transcripts of telephone intercepts and eavesdropping, are handed directly to the trial judge. The intelligence agency then meets the judge in his chambers, without the defence being present, to outline what evidence will be given in open court and what evidence it would prefer to keep secret. It will give reasons why it wants that portion of evidence kept secret, and submits that in its opinion the secret evidence has no bearing on the defence. The trial judge assesses the secret evidence and eventually gives a ruling. If he agrees with the intelligence agency's submission, the trial goes ahead keeping the secret evidence out of court. If, on the other hand, the trial judge rules against the agency, thus requiring the informant's name to be disclosed or some other sensitive issue such as details of eavesdropping to be revealed, the agency invariably walks away and the prosecution is dropped.

Other countries have found ways around the problem. French intelligence agencies have probably perfected the best system. Their lawyers involve the judge at an early stage of an investigation and he makes an on-the-spot decision as to what can be given in evidence at the trial. At the same time, the judge adjudicates on the rights of the individual, which in Britain are only settled after an investigation has been completed.

Other problems for both law enforcement and intelligence agencies are arising from the globalisation of organised crime. Since drug barons and financial crooks are never bound by borders, arresting officers are never certain where they might have to give evidence or what national laws and procedures will apply. In the USA, intelligence officers or agents have to give evidence in open court. In Italy they may be allowed to wear dark glasses, while in Britain they may be allowed to give evidence from behind screens. MI6 officers and agents, who are likely to be involved with even more sensitive evidence, take additional precautions that often end up precluding them from taking part in a trial. This in turn means that suspected criminals and known terrorists either walk free or are not prosecuted at all.

David Bickford's vision of the future, based on the demands of fighting crime and terrorism, predicts greater cooperation between MI5 and MI6 as part of an international effort. His assessment provides food for thought for the law enforcers and for the human rights campaigners who fear further globalisation of law enforcement databases. It highlights the myriad problems looming for both:

> Trying to defeat [crime and terrorism] on national laws, on national intelligence agency, national police bases is failing. There has to be an international focus. In the United Kingdom and the United States, the force of organised crime is coming from without and this creates a common foreign problem to it, and I think that is going to gradually drive MI5 and MI6 to closer cooperation and it may be in the future amalgamation is going to be the better way of coping. It reduces the top-heavy load of directorates and it leads to a sharpening up of operational focus. So that is the first thing that I see for the future: serious discussion on whether or not the foreign and home intelligence agencies should not actually start to amalgamate. It is a myth that they hate each other.
>
> Exchange of information in relation to crime across international borders is extremely difficult. Interpol have had this problem. Unless your information comes through 'the proper channels' your information is much more difficult to turn into evidence. If it comes underneath the table between two individuals you immediately run into problems converting it into evidence. There will have to be greater focus on international information exchange ... and on the harmonisation of laws.

That is taking such a long time to achieve that the debate is now beginning to focus curiously enough in the United States – which is not a party to it – on to an international criminal court and whether or not the international criminal court might actually be the more useful forum to deal with narcotics and terrorism. If that happens then that would also automatically start moving towards an internationalism of the agencies dealing with intelligence and law enforcement.

Harmonisation of laws and investigations could – like the European currency debate – bring its own problems in Britain. Not least among them would be the use of paid informers. The USA, Italy and Spain already make wide use of informants hired specifically to infiltrate a criminal organisation, knowing they will be giving evidence at the end of the day. By using such a system, it has been possible to imprison hundreds of Mafia people in Italy. The USA also uses anti-racketeering laws to allow charges to be brought for involvement with an illegal organisation rather than for a specific crime.

No such legislation exists in the UK; the nearest offence is conspiracy to commit a crime. Compelling arguments for change, however, may yet arise as crime bosses and terrorist leaders resident in the UK remain insulated from arrest and trial through lack of admissible evidence. The same argument is already being put forward by the agencies to allow transcriptions of telephone and Internet intercepts as evidence in British trials. This in turn may lead to the use of electronic evidence of the kind secretly collected by the NSA and GCHQ at Menwith Hill and Cheltenham. David Bickford's view seems to point to that as a racing certainty: 'MI5 has lost a number of senior terrorists through the inability to use telephone intercept. Also [the use of electronic evidence] will have to be seriously looked at; the FBI and NSA are already beginning to enter into a relationship where NSA evidence is going to be made available. GCHQ is going to have to be brought into the fold so their electronic evidence can support intelligence evidence in these trials.'

The spectre of Echelon rises once again.

SECRECY AND NEW TECHNOLOGY

Even so, while the extent of David Bickford's account of MI5's aspirations was not revelatory in operational detail, it was remarkably outspoken on issues that intelligence officers clearly see as constraints in their modernisation attempts. On the one hand, it would be music to the ears of the human rights campaigners who have for years been calling for greater accountability. But on the other, they would abhor some of the thinking about extending the use of evidence gained from telephone taps and other forms of secret information gathering. As to the past, which is still a festering sore with many, Bickford more or less admitted that super-secrecy during the Cold War was brought about by a blinkered approach within the intelligence agencies:

> [They had] a single focus [and] that was the defeat of Communism. They had to defeat Communism through also dealing with subversion. These were very difficult issues. That single focus could be interpreted as being introspective from the outside. From the inside I found that the balances were still there, although I think it is pretty fair to say that the balances were based on what would be awkward if it became public rather than the civil rights balances that the European Convention on Human Rights provided.

Now, the focus is more widespread and efforts are being directed towards the threats already outlined: terrorism, crime and illicit weaponry. The Internet, too, is altering attitudes towards secrecy. So much material about law enforcement and intelligence services is available on-line that the secrecy argument is rapidly diminishing. Former government servants, including law enforcement and intelligence officers, are peddling their services on the Internet to gain and provide information about their own and other countries and businesses there. The information explosion is piercing the secrecy safeguards of states and they are unable to regulate or control it.

Secrecy, Bickford suggested, will be eroded by the demands of the media and public as organised crime – already admitted by British and American authorities to be out of control – becomes even more of a threat. His is a gloomy portrait of life in the twenty-first century. Threats to states are fluid, transient, international and obscure. They come not only in the identifiable shape of state terrorism but also in the dim images of iconoclastic groups and anarchic gangs, and spill over into narcotics traffickers, extortionists and information warfare computer hackers. Organised crime, operating in chameleon form, crosses geographical and financial borders with ease. Money laundering and narcotics trafficking in turn are leading to the stealthy corruption, not only of law enforcement officers and court officials, but also of entire governments. Fraud is becoming more prevalent and increasing rapidly via the Internet, through which unidentified, sophisticated hackers are breaking into banks, and equally sophisticated users are promoting scams of all kinds. In addition to this are the gathering pace of juvenile drug abuse and the ghettoing of the wealthy and middle management into secure compounds. Society will increasingly demand to know why its quality of life is not being adequately protected by the state.

Bickford went on to make projections and express personal thoughts on the future which, for an ex-MI5 man, were again surprisingly frank. He foresaw a future in which governments would finally have to accept that old concepts of Cold War secrecy are dead and be prepared to cut government secrecy to a vital minimum. Secrecy is already being prised open 'like a knife into an oyster' by the information explosion and the fight against crime and terrorism. The extent of the erosion is such that governments are no longer able to protect secrecy in the ways in which they have done in the past, and society is still only at the threshold of this phenomenon.

A reassessment of which elements of secrecy are no longer viable and which really need to be protected is essential. It will be no easy task. In a recent internal exercise the US military found that its combat effectiveness was destroyed by the simple ability of the enemy to hack into the unprotected computers dealing with military supplies. Supplies were rerouted, countermanded or simply made to vanish. Chaos and defeat ensued. The answer to that problem lay not in making the supply system secret, but in protecting the on-line system from hacking.

Many areas of current secrecy are easily identifiable as being unnecessary and vulnerable in the new information age. By abandoning secrecy in these areas, states will no longer have to protect themselves against information loss – except to protect the privacy of individuals. David Bickford concluded his memorandum with one last prediction: 'If states accept that secrecy must be diminished to a vital minimum then society will prosper. If not, state secrecy will be pierced by the needs of society and organised crime will plunder sovereignty.'

PART III

■

THE GADGETS – TECHNOLOGY AND THREATS TO THE INFRASTRUCTURE

CHAPTER 12
BUGS AND THE FIGHT AGAINST CRIME

IN THE WORLD OF SURVEILLANCE technology, one form of gadgetry has remained remarkably popular over the years. Despite many attempts to detect and eradicate them, bugs remain a force to be reckoned with. This chapter examines their use in the fight against crime.

In the dying days of the 1990s, there was a brief flashback to the Cold War era. Bugs were found in Moscow and Washington and, for good measure, Northern Ireland, that produced some forthright diplomatic exchanges during particularly sensitive times. It was a reminder to the world that espionage is not dead.

THE USA VERSUS RUSSIA

The sequence of events began in the first week of December 1999 when officers of the former KGB, now the FSB, apparently caught a US diplomat in the act of obtaining secret military papers on the Russian nuclear capability. Coincidentally, Boris Yeltsin had just reminded the West that Russia was still a nuclear power after the USA had warned the Russians of Western disgust at the bombardment of Chechnya. This warning had been conveyed to the Russian leadership only the day before in a person-to-person call by US Secretary of State Madeleine Albright with her opposite number in Moscow.

Cheri Leberknight, officially a second secretary in the US Embassy's military-political section, but according to the FSB a CIA station officer, was arrested with a number of incriminating objects in her possession, such as bugs and papers. It was the first time in five years that spying allegations had been made against an American diplomat. Her arrest came just hours after the US Navy announced in Washington that a petty officer had been charged with passing secrets to Russia in 1994. Daniel King, forty, described as a code expert with an eighteen-year service record, was taken into military custody at the Quantico Marine base in Virginia, charged with espionage and with disclosing classified information. He had allegedly sent a computer disk loaded with top secret information, including the bugging of Russian submarines, to their embassy in Washington. At the time of writing he has still to come to trial. As ever, there was a good deal of political posturing over the arrests, given the delicate international situation.

Less than a week later, on 11 December 1999, there was another remarkable development. A Russian diplomat was arrested in Washington and accused of an act of espionage. In fact, he was a one-man technical team who had managed to penetrate one of the most vital inner sanctums of the US corridors of political power – the State Department headquarters. It was the first time in history (as far as is known) that it had been bugged. He installed an exceedingly effective bugging device in a seventh-floor briefing room used by Madeleine Albright, and just a few paces from her own office. The microphone and transmitter had ample capability to relay all conversation that went on in that room during a crucial period in recent history, as the Russians prepared for a further invasion of Chechnya. The highly sophisticated bug and transmitter, which would have taken considerable effort and risk to install, were actually discovered long before the invasion occurred – though several weeks after their installation.

The Russian who planted the device, Boris Gusev, had arrived from Moscow in the late summer and was the subject of an FBI 'constant surveillance' order from the moment he landed. But they lost him, and did not pick up his trail again until he was seen driving in and out of the State Department car park. He had been picking up signals from the bug on receiving equipment installed in his car, a Russian Embassy vehicle with diplomatic plates. It later became known that Gusev had made between thirty and forty visits to the streets outside the State Department, always in a car identifiable as belonging to the Russian Embassy. There was no evidence to indicate that he had a mole within the department to supply him with times of important meetings in the bugged room, so he must have inserted the device himself.

The whole business was hushed up while the FBI's red-faced counter-espionage unit was rolled out in great numbers to conduct a security sweep of the entire building. The head of the Washington Intelligence Committee raged in colourful language about the 'inability to protect sensitive and classified information from serious compromise'. The FBI tried to put on a brave face, describing the bugging as 'a classic counterintelligence operation', but this was hardly the case; it had never been ahead of the game in this instance. Thus when Gusev made another appearance outside the State Department, he was arrested while sitting outside in his car, where he had been observed adjusting equipment believed to be used for receiving signals from the transmitter inside the State Department. By the day's end Gusev, under normal procedures involving diplomats suspected of spying, had been handed over to Russian officials with instructions that he should leave the country within ten days as persona non grata.

BUGS IN NORTHERN IRELAND

The Cold War is long gone, but the bugging continues – as indeed it does in Northern Ireland, in spite of the Good Friday Peace Agreement. Gerry Adams, leader of Sinn Fein in Northern Ireland, looked suitably annoyed at a press conference on 8 December 1999, when he announced he had discovered a bug in the car used to transport him during sensitive peace negotiations. Even as he demanded an inquiry and an apology for this 'serious breach of faith', Adams knew it was no less than he might have expected. His team probably checked all vehicles and rooms with anti-bugging devices as a matter of course. Indeed, only a couple of weeks earlier the Royal Ulster Constabulary had been called in to investigate after members of the Sinn Fein security team claimed to have detected a signal during a routine sweep of the room that Adams and his colleagues were using at Stormont, although on that occasion British involvement was categorically denied.

There was little doubt that the tracking and listening bug fitted into the lining of the car, however, had been authorised in the interests of national security at a crucial time when the Good Friday Peace Agreement could quite easily have been thrown to the winds. Prime Minister Tony Blair's spokesman repeatedly refused to comment to newsmen; instead he praised the work of the security services and said: 'It is right that the police, security and intelligence agencies take prudent steps to protect the public from the threat of terrorist violence.' He emphasised several times that the security services worked under ministerial control. Indeed Mo Mowlam, the former Northern Ireland Secretary, admitted to the BBC in July 2000 that she had sanctioned the bugging of a Sinn Fein car 'to save lives'.

The car in which the device was found had been used for driving to meetings with IRA leaders for talks on decommissioning of weapons. The announcement of its discovery was made as the IRA were being asked to sign up to the decommissioning process. It is likely to have been discovered much earlier, however, because Adams and the Sinn Fein leaders were well aware that they were under regular surveillance Adams himself demonstrated a descriptive fluency with the technology itself, stating that the bug had been built to the specifications of the car and was colour-coded to the vehicle. He said that it was digitally enhanced, ran with 20–30 watts of output, and had digital tracking ability that could probably be picked up by satellite. 'It is linear amplified,' he told a press conference of political journalists who had no idea what he was talking about, although he clearly did. 'The device was built into the entire infrastructure of the car. The listening device, which is about the size of a match-head or smaller, was at the centre of the roof of the car. There was also a transmission aerial.' Adams said that another ingenious feature was an input aerial which allowed the bug to be switched on and off remotely. There were also rechargeable batteries. Such devices are available on the open market in London spy shops for around £16,000 each, and are part of the arsenal of equipment now used by security firms to provide protection for their clients.

Some time earlier, the home of a senior Sinn Fein official who had been involved from the outset in the Northern Ireland peace talks was bugged for more than three years by the security services in an attempt to obtain intelligence on the IRA. Listening devices were placed in the home of Gerry Kelly in 1994 before the IRA's September ceasefire was announced. According to Belfast MP Peter Robinson, transcripts were passed to the office of the then Prime Minister, John Major, and played a key role in helping his Cabinet decide if the IRA ceasefire was genuine. Peter Robinson claimed that what had been one of the most successful bugging operations against the Republican movement was botched by something said at Stormont to Sinn Fein which alerted Kelly to the surveillance. Robinson said: 'The bugs provided top-grade intelligence, and the top-grade information went straight to the Cabinet Office and John Major.'

This scenario was nothing new in Northern Ireland. The only surprising factor is that the bugging of Kelly remained undetected for so long. The perceived need for all of the bugging and burgling carried out by intelligence and law enforcement agencies and private security firms in the interests of national and economic security and public safety seems to grow ever larger. Campaigners against abuses see the legislation for bugging, even in the world's most democratic nations, as something of a blank cheque for practitioners of this multifaceted art.

In Britain, for example, there is no law which prevents the sale or purchase of the kind of bugging equipment used against Gerry Adams; it is simply unlawful to use it. But the manufacture of bugs in myriad forms is one of the world's growth industries. Thousands of new products come on to the market every year, many of them originally developed for military use and eventually finding their way on to the global scene.

Years earlier, the Vietnam War had inspired a range of military-based products for use against the Viet Cong and these were eventually transferred to the commercial marketplace. Later Northern Ireland became the place where technical wizardry designed for covert surveillance was invented. For almost three decades, these new tools of the trade were tried and tested in virtually every conceivable terrorist and criminal situation. As a senior officer who served in the Special Forces in Northern Ireland for several years told me: 'Wars tend to produce the implements that become necessary to meet emerging situations. In Northern Ireland it was just ongoing, a continuous flow of situations to be confronted and, on our part, ideas to combat them. The new technology that we asked for began to come on stream in a big way in the 1980s and just became progressively better and better from an intelligence point of view.'

As things settled down, the learning curve produced some dramatic results in new intelligence-gathering techniques and equipment. Captain D (not his actual rank or initial), who arrived in Northern Ireland for service in a Special Forces covert operations unit, told me: 'In the beginning intelligence was really a joke, both in terms of people running it and the gear they provided us with. We were all given some kind of training at the Joint Services Intelligence School at Ashford, but they were still in the Cold War mode – sending us out on exercises and tests with rolled up newspapers for clandestine meets, like we were in Berlin. They had absolutely no bloody relevance at all to the situation in Northern Ireland. This situation existed almost into the 1980s. Of course, few people had had any experience of the kind of things that were to confront us, with horrendously hostile communities and an underground counterintelligence operation run by the Provisional IRA that was frankly beating us on many occasions. They even bugged our military base. Our databases were piss-poor for years, security was lax and agents were being picked off like flies. We simply had to start from scratch and necessity, as they say, is the mother of invention. Northern Ireland became the testing ground for all manner of stuff ... lots of new bugging equipment with enhanced capabilities which were incredibly easy to attach to a property and could provide massive amounts of information for less man-hours. It also became much easier to tap or scan modern telephone systems which once needed to be done manually, either by connecting into the line or actually getting into a property and putting a bug inside the equipment. By the 1990s, none of that was necessary. It could be done by other means, although in some situations we still had to implant a bugging network to be sure of our service.'

Many of the instruments used in what were known as 'tech attacks' in Northern Ireland were pioneered by top secret elements of the British Army such as the FRU (Force Research Unit) and 14th Company, a Special Forces group which developed into the most skilled bunch of surveillance operatives and agent-handlers anywhere in the world. Their field work, coupled with the overhead capabilities of satellite imagery and communications facilities, made it possible to see and hear at a distance, to photograph the bandit country of South Armagh from the sky. These techniques were soon to be adopted elsewhere, among military and civilian spy agencies.

The whole approach to intelligence gathering on the ground – as opposed to the ease of the Echelon electronic info-grabbing techniques – was being rethought and the parameters redrawn. Out of initial experiments in Northern Ireland secret political and paramilitary operations proliferated and expanded, their methods copied and their surveillance armoury moved out into the international marketplace by the electronics companies which devised and manufactured them to original army specifications. The model of 14th Company as a covert unit staffed by super-specialists skilled in both military and intelligence operations has, according to a source, 'proved to be an invaluable tool against terrorism and has been copied by the Americans and by NATO, which has its own similar unit placed at the helm of rapid reaction forces'. It has also provided a number of techniques and a good deal of equipment that civilian intelligence services can incorporate into their own activities.

These developments, together with the burgeoning information gathering of Echelon, produced computer-based storage and retrieval systems of mammoth proportions in which data is available on demand. Northern Ireland thus became a testing ground for the physical surveillance units. Equipment that was tried out there included image amplification devices; infra-red binoculars; light amplifiers; satellite cameras, which now are not far from being able to tell the time from a soldier's wristwatch as he walks down the Falls Road; sound amplification devices; directional microphones; and image and sound recording devices. Later, other inventions were introduced such as miniature video cameras; parabolic microphones to detect conversations over a kilometre away; a laser version that can pick up conversations through closed windows; stroboscopic cameras capable of taking hundreds of pictures a minute and individually photograph every member of a crowd at, say, a demonstration or football match; and automatic vehicle recognition systems which can identify a car number plate and then track it around a city. All these implements of surveillance, developed over a number of years, could eventually be matched with the databases for voice and visual recognition; thousands of faces whose images could be scanned in a moment. The latter development was immediately picked up and moved into public usage for another area of British and European life – that of football hooliganism. As this particular brand of violence spread in the 1980s, Margaret Thatcher demanded that it should be matched by an intelligence effort akin to a military-style operation in Northern Ireland. The police began the mass filming and photographing of crowds of spectators in the same way that they would film and photograph demonstrators and political agitators. MI5 even managed to get agents into the organised groups intent on causing trouble at football matches. Several prosecutions resulted from the identification of soccer hooligans from videotapes as image-scanning from stored databases of photographs and videos moved from military to civilian agency usage.

It came at a time when computer and electronics companies in the UK, USA and Far East had begun to expand into new markets with equipment originally developed for the military. Companies such as E Systems, Electronic Data Systems and Texas Instruments, soon to be followed by the Japanese giants such as Sony and Mitsubishi, began selling advanced computer systems and surveillance equipment not merely to intelligence agencies and private security services but to state and local governments. As Steve Wright of the Omega Foundation pointed out in his report to the European Parliament: 'Surveillance technology [with an array of] devices or systems which can monitor, track and assess the movements of individuals, their property and other assets was soon being used against human rights activists, journalists, student leaders, minorities, trade union leaders and political opponents.'

It was already a far cry from the 1970s, when the British Society for Social Responsibility in Science first warned that a new technology of repression was being spawned in an effort to contain the conflict in Northern Ireland. Since then, several non-government research organisations have agreed with those findings and have periodically warned against the application of science and technology to the problem of 'neutralising' troublesome members of society. Such warnings fell largely on deaf ears and, by the 1990s, the new forms of electronic surveillance originally devised to target individuals or small groups of people in specific situations were emerging for use against the general public.

The overall trend was towards miniaturisation, with more precise sound and images being gained through digital technology. The down-sizing continued into the micro-developments. Where once 'tube' microphones were inserted into the walls or window frames of buildings, they could now be replaced with 'needle' mikes. Bugging therefore became significantly easier. Many systems do not require physical entry into the target property. If access can be achieved there is a plethora of devices available, many pre-packaged to fit into phones, light fittings, smoke detector units and wall clocks, and which can be tuned into from a suitable radio.

The next generation of covert audio bugs is already arriving, such as Lorraine Electronics' multi-room surveillance system called DIAL (Direct Intelligent Access Listening) which allows an operator to monitor several rooms in a single building from anywhere in the world. Up to four concealed microphones are connected to the subscriber's line and these can be remotely activated simply by making a coded telephone call to the target building. Neural network bugs go one step further. Built like a small cockroach, as soon as the lights go out they can crawl to the best location for monitoring purposes. Meanwhile, specially programmed laptop computers can capture all the mobile phones and cordless telephones active in a particular area by cursoring down to their number. The machine will even search for numbers of interest to see if they are active.

One of the most significant developments was the way the new technology was adapted by civilian intelligence agencies as they began searching for new missions to justify their budgets, transferring their resources to combating organised crime and terrorism. An operation which demonstrated what the drug dealers and suspected terrorists might face in the future was among the last major IRA investigations on the British mainland before the paramilitary ceasefire which led to the Good Friday Peace Agreement came into effect. It involved a network of police and MI5 officers and went down in history as the largest, longest and most expensive anti-terrorist operation ever mounted, involving more than three hundred officers engaged in the intense monitoring of just five men. They notched up fifty thousand hours of surveillance and studied thousands of hours of CCTV footage, the greater part of which was concentrated over a period of six weeks, to trap a Provisional IRA active service bombing unit in September 1996.

OPERATION TINNITUS

The MI5 and police operation, codenamed Tinnitus, began after two IRA suspects were routinely picked up by CCTV security cameras at Hammersmith Broadway station and recognised from database scans. The planning and clandestine observation of them immediately swung into action – a labour-intensive Humint operation that went some way to proving the point made by experts such as Stephen Lander and CIA boss Tenet: that although there is no going back to the cloak and dagger days, often there is no substitute for legwork and people on the ground.

Teams of men and women joined a rota to perform a twenty-four-hour watch, some conducting mobile surveillance from vans, cars and even milk floats, some on foot, some positioned at observation posts for days at a time. They used videos, traffic cameras, digital cameras for computer databases and ordinary cameras for still photos. They planted listening devices in vehicles and property, took hundreds of rolls of photographs and recorded miles of tape in monitoring the movements of the five men, two of whom came directly from Dublin for the job.

Surveillance was difficult when tracking a group who were themselves ultra-sensitive to such methods, having undergone their own intensive IRA training in anti-surveillance techniques. The bombing team used codewords for their names and rendezvous points. They switched transport often. They communicated with each other and their Dublin base only from public phones and pagers, never from residential or mobile telephones. To avoid being followed, they took all the classic precautions such as doubling back on their routes, meeting in parks or crowded places and having lookouts behind them for anyone tailing them. The two who came from Dublin, Brian McHugh, thirty-one, said to be the unit's commander, and Patrick Kelly, also thirty-one, were so determined to protect their identities that they had no dealings with staff at the Hammersmith hotel where they stayed. One of their number paid all the bills and moved their belongings. In spite of these precautions, however, MI5 bugged their rooms at the hotel and planted listening devices in at least two cars they used regularly.

Kelly was tailed to North Wales where he rented a self-catering chalet at a Butlin's holiday centre. From that base he made several trips to Yorkshire, where he was apparently awaiting delivery of a lorry which the gang intended to pack with explosives and leave somewhere in London to create mayhem and cause death on a large scale. Eventually one was delivered to a lorry park in Beignton, left by a man whom the surveillance team gave the codename of Base Metal because they could not establish his true identity. After he had delivered the lorry, he was followed to Manchester Airport where he caught a flight to Dublin. Neither MI5 nor British police are allowed to operate in the Republic of Ireland, but no doubt an MI6 agent was waiting at the other end. The suspect would have been followed and, eventually, his identity discovered to be logged for future reference.

Meanwhile, the MI5 and police teams followed the men to numerous meetings in a 'vast number of pubs', a lock-up garage and a lorry park. McHugh was observed on several occasions making calls from a phone box, and the officers were able to trace the number he dialled to a public telephone in Castle Blaney in the Irish Republic. He was monitored making a brief trip to Ireland to get more money from the IRA paymaster general. The appearance of the lorry, driven back to London by Kelly, presented the police and MI5 with a great dilemma. If the surveillance team had moved in too early, they might have had insufficient grounds for arrest and prosecution. If, on the other hand, they had left it too late the bombers might have carried out their task and many people might have died.

Further information was needed. MI5's breaking and entering specialists picked the lock on the gang's store and discovered it contained four massive bombs in an 'advanced state of readiness' and a hundred bags of ammonium nitrate and sugar – the explosive mixture – hidden underneath bags of compost. This was enough for a devastating bombing campaign in the capital. There were also detonators, timers, boosters, car booby traps, three Kalashnikov rifles, handguns and a large amount of ammunition. The man who rented the lock-up, using a false name, was twenty-seven-year-old Dairmuid O'Neill, a committed IRA man and key member of the team, who had lived in London for several years. MI5 managed to plant a listening device in his car. From information gathered, the investigators decided it was time to move in and arrest the men. Armed units made their move and in the process

Diarmuid O'Neill, mistakenly believed to have been carrying a gun, was shot dead by a police marksman.

The remaining four were arrested and charged with conspiracy to cause explosions. McHugh was sentenced to twenty-five years in prison, Kelly to twenty, and a third and lesser accomplice, James Murphy, twenty-six, a school groundsman with an Irish background who lived in Chelsea, was jailed for seventeen years. The fourth man was found not guilty and was discharged. But there was a sting in the tail which demonstrated that even the most modern types of surveillance cannot gather up all the secrets of such a gang. Two months after their arrest, the manager of a lock-up storage depot in Shepherd's Bush, West London, was attacked by three masked men demanding to know which was the unit rented in the name of Murphy. None of them was, because he had used an alias, but the men broke open several storage units until they found what they were looking for – a cache of explosives which they carted away. Traces of these substances were found on the floor by MI5 forensics, and staff later identified Murphy as the man who had rented the unit.

And still there was one more twist to come. Almost a year after the arrests were made, another rented lock-up a hundred yards from Chelsea football ground in London was repossessed by the owner because no rent had been paid since September 1996 – the time the gang was arrested. The owners found sacks containing four blocks of Semtex, bullets and timers. Murphy's fingerprints and a photograph of him were also discovered in the lock-up. It had been rented by O'Neill using a false name, and keys to fit its lock were found at Murphy's home, along with a bag which bore traces of explosives.

MOVES TO WIDEN SURVEILLANCE POWERS

In the 1990s widespread legal and illegal bugging, tapping and burgling by police or internal security forces became an issue across Europe and North America – anywhere, in fact, that civil rights groups had both the knowledge of what was happening and the clout to attempt to bring it into the public arena for debate. The increase – demonstrated in figures released for the number of annual wire-tapping operations admitted by the various agencies under the law of their own countries – ran parallel to those agencies taking on board new areas of operation and new equipment to monitor them. This activity, in several countries including Britain and the USA, required a change in the law to give the agencies more powers as they switched their resources from counterespionage and anti-subversion to crime fighting. In Britain, it was the extension of bug and burgle powers for MI5 which caused most controversy. The Security Service Act of 1989, which was the first legislation to acknowledge the existence of MI5 since its formation in 1909, allowed the service to apply to the Home Secretary for a warrant to enter and/or interfere with property, to enter a home or office secretly, to collect material or documents and to install listening devices; it was merely the formalising of activities carried out for years. Bugging warrants could be applied for against individuals, groups and organisations, and MI5 was also allowed to 'front' applications for entry warrants on behalf of MI6 who were, in theory, prohibited from operating on British soil against British citizens. The wording of the new powers to allow bugging against 'a large number of persons in pursuit of a common purpose' caused more consternation among the civil rights campaigners, who saw it as a back-door method of legalising surveillance against political and human rights activists, over and above the criminal element. The changes meant that MI5, MI6 and GCHQ were aligned with the police and the NCIS to tackle organised crime, using extensive powers under warrants – which can remain in force up to six months – to enter, place bugs or audio-visual equipment in homes, offices or public places and to bug vehicles. The police themselves also sought an extension of their powers to enter property, to place bugs, to carry out covert searches and to place tracking and listening devices on cars.

Various police groups put their case to a Commons Select Committee on Organised Crime and argued a case for legal backing that recognised a distinction between telephone tapping and other forms of surveillance activity, for example listening into conversations held in a bugged room or office. If such a power was granted, the police recognised that they would also have to have legal provision on the question of evidence obtained in this manner being admissible in a court of law 'to protect them from having to disclose details as to how it was acquired'.

Additional armoury in the fight against crime and terrorism was rolled in with new home-based powers awarded to MI6 and GCHQ under the Intelligence Services Act 1994 which allowed them to intercept 'wireless telegraphy' – telephones, faxes, e-mails and so on – in cases where 'there is no information-gathering aspect'. Their involvement in crime fighting was further enhanced when the New Labour government came to power in 1997. Foreign Secretary Robin Cook, whose department includes MI6 and GCHQ, ordered both organisations to move to the forefront of the war against drugs. Cook singled out Burma, the world's largest producer of opiates, as a particular target and accused its military junta of 'conniving' with the drug barons.

THE WAR AGAINST DRUGS

Although drugs intelligence is moving up in the order of priorities, MI6 still focuses heavily on other international concerns such as the proliferation of weapons of mass destruction and the protection of British interests overseas. In fact, the service was already short of manpower in dealing with its more traditional roles of running covert activity in a large number of political hot-spots around the globe, not least in the Balkans and Russia itself. The Global Issues Controllerate of MI6 was given the task of running the anti-drugs operations, linking up with MI5, British Customs or the police. There was, however, considerable scepticism among the latter two organisations which felt that, given existing demands on their agents abroad, MI6 could make little more than a piecemeal contribution to the anti-drugs effort. Even so, there were several spectacular successes involving the collective input of police, intelligence services, GCHQ and agencies across Europe in which modern surveillance techniques were to the fore. One case in particular demonstrated the potential of operations in which close surveillance of the targets featured strongly.

In the summer of 1997 Curtis Warren, a thirty-four-year-old multi-millionaire from Toxteth, Liverpool, was finally unmasked as an international drugs trafficker. A year earlier he had featured in the *Sunday Times* list of Britain's five hundred richest people, coming in at joint 481st with an entry which read: 'Warren is a major property player and trader in the North West, particularly in the Merseyside area where he is a well-known figure in the local community. He also has extensive interests on the Continent.' By the time the list was published he was sitting in a top-security prison cell in the Netherlands, and his 'extensive interests on the Continent' were being taken apart by drugs investigators who had codenamed him Target One.

In a Dutch court in June 1997 Warren was said to have amassed his fortune through his connections with the drugs cartels in Colombia, from which country he organised a worldwide operation dealing in cocaine, eventually extending into the trafficking of all major drugs including heroin, cannabis, Ecstasy and amphetamines. He had begun his operations from the north of England, supplying wholesale to drug dealers in Liverpool and other major cities, and had been under regular surveillance since he and eight other men were acquitted at Newcastle upon Tyne in 1993 of smuggling 1980lb of cocaine. He had been monitored under a joint drugs-busting operation, codenamed Crayfish, involving customs, regional crime units, MI5 and GCHQ. In November 1995, aware that he was under close watch on his home turf, he switched his headquarters to a secluded £1 million villa on the outskirts of Amsterdam.

From there he built up a massive supply business, running in shipments of cocaine from Colombia, heroin from Turkey and cannabis from Morocco, and arranging the local manufacture of Ecstasy and amphetamines in massive quantities from illegal drugs factories in the Netherlands. Warren and his aides concentrated strictly on wholesale distribution, supplying a network of major dealers across the United Kingdom and in other European cities. He set up an intricate anti-surveillance system, but it fell apart when a 700lb shipment of cocaine was offloaded by mistake at Rotterdam. While Warren's people were attempting to reload the drugs aboard a ship bound for Bulgaria, numerous mobile telephone calls were intercepted. The police then had sufficient evidence to move and, in a series of armed raids around Amsterdam, they took possession of a ton and a half of cannabis resin, 150lb of heroin and 3740lb of hashish, along with a small arsenal of handguns and rifles, several hand grenades and 980 CS gas canisters.

Warren was charged with masterminding a drug-trafficking operation from his villa and with the illegal possession of weapons. He denied everything and in court his defence lawyer moved to have the case dismissed, claiming that the evidence was 'contaminated by illegal phone-taps' conducted from Britain. The Dutch judges rejected the argument and sentenced Warren to twelve years' imprisonment. One of his senior lieutenants, Stephen Mee, thirty-eight, also from Liverpool, and another member of the gang, Stephen Whitehead, thirty-five, from Oldham, were each jailed for seven years. Mee was already wanted in Britain after escaping from a prison van while being taken to Manchester Crown Court in 1993 to be sentenced for his part in a £1 million drugs operation. He had fled abroad and had been sentenced in his absence to twenty-two years in jail for smuggling cocaine from Colombia. Three other members of Warren's gang, William Fitzgerald, fifty-six, from Liverpool, Raymond Nolan, twenty-nine, and William Riley, forty-eight, both from Merseyside, were jailed for three years by the same court. Nolan remains wanted in Britain for questioning in connection with a £1.7 million Security Express robbery in Huyton in February 1996. Warren's departure from the European drugs scene was regarded as a triumph for the British investigation team which had been tracking him for five years. Detective Chief Inspector Mike Keogh, coordinator of the North West regional crime squad, said: 'He and some of his friends in Liverpool thought he was untouchable, but that has proved not to be the case.'

Another unheralded surveillance and interception project concerned the tracking of the man who, at one stage, was described in the press as 'Britain's most wanted': the burly Londoner Kenneth Noye, whom police wanted to question about the 1996 roadside knife killing of a motorist in what appeared to be a road rage attack. Some years earlier, Noye had been cleared of the manslaughter of an undercover policeman, whom he had stabbed to death in his front garden. He had claimed he thought he was being attacked. After the death of the young motorist Noye vanished from his home and, following a two-year world-wide hunt, was eventually traced to Spain in what a source would only describe as a 'surveillance operation supported by GCHQ at Cheltenham'. Spanish police and intelligence officers began a month-long watch, in which British officers also took part. Noye's house near Cadiz was bugged, his telephone calls and those of his associates were tapped, his callers photographed and a device was fitted to his car.

In Britain, Noye's wife Brenda was also under surveillance at their home near Sevenoaks in Kent. In a simultaneous operation, Noye was arrested in Spain on an international warrant while police called at the £5 million Kent home and removed a number of possessions. Noye was eventually extradited to Britain, and convicted of murder and sentenced to life imprisonment.

FIGHTING THE MAFIA

The exact nature of the surveillance techniques used in the Noye case were never revealed, nor would they be; as ever, the British liked to keep things under wraps. The Italians are less secretive, or at least they were on the occasion when I was in the company of one of the country's leading anti-Mafia figures, Judge Liliano Ferraro, while researching my book *The Walking Dead* which concerned her own activities and those of two close associates, Judges Borsellino and Falcone. Both the latter had been killed by a bomb in Palermo. Through this link, I was party to details of a particularly successful surveillance operation which demonstrated the power of the tools of interception and which began to become available to police and security forces across Europe throughout the 1990s. In Italy that was progress indeed, and a dramatic advance. In the mid-1980s the police and security forces in Sicily – beating heart of the Italian Mafia – did not possess a single computer. A decade later, they were very well equipped as the war on the Mafia intensified.

The classic surveillance sting to which I was witness occurred at Linate in the north of Italy, where Giacomo Riina, ageing uncle of the imprisoned head of the Sicilian Corleone family, Toto Riina, was in command of a massive cocaine distribution network, running huge shipments into Germany. Not long before, Paolo Borsellino had been blown up one Sunday morning, shortly after returning from discussions with the German authorities in Mannheim. It was rumoured among informers that the Corleonesi had ordered Borsellino's death and, as a matter of course, Giacomo Riina was placed under surveillance in a joint operation with the Italian anti-drugs agency and the Italian secret service. This led them to the discovery of another leading

Mafia boss, Giuseppe Madonia, and it became evident there was something big in the offing. Madonia's car was fitted with a tracking device which led the officers to a massive warehouse near a football ground in Linate. An undercover unit established an observation post 350 metres from the warehouse, where they were able to film every movement to and from the building, twenty-four hours a day. Meanwhile, the Italian secret service installed micro-spy equipment inside, with time-lapse cameras and a dozen microphones through which they were able to eavesdrop.

The information obtained through this remarkable operation confirmed the importance of the warehouse to a criminal network involving an alliance of the Catanesi (a group of Mafia families from Catania) and the Corleonesi, represented by Toto Riina's uncle. They were wholesaling a huge range of merchandise, including drugs, small arms and heavy weapons acquired from former Soviet bloc countries, with a turnover of $600,000 a week. The Italian police could have pounced at any time and arrested all concerned, but the intelligence being gleaned from the conversation inside the building was so good that they let the situation run. Through the micro-surveillance equipment the agents listened to the mafiosi setting up deals, along with talk about the elimination of rivals and rooting out unreliable connections. A fountain of information flowed during weeks of monitoring and at last a major event in the gang's calendar approached – the imminent arrival of a consignment of 1000 kilos of cocaine from Colombia. The two Italian judges in charge of the investigation – and who were kept abreast of every operation by the surveillance teams – Giuseppe Nicolossi from Florence and Antonio Ferrara from Catania, prepared to gather their forces and arrest the men when the shipment arrived, aware that money and bosses would be on hand for the division of the cargo and finances. Ferrara prepared to move up to Linate from Catania. He planned to fly by police aircraft to Milan and then travel by armoured car to Linate. Two days before he was due to leave Sicily the Linate group received a hand-delivered letter from a Mafia boss in prison, and his message was relayed over the telephone to the Catanesi. Their instructions were to murder Ferrara immediately: 'Blow him up ... do it as he goes to Mass on Sunday because he will be leaving immediately afterwards to fly to Milan.' The Mafia boss clearly knew the judge's immediate plans from an informer. The men of the Italian secret police filmed this entire episode – the delivery of the note, the mafioso reading it over the telephone, first with the letter in his hand and then burning it.

The plan to swoop on the warehouse at the time of the delivery of the cocaine shipment was abandoned. That night, all judges in Catania were brought into protective custody or given guards. The warehouse was raided by 150 armed security men and twenty people were arrested. From the documents inside and from telephone records, the anti-Mafia forces gleaned much useful information. The list of telephone numbers included that of a highly placed Mafia contact in the Ministry of Defence. The bugs had saved the life of at least one Italian judge.

The Linate operation also demonstrated a system widely used in Europe, but not in Britain, in which judges themselves are involved at the front end of major investigations where surveillance is to be used. This can have benefits in guarding against any abuses or errors. In July 1999 in the UK for example, the Attorney General John Morris announced an inquiry into a major drug prosecution which collapsed after customs and excise officials were said to have broken the law in regard to bugging and lied about it in court. The targets were a group of five men who were suspected of attempting to smuggle £34 million worth of cocaine into Britain from the Caribbean aboard a catamaran. At their original trial in Bristol in 1997, Brian Doran and Kenneth Togher were described as the ringleaders and were jailed for twenty-five years. Defence lawyers later lodged an appeal, claiming that it had since emerged that customs officers had bugged Togher's hotel room without getting permission from the hotel or their superiors. A retrial was ordered by the Court of Appeal but it was eventually aborted when the trial judge Mr Justice Turner branded the prosecution of five men for the cocaine smuggling operation a 'debacle.' In his judgment delivered to the Attorney General in July 1999, he said 'It would not be right to leave this case without expressing a deep sense of judicial concern over what may be considered to be a scandalous result. This arises out of the undoubted commission of a crime which is as socially corrosive and destructive as the importation of a massive amount of high purity cocaine which will in effect go unpunished.'

The inquiry ordered by the Attorney General would look into the conduct not only of customs officials and prosecuting counsel but also the flouting of the rules in regard to bugging which could be catastrophic for a long, costly and painstaking investigation.

CHAPTER 13
TAP ... TAP!: THE USES AND ABUSES OF PHONE TAPPING

TOGETHER WITH BUGGING, phone tapping is one of the best known forms of surveillance. This chapter explores the abuses of phone tapping in the past, and how, even today, our privacy is not adequately protected by law.

First, a couple of statistics: 1329 legally authorised wire-tap operations were conducted in the USA during 1998, and 2031 telephone or mail interception warrants were approved in the United Kingdom during the same period. They seem modest enough figures; in fact Louis Freeh, director of the FBI, boasted about their modest nature in a speech to college students in the USA in the summer of 1999. But as everyone knows, statistics can be applied to suit.

The number of taps in the USA only covers surveillance by state and federal investigators within the country itself, through the act of tapping the telephones of individuals or groups of people connected with criminal investigations. The figure excludes all interceptions by the methods employed by the National Security Agency, all external operations and all intelligence and counterintelligence missions by the eighteen groups in the US intelligence community or the dozens of US military intelligence formations, which for reasons of national security remain classified. Nor does it include bugging by other means. In other words, it is straightforward telephone tapping for the purpose of listening in to the conversations of specifically targeted people, usually suspected criminals.

In the United Kingdom the figures exclude all warrants issued by the Northern Ireland Secretary (because the totals in the past have been rather substantial), and all the routinely operated sweeps of the global telecom networks operated by GCHQ, Menwith Hill and general signals intelligence interceptions. Nor does it include operations under the 'bugging and burgling' facility allowed to the various intelligence services by means of other electronic devices. The British government does not publish a detailed analysis of telephone-tapping activities approved under warrant. So we have to go with the figures gleaned from the USA where, under the Freedom of Information Act, they have become much more open about their operations. There, a more revealing picture emerges, at least in regard to wire-taps carried out under warrants approved by judges.

The number of telephone communications intercepted under these 1329 warrants in the USA during 1998 totalled 2,469,282; the number of individuals actually 'listened in to' was 252,510 and the human resources engaged on each wire-tapping operation can perhaps be judged from the cost: the average for *each* of the federal wire-taps in 1998 was $73,404. This was on the basis that the maximum period for each interception operation in the USA is thirty days (although this may be extended further upon application, and frequently is) while in Britain the initial warrant runs for sixty days for police and customs and for up to six months for MI5.

Wire tapping and mail opening are conducted in nearly every country in the world and are frequently abused. The US Department of State, in its annual *Country Reports on Human Rights Practices*, reported widespread, illegal or uncontrolled use of wire-taps by both government and private groups in more than seventy countries. That was some statement from a nation which taps the telephones of the world with the most phenomenal array of bugging and tapping hardware known to mankind and employs the world's largest army of eavesdroppers. The ability of state-run agencies in most of the democratically governed nations of the world to make their 'holier than thou' claims of abuse by other nations lies in the wording of such statements, the use of words such as 'illegal or uncontrolled'. They argue, to a man, that wire-tap interceptions against the general public and organisations are governed by warrants and supported by a strict code of practice and oversight.

That is certainly the case in regard to telephone tapping in the USA, though the oversight is far less apparent in the UK.

Historically, the intelligence agencies do not have a good record in abiding by the rules. Wire-taps have been an essential part of their armoury almost since the first telephone exchanges were established in 1879. By then, telegraphs and subsequently telegrams were being read and monitored, but the extent of these activities did not become publicly known until 16 December 1920 when the president of Western Union, Newcomb Carlton, was forced under oath to reveal to a US Senate committee that the British government secretly required his company routinely to turn over to British Naval Intelligence copies of every telegram that went out of Britain or came in.

Pressured, the Western Union boss refused to answer the question of whether these included US government communications – which the committee took to mean yes. Of course, the US government was doing exactly the same with its own in-and-out cables, copies of which were delivered to what was known in the USA as the Black Chamber. In 1928, Judge Louis Brandeis commented during a US Supreme Court hearing: 'Subtler and more far-reaching means of invading privacy have become available to government; discovery and invention have made it possible for government, by means far more effective than stretching upon the rack, to obtain disclosure of what is whispered in the closet.'

Seventy years later, the pattern remains unchanged except that the Black Chamber was long ago supplanted by the National Security Agency and the British Admiralty communications intelligence arm by GCHQ. They and their colleagues in other agencies who joined them in the intelligence war denied they were doing anything illegal then, and still do – but there is a wealth of ammunition for the privacy and human rights campaigners to draw upon. Only in comparatively recent times have oversight laws forced them to clean up their act, but great suspicion remains about the whole practice – a suspicion which has merely been heightened by the astonishing pace of the arrival of new technology in the telecommunications industry in the 1990s.

The words 'legal and controlled' point up two other factors: in many countries where human rights are not high among their governments' concerns, wire tapping is widespread and out of control; and there has been a large increase in the use of wire tapping by non-governmental organisations, ranging from crime and terrorist groups, through practitioners of economic and industrial espionage, all the way down to the level of gumshoe private detectives tapping the telephone of an errant wife or husband.

J. EDGAR HOOVER

Perhaps the most infamous figure in the world of illegal surveillance was the former director of the FBI, J. Edgar Hoover. For many decades of the twentieth century while the Soviet Union had the KGB, East Germany the Stasi and the UK MI5, America had J. Edgar Hoover. He was a one-man NSA, only worse; a bundle of nastiness and sheer evil. Hoover believed knowledge was power (which he undoubtedly proved) and that knowledge came largely from wire-taps, bugs and mail openings, many of which were illegal and authorised by no other authority than himself. It is worth recalling some of the bugging and tapping activities conducted under his command to remind ourselves how corrupted power can run right out of control.

America only began to come to terms with the full extent of his abuse of power on his death in 1972. His *personal* files on practically everyone who was famous or notorious in the previous half-century – including dozens from the world of show business – weighed four tonnes. They were an appalling catalogue of indiscriminate spying on private lives, often by wire-taps, on anyone he cared to select, ranging from Mafia bosses to Presidents, from New Left to black nationalists, anti-Vietnam protestors to Ku Klux Klan. And what Hoover failed – or refused – to accept was the distinction between criminal conduct and free expression.

The most infamous of all his wire-taps occurred under the FBI's COINTELPRO operations, which actually stepped across the line from investigation to covert action. Frustrated by the bureau's legal mandate and limitations placed on the admission of tapped evidence in court, Hoover set up a programme of illegal wire-taps, the aim of which was 'to disrupt, disorganise and neutralise' chosen targets. The tactics, which Hoover encouraged to be as 'imaginative' as possible, included character assassination by placing false stories with friendly media contacts, concocting spurious stories alleging anything from rape to embezzle-ment, drug addiction or sexual deviance. Coming from the FBI, these stories usually appeared in print. He used harassment; poison pen letters; informing on left-leaning targets to employers, banks and friends; and what he termed 'selective law enforcement' by encouraging other state agencies such as the tax authorities to institute investigations.

He poured thousands upon thousands of man-hours into the COINTELPRO operations and general wire-tapping activity. He ran surveillance against – and 'against' is the operative word – national figures in virtually every sphere of public life, running to millions of pages of transcripts, many demonstrating his obsession with the belief that Communist influences were being brought to bear upon the American nation by high-profile people; this, coupled with his other obsession, sex, claimed the working days of many an agent.

Most famous was his onslaught against the Kennedy brothers. Most despicable was his campaign against civil rights leader Dr Martin Luther King. He persuaded the then US Attorney General to approve a wire-tap warrant on the basis that 'dangerous Communist influence is being asserted on the Negro ...'. King was no saint, but what followed remains one of the most shameful episodes in modern American history.

Hoover resorted to the vilest of methods and leaked information to try to influence media and politicians – even attempting to halt the award of the Nobel Peace Prize by arranging delivery to Sweden of a thirteen-page memorandum headed, 'Dr Martin Luther King: His Personal Conduct'. The same document was delivered to Westminster when the enraged Hoover learned that King might be received by the then Prime Minister, Harold Wilson. When King returned from Europe to the prospect of numerous accolades and receptions in his home country, Hoover attempted to discourage the attendance of leading politicians by circulating details of the man's private life. He leaked material to newspapers, which generally refused to touch it. When that failed, a plan, emanating from the FBI's creative thinkers in the COIN-TELPRO department, was launched to try to force King from the national scene by plunging him into a deep depression. A compilation tape of telephone intercepts was mailed to him anonymously with what amounted to a threatening letter: 'King look into your heart. You know you are a complete fraud ... your honorary degrees and Nobel Prize will not save you ... you are done. There is only one way out for you. You know what it is. You had better take it before your filthy, abnormal fraudulent self is bared to the nation.' The unsigned letter now lies in FBI files.

The FBI director, in office from 1924 to his death in 1972, kept up illegal surveillance on politicians and showbiz people for his personal files which he used for his own ends when the occasion arose. When the FBI was threatened with a congressional inquiry during the presidency of Richard Nixon after tapping the telephones of the CIA headquarters, Hoover had it blocked by threatening to tell what he *really* knew. He used illegal wire-taps to destroy anyone who opposed him, helped create McCarthyism, blackmailed the Kennedys and ran a massive personal and internal campaign to damage the civil rights movement; while his investigations into the assassinations of JFK and Martin Luther King were so flawed as to invoke conspiracy theories that such incompetence could only have been deliberate, perhaps to hide his personal involvement. He delighted in letting people know he knew their secrets – even down to minutiae. He discovered JFK's affair with Marilyn Monroe when he began tapping her after she married left-leaning playwright Arthur Miller. Yet his 'knowledge' included incredibly low-grade and personal data that had no place in the intelligence-gathering operations of what was supposedly the world's most renowned police force. He once rang bandleader Desi Arnaz to tell him his wife, Lucille Ball, was expecting a child, ten minutes after she had received the news herself from her doctor. Through such insidious methods Hoover managed to remain director of the FBI throughout the administrations of ten Presidents of the United States.

Several attempts to force an investigation into FBI wire-taps were thwarted and those campaigning for them 'neutralised' – Hoover loved that word. In April 1971, however, Hale Boggs, majority leader of the US House of Representatives, stunned his colleagues by calling for Hoover's resignation: 'When the FBI taps telephones of members of this body and of members of the Senate ... when the FBI stations agents on college campuses to infiltrate college organisations ... when the FBI adopts the tactics of the Soviet Union and Hitler's Gestapo then it is time – it is way past time – that the present director no longer be the director.'

Gerald Ford, soon to be President of the United States after Nixon's resignation, made a stumbling rebuttal of the charges, while Hoover himself marshalled his forces and leaked material to the newspapers alleging Boggs's perpetual drunkenness. He also falsely claimed that the FBI had discovered that the wire-taps on his house had been placed there not by them but by a private detective hired by Mrs Boggs to get evidence of his 'dalliances with his mistress'.

Continued media reports discrediting Boggs began to appear, and less attention was paid to his next speech in which he insisted: 'Over the post-war years we have granted to the elite and secret police within our system vast new powers over the lives and liberties of the people. At the request of the trusted and respected heads of those forces and their appeal to the necessities of national security, we have exempted those grants of power from due accounting and strict surveillance. Liberty has yielded ... I submit that 1984 is closer than we think. ...'

Only then did the public disquiet about Hoover begin to crystallise. *Newsweek* ran a poll which showed that 51 per cent of those interviewed thought he should retire. Hoover responded with a speech to ex-FBI agents, who cheered wildly when he declared: 'The FBI has no intention of compromising its standards to satisfy journalistic prostitutes ... to accommodate kooks, misfits, drunks and slobs ... it is time we stopped coddling the hoodlums and hippies who are causing so much serious trouble these days. Let us treat them like the vicious enemies of society they really are.'

The 'hippies' included John Lennon who, like Jane Fonda et al, was put under constant FBI surveillance over his support for anti-Vietnam protesters. Hoover ran a COINTELPRO-style operation against Lennon and invoked the assistance of the US drugs and immigration agencies in an attempt to get him kicked out of the USA. Many of the files relating to Lennon in FBI and Immigration Service vaults are still classified and repeated attempts, including my own, to have them released under the Freedom of Information Act have been refused – not necessarily because of the secret material they contain but because of the deep embarrassment they might cause to the FBI and the American nation as a whole.

Another target was actress Jean Seberg, against whom Hoover launched an incredibly vitriolic campaign, alleging that her expected child had been fathered by a leading member of the Black Panthers, a cause for which Seberg had spoken in support. When the child was born prematurely, stillborn, it was discovered to have white skin. Seberg had the child buried in a coffin with a glass lid so that people could see for themselves. Driven to despair by continual media references planted by the FBI director, she committed suicide soon afterwards.

Hoover eventually began to come under increasing media scrutiny, especially from Washington columnist Jack Anderson, who risked his wrath by being among the first to challenge his appalling tactics. Unfortunately, Hoover did not live to face the ignominy of fuller disclosure about his scandal-ridden forty-eight years in office or his own sexual proclivities. As one of his opponents long ago attempted to reveal, he and his deputy Clive Tolson had 'lived as husband and wife' for years. When Hoover died of a heart attack in May 1972 President Nixon gave a glowing eulogy at his funeral, saying that the FBI would remain a memorial to him. In private, as the White House tapes showed, Nixon opined: 'He had files on everybody, God damn it.'

WIRE TAPPING TODAY

Thereafter, controls and oversight on wire tapping began to get on to the statute books in the USA and more or less ensured that no single individual in a state-run organisation could amass such power again. Even so, there is throughout the world a deep suspicion of wire-tapping operations, which constitute one of the most invasive, flesh-crawling types of surveillance and go to the very heart of the basic human right of privacy.

Wire tapping also remains, however, the principal weapon in today's fight against crime, terrorism and other modern ills in society. The FBI's cumulative eye on the American people was no less apparent in the 1990s, when once again it – and its British counterparts – began pressing for extended power to cover new technology (see Chapter 14). Controls which still governed wire tapping towards the end of the century became effective in both the USA and the UK in 1986. In America, they define what is termed a baseline for all wire-taps performed by federal, state and local law enforcement agencies. However, although the tactics of J. Edgar Hoover are long gone, the number of legal wire-taps in the USA continues to rise, as do those interceptions about which no information is published. In the ten years up to 1998, the last figures available at the time of writing, wire-tapping interceptions by warrant doubled in the USA – as indeed they did in the UK. The upward line on the graph more or less matched the increased activity in the areas of organised crime and terrorist organisations.

America is the only country in the West where data is available on wire-tapping operations by state and federal investigators, and the 1998 summary provides a fascinating glimpse of present operations under a system that has some similarities with many of those run by other Western nations. In the USA, every federal or state judge is required to file a written report to the Administrative Office of the United States Courts on orders authorising the interception of communications. They show that the number of intercepts on drug-related investigations has seen the most significant growth, largely in New York where a quarter of all US wire-taps occur.

The average length of listening in is twenty-seven days, but during any year a thousand or more applications for extension might be granted. The longest federal intercept during 1998 occurred in the Eastern District of New York, where the original thirty-day order was extended seven times to complete a 240-day wire-tap used in a criminal investigation. Even that was nothing compared to a drugs-related investigation by the New York Organised Crime Task Force. When the investigation was finally terminated in 1998 wire-taps had been in place for almost six years, nearly three times longer than any wire-tap reported since tracking began in 1968 in the wake of the assassinations of Robert Kennedy and Martin Luther King. The original order was extended 146 times and was in operation on 2073 days. (Because its duration would distort the 1998 summary information, data from this wire-tap is excluded from computations of averages quoted here.)

The next longest state wire-tap was used in a narcotics investigation in Los Angeles County, California. It required a thirty-day order to be extended nineteen times and kept the intercept in operation for six hundred days. The most active federal intercept also occurred in California, where a fraud investigation involved more than 120 agent-workdays over an intensive fourteen-day period when they were intercepting an average of 818 calls per day. Nationwide, almost a quarter of the wire-taps were placed in what were described as single-family dwellings and only 7 per cent in business premises such as restaurants and hotels. By 31 December, 3450 people had been arrested as a result of electronic surveillance in the USA during 1998; 911 people were convicted during the year on charges arising out of wire-taps.

A wire-tap in Ohio was the most successful single federal intercept: it resulted in the arrest of fifty-nine people, of whom fifty-four were convicted of drugs-related offences. Forty-four per cent of intercept applications, however, were specified as 'other locations' which include mobile telephones, electronic pagers and cellular telephones. In recent years, state statutes have been modified to keep pace with rapid technological advances in telecommunications. New Jersey, for example, amended its electronic surveillance statute in 1993 to include cellular telephones, cordless telephones, digital display beepers, fax transmissions, computer-to-computer communications and traces obtained through caller-ID systems. In that state, the use of wire-taps can only be used in investigations for serious crimes such as murder, kidnapping, forgery, narcotics trafficking, firearms racketeering and any form of organised crime.

In fact America's published telephone-tapping figures relate almost entirely to criminal investigations, and in reality the full extent of state surveillance on its population is generally unknown. Perhaps the only individuals to know are the oversight generals of the intelligence community, because of the complexity of the network of organisations which are able to perform snooping operations by warrant and general intelligence-gathering techniques, the details of which generally remain classified.

For instance, there are never any details published or made available through any other channels on the Foreign Interception Court, which exists to give formal approval to a range of interception and wire-tap operations under the Foreign Intelligence Surveillance Act (FISA). 'In a highly restricted room inside the Department of Justice Building in Washington DC resides a federal court that meets in complete secrecy,' according to Patrick S. Poole, former Deputy Director for the Center for Technology Policy, a division of the Washington-based Free Congress Foundation. This court handles wire-tap and bugging approvals for the US intelligence community and the Department of Justice. It originally came into being during the 1970s' era of terrorism, chartered by President Jimmy Carter, and appears to give authority for initiating wire-taps by bypassing the system in cases involving national security or the safety of the nation's secrets; a deliberately vague and wide channel. 'During the twenty-year tenure of the FISA,' Poole insists, 'the court has received over ten thousand applications for covert surveillance ... to date, not a single application has been denied ... The FISA court issues more surveillance and physical search orders than the entire federal judiciary combined.'

WIRE TAPPING IN THE UK

The secrecy of the FISA court is in line with that surrounding Britain's officially approved wire-taps. No breakdown of figures is ever released, even for criminal investigations. No details at all were released into the public domain until the 1980s, and even then the figures were a straight-forward confirmation that 429 interception warrants had been issued in the previous year by the Home Secretary for the police and MI5. It was not deemed necessary to mention the activities of the eighty-nine sections then in existence under the Defence Intelligence banner, or GCHQ and MI6 operations. Ironically, responsibility for the latter eventually came under the control of Robin Cook when he was appointed Foreign Secretary in the New Labour administration in 1997.

He did not, however, attempt to reactivate his failed campaign as a young Member of Parliament eighteen years earlier to change the law so that 'warrants for any form of interception should be given by a High Court Judge and that the grounds for doing so should be strictly defined, e.g., no general warrants and a strict definition as to what constitutes subversive activities'. Indeed, he came to rely heavily on the intelligence assessments of MI6, especially in the Balkans and Africa.

Cook's attempts at closer controls of telephone tapping in 1979 came during a time of increasing concerns in Britain about the extent of surveillance of left-wing politicians, activists, trade unionists and other groups, as described earlier. The fact was that, even at that stage, controls were not especially tight and the largest customer for the telephone-tapping engineers supplied by the Post Office was MI5.

Controls of wire-taps and bugging have never been a great priority in Britain. Until 1937, the Post Office intercepted calls at the direct request of the police, the Special Branch or MI5 without reference to any government minister. In that year, the then Home Secretary decided to regularise the system by bringing tapping into line with mail opening, in that it was to be done only on the issuing of a warrant by himself.

That situation remains, and was amended to empower the Foreign Secretary and the Defence Secretary to issue warrants which are not covered by the current rules laid down by the Home Office – that is, wire tapping and interceptions by GCHQ, MI6 and Military Intelligence. Warrants for Northern Ireland and Scotland are also separated out, signed by the relevant Secretary of State. The major loophole in these conditions in post-war Britain has been that the minister responsible for signing warrants has been dependent on the submission of the agency seeking permission to intercept that it was 'entirely necessary and that all other methods had been exhausted'.

As history now shows us, quite clearly this was not the case in hundreds of instances, certainly during the 1970s and 1980s. MI5 investigators could always roll out their favourite reason for tapping – in the interests of national security. In fact, MI5's relationship with Whitehall was for years much more arm's length than that of the police – especially when peaks in the Cold War clashed with 'the usual suspects' in the Labour Party and trade union movement. MI5 clung on to an earlier dispensation which allowed them to withhold certain matters from the government of the day if it felt so inclined, having lobbied heavily to secure a directive that ministers, including the Home Secretary, should be subject to the 'need to know' principle which governed all matters concerning the security service and MI6. This concern dated back to 1947, when MI5 was worried that records held at the Home Office were too available to prying eyes. All records held there were subsequently destroyed and only a list of serial numbers, which it needed MI5 to unscramble, was held thereafter.

Official figures for the number of warrants issued for telephone tapping and mail opening were issued in 1980 for the first time – and only then after Judge Megarry, rejecting a complaint over wire tapping, none the less said it was 'abundantly clear' that British practice failed to meet the standards laid down by the European Convention on Human

Rights. Years later, Britain had still not conformed when Alison Halford, the former Assistant Chief Constable of Merseyside, was awarded compensation when the European Court ruled that her human rights had been breached.

Anomalies still existed in the UK at the end of the 1990s. Another discrepancy lay in a key element in the British system which was supposed to provide a built-in safeguard against abuse: a wire-tapping warrant had to name just one individual at one address and telephone number. There was a get-out clause for this stipulation which MI5, MI6 and GCHQ have since used to their benefit, in that it was prefaced by the phrase 'as a general rule' and openly confirmed further that warrants could be issued for surveillance on organisations.

Only by some careful reading between the lines – as is necessary in all statements by the intelligence services – could it be established that, as in the USA, the bland statement about the number of warrants issued each year was never a true reflection of what was really happening in the world of wire tapping, let alone the bugs and general surveillance techniques coming into play as the technology progressed. Nor would it ever show the many areas where it was not necessary for the police and intelligence agencies to apply for a warrant.

These included the unregulated use of 'metering' in the 1990s – a system by which police forces throughout the United Kingdom could apply to telephone companies for lists of calls, giving time, date, duration and the numbers called. This facility could be granted to the police and MI5 long before itemised billing was introduced. British Telecom and major mobile phone companies provide this information on request, subject only to guidelines such as that the request should be made only in investigations into serious crime or where no other method of investigation can be utilised. No figures for metering by UK police forces or intelligence agencies have ever been published because Home Office lawyers have ruled that there is no requirement in law to do so. They regard it as an 'operational matter'.

Then there was the unresolved question of the potential use to the police and intelligence of the new generation of British digital telephone exchanges which came into use from the mid-1980s. One of them, System X – mentioned in Chapter 8 – was still a cause for major concern in 1999, in spite of being highlighted in three reports to the European

Parliament which focused on wire tapping. The Omega report to the European Union pointedly accused some of the most 'respectable' nations of indulging in dubious wire-tapping practices. In recent years, supposedly to the European Union's embarrassment, illegal and legal interception of telecommunications traffic has become widespread in many European states, including Norway, the Netherlands, France, Sweden, Belgium, Germany, Italy and the UK. The report added that the 'level and scale of some of these activities is astonishing'. Omega quoted an instance in France in 1996, when an anti-terrorist intelligence unit was tapping the telephones of six former officials of the Mitterrand administration. An investigation by an Independent Commission for the Control of Security in France came to the conclusion that at least one hundred thousand telephone lines were illegally tapped across the country each year, and that state agencies may have been responsible for most of the eavesdropping.

Chapter 14
Back-door Key?:
Fighting Encryption

IN **THE LAST DECADE** of the twentieth century the great campaigns by intelligence forces across the world against their assorted foes threatened to falter. How could this be, with so much physical, human and technical expertise throughout the Western nations? FBI director Louis Freeh revealed the crisis being faced by law enforcers everywhere, a crisis brought about by technological advancement: 'No one actually perceived that telephone systems could become untappable, that virtually unbreakable security ciphers would become commonplace in electronic communications, that people using powerful laptop computers in distant lands could steal in seconds sensational amounts of money, or that the marvels of the Internet could be used for evil against children.'

This chapter explores the technological revolution that seemed to threaten the traditional tools of surveillance, and the attempts by governments to regain the advantage.

The IT explosion and the frenzy of mobile telephone buying certainly put international law enforcers into a flat spin. Technology that in 1985 was still the sole preserve of the state was, half a decade later, in the hands of ordinary folk. And from then on it was a non-stop power surge, new development after new development. The capacity of computers, personal and business, was expanding by the month; laptops with memories bigger than those fitted to sections of the Hubble space telescope were soon to be available in every high street at very afford-able prices. State-employed computer specialists, who had led the way in the eighties, were left standing in the UK, the USA and elsewhere by the heavily resourced universities and Silicon Valley whizzkids of the 1990s. Every aspect of computer technology was being pushed beyond imagined boundaries. Search engines not dissimilar in principle to those used on the Echelon project were available on the Internet for everyone, and we would marvel that 50 million documents could be scanned in the bat of an eyelid and produce on screen, in a trice, ten thousand recipes on how to make apple pie or a nerve gas bomb, or take you directly to the office of Louis Freeh himself. The development that really upset Louis Freeh and his fellow law enforcers, however, was the concept of encryption.

ENCRYPTION

Encryption is the technology that scrambles a clear readable message or signal in complex ways to make it unreadable to a third party who is listening in; in other words, eavesdroppers. Like so many other things in the modern age of electronics, encryption was once the preserve of the decoders and decipher specialists of the National Security Agency and GCHQ or military agencies. Then it became a crucial building block in the digital economy. Apart from mobile phone security, it was an essential element in providing security for all Internet transactions, e-mail, e-commerce – e-everything.

The international crime syndicates with their vast resources, counted in billions per month, latched on to new technology quicker than most, initially in the area of electronic money laundering and then in using heavily encrypted systems for drug deals, thus avoiding inter-ception. Encryption was also discovered by paedophile networks, who moved vast amounts of child porn around the globe and stored it safely in personal computers that generally eluded the search powers of inves-tigating police forces. Louis Freeh again:

> Crime and terrorism developed in unimaginable ways. The
> issues are critical and immediate ... new technology, new

threats, new kinds of crime and a shrinking globe are continuously creating new issues. Complex frauds perpetrated in the US are controlled from Eastern Europe. Russian and Asian organised crime activity has become commonplace. New corridors have opened to continue the flood of drugs into America, and drug lords are now supported by the best technology money can buy. Terrorism, both international and domestic, threatens us like never before. The country has for the first time suffered catastrophic attacks. In some parts of the world nuclear material floats across the black market to the highest bidder. We have arrested people here who possessed anthrax or ricin, an extraordinarily deadly chemical. Reliance on computers and other amazing technologies has inadvertently created vulnerabilities that can be exploited from anywhere in the world and give terrorists abilities unheard of only a few years ago.

This argument, it must be said, was already a familiar one to the civil liberties groups. It had been made by the heads of intelligence and law enforcement agencies around the world for some time. As noted in earlier chapters, the agencies were emphasising new dangers both as a warning to governments against cutting too deeply into post-Cold War budgets and as a way of finding additional employment for the operatives left high and dry with the collapse of the KGB.

None the less, by the mid-1990s, it was quite evident that there had been no exaggeration on the scope and extent of the mounting threat of international crime organisations, terror groups and nationalist guerrillas. As to the effect of 'untappable' communications on the ability of the agencies to fight them, there were conflicting opinions on how serious the effect would be. To some extent, Freeh and the prophets of doom held sway. There was good reason to emphasise the most dramatic, frightening examples that were to hand. From a standing start in the late 1980s, 100 million mobile telephones and 200 million e-mail addresses on the Internet had become active in less than a decade. Encryption became a big issue – and outside of existing laws.

In 1992, the FBI initiated what became a long-running campaign to achieve international agreements to ensure that all telephone and e-transmissions could be intercepted by law enforcement and intelligence agencies, and that the hundreds of mobile telephone companies and new-breed satellite communications not previously covered by the warrant mandates for tapping were brought into line regardless of cost and, by law, installed with technology to enable all the telephone systems to be tapped. Freeh toured Europe in 1992–3, trying to drum up support for cooperation in introducing a state-of-the-art microcircuit, nicknamed the Clipper Chip, which was eventually revealed to the public by President Clinton in April 1993.

The Clipper Chip

The Clipper Chip was to the FBI and associated agencies what the Enigma machine was to World War II intelligence. Enigma provided the experts at Bletchley Park with the back-door key so that they could listen to everything the Nazis were saying to each other; the American-sponsored chip would have the same effect on the world's telephone systems, over and above the interception capabilities of agencies such as GCHQ and the NSA. This was to be telephone tapping in its most modern form; the Clipper Chip could be installed in relatively inexpensive encryption devices attached to ordinary telephones or computers to scramble transmissions, so that they were essentially secure against all eavesdroppers except those authorised by legal warrant – the back-door key holders.

AT & T, which had been on the brink of marketing its own highly secure telephone, announced that it would be prepared to incorporate the new standard into its products, which were marketed worldwide, if so instructed by law. One of the co-investors of the chip spelled out the intended parameters:

> It can be used to protect the privacy of personal phone
> conversations but at the same time protect the ability of law
> enforcement agencies to lawfully intercept the phone
> conversations of criminals, terrorists or drug dealers. There are
> so many different encryption devices in use to protect business
> communications from eavesdroppers that these systems also foil
> traditional means of wire tapping. The Chip would have two

unique numbers, or keys, needed by authorised government agencies to decode the transmissions.

Not unexpectedly, there was uproar from US civil liberties and human rights groups, soon to be joined by those in Britain and Europe as Louis Freeh announced the scheme overseas and sought international cooperation. In the USA, challenges to the FBI proposals soon began to bite. Although $500 million was allocated to compensate US mobile phone companies, the whole business quickly fell into disarray and confusion; dozens of companies launched hundreds of queries. Meanwhile, export of strong encryption technology by software companies was banned and organisations such as Microsoft and Lotus had to write two sets of their most popular products, one with strong encryption for the home market and the other with weaker encryption for the rest of the world, so that US law enforcers, including the FBI and the NSA, could if necessary break into foreign transmissions without too much effort.

As far as the FBI and the European agencies were concerned, they wanted nothing short of total compliance by the new media companies; but under pressure from campaigners that goal began to slip away.

Freeh and his experts assessed that uncrackable encryption would allow drug barons, terrorists and violent gangs to communicate with impunity. He predicted that the impact on public safety and national security of a 'wait and see' policy or voluntary market force approach would be too great a price to pay. He argued that if 'narrow interests prevailed' law enforcement would be unable to provide the level of protection that people in a democracy expect and deserve. He went on:

> Congress has on many occasions accepted the premise that the use of electronic surveillance is a tool of utmost importance. There have been numerous cases where law enforcement, through the use of electronic surveillance, has not only solved and successfully prosecuted serious crimes and dangerous criminals, but has also been able to prevent serious and life-threatening criminal acts. For example, terrorists in New York were plotting to bomb the United Nations building, the Lincoln and Holland tunnels, and 26 Federal Plaza as well as conduct

assassinations of political figures. Court-authorised electronic surveillance enabled the FBI to disrupt the plot as explosives were being mixed. Ultimately, the evidence obtained was used to convict the conspirators. In another example, electronic surveillance was used to prevent and then convict two men who intended to kidnap, molest and then kill a male child.

Most encryption products manufactured today do not contain features that provide for immediate law enforcement decryption. Widespread use of unbreakable encryption or communications infrastructure that supports the use of unbreakable encryption clearly will undermine law enforcement's ability to effectively carry out its public safety mission and to combat dangerous criminals and terrorists.

In fact, those so-called 'narrow interests' won the first few rounds in the battle for encryption and the Clipper Chip did not make it on to the statute books in the USA or indeed anywhere else. Secret agreement was given by elements of the European Union, but it soon became apparent that there was no legal base anywhere in the world for the installation of such technology. New laws were necessary.

The Communications Assistance to Law Enforcement Act

In 1994 Congress passed the Communications Assistance to Law Enforcement Act (CALEA) to extend phone-tapping powers to cover cellular phones. However, the Act, which was supposed to be the fore-runner of numerous pieces of legislation aimed at getting the new technology within the 'tap' laws, ran into difficulties of its own. The key problems presented by cellular phones for law enforcement agencies were identified by James Dempsey, Senior Staff Counsel for the Centre for Democracy and Technology:

The most common was lack of adequate capacity in cellular systems to accommodate multiple surveillance systems at the same time. This accounted for 30 per cent of all problems law enforcement could identify. The second most common problem was the inability of certain cellular systems to provide law enforcement with immediate call-identifying information. [The cellular system collected dialling information, but there was a delay before the information could be accessed.]

The third most common set of problems related to special dialling features. Basically, when a person uses speed dialling, voice dialling or automatic re-dial or call-back, the pen register on the customer line only picks up the coded command, not the full number that it represents. The fourth most common problem was call forwarding. Law enforcement could not capture incoming calls to the target's line that were forwarded at the central office using a service provided by the telephone company. Like the other problems, call forwarding was not a uniquely 'digital' problem; it had existed in the analogue world. There were other miscellaneous problems.

The CALEA was intended to balance three key policies: to preserve a narrowly focused capability for law enforcement agencies to carry out properly authorised intercepts; to protect privacy in the face of increasingly powerful and personally revealing technologies; and to avoid impeding the development of new communications services and technologies. The essential features of the balance that Congress struck in CALEA were:

- telephone companies would be required to ensure that their systems enabled government agencies to intercept communications and associated call-identifying data;

- law enforcement's ability to wire-tap would be preserved but not expanded;

- law enforcement would not be able to dictate system design; rather, industry would develop the technical specifications for implementation, with an appeal to the Federal Communications Commission (FCC) if the standards process failed;

- privacy protections would be strengthened to protect the communications not authorised to be intercepted;

- carriers would be reimbursed for expenses in retrofitting existing equipment and adding additional capacity for law enforcement;

- there would be oversight by Congress and ultimately by the public.

However, critics claimed the FBI was playing dirty. James Dempsey argued:

> Since CALEA was enacted in 1994, the FBI has tried to enforce the statute that it wanted, rather than the balanced and narrowly focused statute that Congress enacted. Early versions of digital telephony legislation would have given them design control over the nation's telecommunications system. FBI has rejected reasonableness. It has sought to dominate the industry standards process and has sought to assume for itself the type of design control over the nation's telecommunications system that Congress expressly denied it. The FBI has tried to use the statute to exploit the potential of the new digital technology to enhance rather than merely preserve its surveillance capability.
>
> Conclusive evidence that Congress's assumption was correct is found in the fact that since 1994, although CALEA has been stalled and the industry has continued to install equipment not designed with law enforcement's requirements in mind, electronic surveillance continues to be carried out. In the years since CALEA was enacted, the numbers of wire taps, trap and trace devices have remained at all-time highs, while the number of persons intercepted and the number of conversations monitored have gone up. There is no need for a comprehensive redesign of the telecommunications networks. Most equipment and services in place today are CALEA-compliant.

In spite of the claims by the Centre for Democracy and Technology and a rising tide of other protesters against more stringent FBI tapping capabilities, in the autumn of 1999 the US Federal Communications Commission gave way on key points that Louis Freeh and the FBI had argued for. The Commission was empowered to force all telecommunications carriers to:

- enable electronic surveillance of customers by the FBI when legally authorised to do so;

- define the location of a cell phone at the beginning and end of a mobile call;

- ensure the ability to monitor conference calls initiated by a subject under surveillance;

- confirm the identity of the active parties to a call and specifically, on a conference call, indicate whether a party is on hold, has joined, or has been dropped from the call;

- provide information on a subject's use of features (e.g. call forwarding, call waiting, call hold, and three-way calling); and

- provide telephone numbers dialled by the subject after connecting to another telecom service.

At the same time, the Clinton administration went one step further towards the FBI's aspirations by introducing the Cyberspace Electronic Security Act (CESA) of 1999. This was specifically aimed at encryption and was said to provide for the 'legitimate protection of privacy and confidentiality by business and individuals while helping law enforcement obtain evidence to investigate and prosecute criminals despite their use of encryption to hide criminal activity'.

The new law, it was said, recognised that existing methods of electronic surveillance of illegal activity were rendered useless when encryption was used to scramble evidence so that law enforcement could not decipher it in a timely manner, if at all. Clinton insisted: 'Timely action against terrorists, drug dealers, or kidnappers may require rapid access to electronic information that must not be thwarted by encryption. CESA balances the needs of privacy and public safety. It establishes significant new protections for the privacy of persons who use encryption legally. CESA also provides mechanisms to help maintain law enforcement's current ability to obtain usable evidence as encryption becomes more common.' And so the FBI was granted limited power for 'back-door' access by use of a decryption key obtained using court process. CESA also provided an $80 million working fund over four years for the FBI's Technical Support Centre, which would act as a centralised base for the attack on the increasing use of encryption by criminals.

THE BRITISH RESPONSE

As these adjustments were confirmed by the American authorities, the British government initiated its own proposals to bring in new measures governing the interception of communications. In June 1999, Home Secretary Jack Straw launched a consultative paper aimed at establishing a new legal code for the interception of all forms of communication – a document which, he maintained, would strike a balance between the requirements of law enforcement agencies and campaigners on behalf of privacy and human rights. The paper was, however, undoubtedly weighted towards the needs of the former, and Straw's case for expansion was in the same vein as Louis Freeh's:

> Interception plays a crucial role in helping law enforcement agencies to combat criminal activity. On average, one of every two interception warrants which I issue results in the arrest of a person involved in serious crime ... but those who drafted the current legislation fifteen years ago could not and did not foresee the extraordinary pace of change in the communications industry. Faced with dated legislation on interception, sophisticated criminals and terrorists have been quick to put the new technology to use. The law must be

revised if we are to preserve the ability of the law enforcement and intelligence agencies to detect serious crime and threats to our national security.

Since the 1985 Act was enacted there have been enormous changes in the telecommunications and postal market, and a great expansion in the nature and range of services available. The number of telecommunications companies offering fixed line services has grown from two to around 150; the satellite telephone market, while still in its infancy, will evolve rapidly in the next few years; Internet communications have grown and continue to grow, and the postal sector has also developed rapidly, with a huge growth in the number of companies offering parcel and document delivery services.

Straw admitted that disproportionate, or unfettered, use of interception could have consequences for the rights of individuals. Itemised billing, for example, was a great aid to investigative officers and they should be able to access this material while bearing in mind the requirements of the European Convention on Human Rights. He said its use was only justified for clearly defined purposes.

The paper also examined the interception of communications on private telephone networks. This was an attempt to curb the abuse of wire tapping of employers' telephones as figured in the case of former Assistant Chief Constable Alison Halford. Her victory in the European Court demonstrated that there were no laws on the British statute book to cover internal eavesdropping on employees. Jack Straw's document insisted 'that the privacy of those who use these networks is respected, and that they have a means of redress if their communications are intercepted unlawfully'.

Generally, the safeguards in the 1990s are better than they were. It was clear from the opposition and challenges that Louis Freeh experienced in the USA and from the rapid reaction strategy deployed by civil rights and privacy groups in the UK and Europe that close eyes are now being kept on the expansion of surveillance technology. Even so, Jack Straw's Home Office document included some expansions upon existing laws, such as extending the initial surveillance warrants to three months for serious crime and to six months for matters of national security and 'economic wellbeing'.

Interception, of course, is not limited to electronic surveillance. In 1999 the opening of mail reached higher levels during the whole of the twentieth century than at any time outside the war years, even though – as Jack Straw himself noted – the operations of dozens of new document and parcel delivery companies were outside existing laws. Thus his consultative document proposed new laws to cover private delivery services; to cover the interception of all telephone networks, private or public; and for the disclosure of all data held by communications service providers on their customers.

In a nutshell, Britain's proposed changes are designed to update the legislation to take account of communications services introduced since the existing legislation was enacted; to extend the law to cover interception of private telephone networks; to provide a framework for authorising the disclosure of data held by communications service providers; to retain the existing safeguards which ensure that interception is authorised only when it is justified in relation to strict statutory criteria; and to ensure that the use of the power is subject to independent judicial oversight.

Britain was, however, already one step ahead of America and other parts of Europe by having the ability to use existing powers to search for encrypted material on any computer if crime was suspected; the computer could be treated as if it were the store of documents – although as the police, MI5 and the National Criminal Intelligence Service discovered, it could be a long and laborious process trying to unravel skilfully encrypted material stored on computers. NCIS director John Abbott reckoned that encryption remained one of the most difficult issues facing law enforcement throughout the world.

Case histories regarding encryption difficulties were already mounting up. In 1998 police inquiries into an attempted murder and sexual assault were hampered by the discovery of encrypted material on a suspect's computer. The investigation was able to proceed only after the relevant encryption key was discovered by the police among other material seized from the suspect. The NCIS has numerous examples of international paedophile exchange groups using encryption to conceal their activity. In what was then among the first cases of its type, suspected paedophiles were arrested in the UK on suspicion of distributing child pornography on the Internet. Their computer systems were found to contain pornographic images of children and, in the case of the leading suspect, a large amount of encrypted material. The suspects had used encrypted communications to distribute child pornography to contacts round the world via e-mail.

Although members of the ring were subsequently convicted of distributing child pornography, the police investigation into the leading suspect was severely hampered by the fact that he had used encryption. More high-profile cases followed, including that of the former pop star Gary Glitter whose material was decrypted after he had taken his computer base to be repaired. Thousands of pornographic images involving children were discovered, both on the computer and in downloaded form at his home. He was arrested, tried, convicted and given a four-month prison sentence.

The encryption of paedophilia remains one of the most difficult areas for law agencies to break open. One example was discovered during an investigation conducted by the New York Computer Crimes Squad. It focused on a website that offered a free download of a form of pornography. During this download, encrypted software was placed upon the user's system which, unbeknown to the user – because it could not be accessed by them – disconnected them from the current provider and routed their telephone connection through another country at premium rates, resulting in huge bills. Because of the embarrassment of the subject matter, and the fact that the scam was run from a strongly encrypted overseas site, prosecution was impossible.

There are also examples of terrorists in the UK using encryption as a means of concealing their activities. In late 1996, a police operation culminated in the arrest of several leading members of a British-based terrorist group (presumed to be the IRA, though not confirmed by the NCIS) and the seizure of computer equipment containing encrypted files. The files held information on potential terrorist targets such as police officers and politicians. The data was eventually retrieved, but only after considerable effort by GCHQ code-breakers. With so many cases now arising, the British government has ordered a feasibility study on the setting up of a specialist cryptology department to assist the police in cracking computer encryption codes.

This new onslaught on criminal activity via telephone interception was, by 1999, evident throughout Europe, and was largely sold as an issue of public safety, much in the same way it was by the FBI in the USA. Indeed, any similarities in the approach of the law enforcers towards their modern requirements were only to be expected, given that Louis Freeh had personally brought together representatives of European and other international governments for secret conferences on the issue – or, as one put it, 'brainwashing'.

In 1993, the FBI staged its first international conference on tackling the encryption problems presented by advanced telecommunications. Delegates from eleven countries were flown to the FBI Academy in Quantico, Virginia. Since then, this group of states has been working to standardise the requirements for interception on the part of law enforcement agencies. The Quantico gathering established what became known as the International Law Enforcement Seminar (ILETS), whose principal task was to promote, through an 'unseen' group of officials, the standardising of the requirements of law enforcement on telecommunications interception. The ILETS group was soon enlarged to twenty countries: the fifteen EU nations, the USA, Canada, Hong Kong, Australia and New Zealand.

Aims and objects were set out in a secret document finalised at a meeting of ILETS in Bonn; it was eventually ratified by the representatives of all the nations involved in the autumn of 1995. In short, through the FBI's Quantico initiative the ILETS group paved the way for the formation of another global system of surveillance of telecommunications which has become known as the EU–FBI system.

While few could argue against the validity of attempting to foil the activities of terrorists or paedophiles, there remains a deep suspicion – largely because of past excesses – about the underlying intentions of the FBI and the NSA. In April 1999, I discovered that the FBI and the NSA had formed specific channels of liaison over the issues of encryption and electronic surveillance, establishing a level of cooperation unheard of in the history of the two organisations which, traditionally, had been poles apart in almost every aspect of their operations. Now the two foremost agencies of Comint and Humint in the United States were coming together, for the first time ever, in a joint effort by which the NSA's global surveillance system could be interfaced with the FBI's link-up with

Europe. A similar development can be expected in the UK, possibly on an even more vital scale, with the link-up of MI5, MI6 and GCHQ.

Between 1993 and 1998, as Duncan Campbell confirmed in his report *Interception Capabilities 2000* presented to the European Parliament, the United States conducted sustained diplomatic activity in an attempt to persuade EU nations and the OECD (Organisation for Economic Cooperation and Development) to adopt its system. Throughout this period, said Campbell:

> the US government insisted that the purpose of the initiative was to assist law enforcement agencies. Documents obtained for this study suggest that these claims wilfully misrepresented the true intention of US policy. Documents obtained under the US Freedom of Information Act indicate that policymaking was led exclusively by NSA officials, sometimes to the complete exclusion of police or judicial officials. This US deception was, however, clear to the senior Commission official responsible for information security. In September 1996 David Herson, head of the EU Senior Officers' Group on Information Security, stated his assessment of the US 'key recovery' project: 'Law Enforcement is a protective shield for all the other governmental activities ... We're talking about foreign intelligence, that's what all this is about. There is no question [that] law enforcement is a smoke screen.'

The Regulation of Investigatory Powers Bill

British Home Secretary Jack Straw meanwhile pressed ahead and six months after publishing his consultative document on the interception of communications, he revealed the government's intentions to rush through a new Bill to update powers across the whole spectrum of state surveillance in Britain. The Regulation of Investigatory Powers Bill (RIP Bill) was introduced on 9 February 2000 to begin its passage through Parliament to replace the 1985 Interception of Communications Act (IOCA). It encompassed virtually all of the ideas floated in the consultative paper, with a few significant additions. The RIP Bill was clearly designed to match as far as possible the new powers of interception introduced in the USA. It also took account of the proposals concerning interception and covert operations set out in the European Union draft Convention on Mutual Criminal Assistance, based upon the European Union–FBI telecommunications surveillance accord adopted by the European Union in January 1995.

Principal features of the RIP Bill legitimise all-embracing powers of interception by police and the enforcement agencies of all phone calls, e-mails and faxes as well as other forms of surveillance on individuals and groups. Jack Straw stated on its publication that there was 'nothing new' in the Bill, merely an updating of laws to encompass modern technology. This statement was utterly refuted by civil rights watchdogs. Statewatch, in its summary of the legislation published in its March bulletin, said the title of the Bill was deliberately misleading, placing the emphasis on regulation rather than on the extensive new powers that would be legalised.

It said the new powers would introduce far-reaching surveillance and legitimise many existing clandestine – and illegal – practices with controls of encryption which would enable state authority to intercept anything they wished. Liberty agreed and commented that the clandestine nature of operations regulated by the legislation heightened the care needed to ensure that necessary official activities impinged as little as possible on citizens' rights.

As well as telecommunications, the Bill covers general surveillance powers and the procedures by which surveillance is authorised. In most cases, surveillance may be conducted against individuals or groups of people in the interests of national security, for the purpose of detecting or preventing crime, public disorder and public safety. Powers of interception without a warrant are also extended to include cases where one party agrees to the interception or where warrants for surveillance are already in force for covert investigations. Those able to authorise interception or surveillance are also extended to cover 'offices, ranks and positions with relevant public authorities' laid down by the Home Secretary. These 'offices' include police, customs, immigration, tax, health bodies and local authorities.

The Bill also sets out agencies which can request interception warrants for up to six months for investigations connected with national security, six months for 'purposes of safeguarding the economic wellbeing of the nation' and three months in criminal cases. They include MI5, MI6, GCHQ, NCIS, the police, customs, the Permanent Under-Secretary for Defence as well as non-UK states and agencies under mutual assistance agreements. Liberty was especially critical of the new powers of authorisation: 'Executive rather than prior judicial authorisation of interception is fundamentally objectionable. That the executive should secretly authorise itself to commit clandestine interference with important rights is neither acceptable or necessary.'

The Bill leaves virtually no stone unturned in the new arena of communications. Key aspects of the complex and wide-ranging powers include:

- The power to intercept all telecommunications, including exchange of data with other countries or agencies; the power to demand communications data, such as billing information that identifies calls made and to whom, and the power to order the handing over of encryption 'keys' used on all forms of voice and document communications.

- The power to undertake intrusive surveillance, for the installation of a sound or video recording device in residential premises and vehicles (although attachment of tracking devices to vehicles is not considered 'intrusive').

- The power to undertake covert surveillance which also covers the use of 'human intelligence sources' – meaning agents, undercover officers or other informants, paid or unpaid, and 'induced' agents such as criminals or others who are part of a group engaged in criminal activity.

- The power to undertake directed surveillance, which is not part of covert or intrusive operations, but which may fall within 'any purpose' laid down by the Home Secretary. In short, it covers and empowers virtually every form of surveillance that is likely to arise in the next decade and reflects the dramatic changes in the nature of policing across the globe.

As the watchdogs were quick to point out, Britain, along with Europe and the United States, had brought under one roof all the clandestine methods of intelligence gathering employed in the days of the Cold War by internal security agencies for general police practice and use against the public at large as well as the more clearly defined targets of terrorists, criminals and those bent on attacking computers and their infrastructure. Home Office officials could not deny that the Bill will enable the law enforcement agencies to conduct systematic targeting of an individual over a period of time to obtain an overall portrait of his life, activities and his associates. And as Liberty pointed out, the new laws would heighten – rather than reduce – suspicion over motive, need and secrecy because the politicians and officials would henceforth be able to authorise themselves to conduct surveillance rather than seeking the independent assessment of the judiciary. It is fortunate therefore that those who feel they have been wrongly or illegally targeted may at least have redress to the European Court of Human Rights.

MI5 AND THE E-MAIL SURVEILLANCE CENTRE

Meanwhile, British surveillance of the Internet and e-mail was not to be held up by the mere formality of passing new legislation. In May 2000 the *Sunday Times* reported that MI5 was already building a new £25 million surveillance centre that will have the power to monitor all e-mails and Internet messages sent and received in Britain. All Internet service providers, such as Freeserve and AOL would be required to accept links to the interception facility so that MI5 could keep track of all Internet mail and messaging activity. The centre would be governed by the same legislation used to empower interception of telephones and would require Home Office permission or general warrants for an extended operation. The new centre, codenamed GTAC – Government Technical Assistance Centre – will be in operation by the end of 2000, housed within MI5's London headquarters. Caspar Bowden, director of the Foundation for Information Policy Research led a chorus of opponents when he said: 'With this facility, the government can track every website that a person visits, without a warrant, giving rise to a culture of suspicion by association.'

The Home Office officials responded by restating the now familiar plaintive cry that Internet surveillance was necessary to keep abreast of the war against terrorists, criminals and paedophiles.

The new spy centre will decode messages that have been encrypted under new powers assigned to the law enforcers by the RIP Bill.

None could deny, however, that the explosion of Internet-related crime was increasing to a worrying degree.

CHAPTER 15
CRIMINAL TENDENCIES AND THE INTERNET

THE INTERNET ENCAPSULATES THE KEY issues in the debate over privacy versus the need for surveillance. Should there be controls? How can it be controlled? Should it be monitored? Who should monitor it? And what are the legal implications for doing so? How secure is it? How safe is it? In fact, surveillance is as prevalent among criminal groups – but now the emphasis changes.

PAEDOPHILES AND THE INTERNET

On 3 November 1999 more than a hundred members of the International Association of Police Chiefs at its convention in Charlotte, North Carolina, were shocked to witness first-hand Internet crime. An FBI agent running a seminar for law enforcers on child pornography sat down at a computer, logged into a user-created chat room through a leading international Internet service provider and posed as a twelve-year-old girl who was away from school because she had flu. Within minutes the 'girl' was being stalked. She began to receive messages from a number of men asking what she thought of older men, whether she had a boyfriend and how far she had gone sexually; two asked if she had a picture to put on-line. The 'girl' said she did not have a picture, but invited any of those present on the chat room to send theirs. One of them sent a digital image of his genitals. It was a live example of digital cameras and encryption software as key elements in the traffic of on-line child pornography. Paedophiles have developed their own information network where they share and exchange information about police activity, how to lure children, how to court them using erotica and Disney characters in sexual poses, and what to do if caught.

Some, known as 'travellers', stalk children on the Internet for the purpose of setting up a meeting. In one recent case, a sixteen-year-old boy suggested meeting a fourteen-year-old girl after making contact in an America Online chat room. The girl's mother agreed, provided that she went along and that the meeting would take place at a local library. The parent, assuming nothing could go wrong in such a venue, left her daughter to meet the date, but came back to discover that the sixteen-year-old boy was really a fifty-year-old man who had persuaded the girl to accompany him out of the building. When the parent called out, the man disappeared, but an FBI agent assumed the girl's profile on America Online and made contact again. The man travelled back to a second supposed meeting with the girl and was arrested. An almost identical case occurred in Milton Keynes in May 2000.

More seriously, on 20 December 1999, two men trapped through on-line contact by police officers posing as children were given prison sentences. In separate cases, both were charged with using the Internet to lure teenagers into illegal sex acts. One of them, a twenty-eight-year-old man from Alabama, was given a ten-year sentence for attempting to meet a 'fourteen-year-old girl' with whom he had made contact in a chat room. He had turned up at a prearranged meeting place, a local shopping centre, where police arrested him and found in his car handcuffs, a handgun, rope and a video camera. In addition to the prison sentence, he was fined $3000. The other 'traveller' thought he was going to meet a fourteen-year-old boy but was confronted by undercover federal agents. He was given a sixteen-month prison sentence and fined $6000. Both men were also ordered to forfeit all their computer equipment.

What happens in America – which is generally believed to be four or five years ahead of the rest of the world in Internet activity – is a forerunner of what law enforcers across the globe may expect to occur in their territories. The Internet stalking of children is an increasing problem, allied to the growth of child pornography sites.

American statistics, which are the most up to date available, do not augur well for Europe and the rest of the world. In 1999 the FBI's Innocent Images programme, set up to pursue child porn on the Internet and the stalkers who lurk on the edge of the chat rooms, recorded its highest number of cases: 1497 by November, compared with 698 in 1998, 301 in 1997, and 113 in 1996, the year when it was launched. Two-thirds of the cases dealt with on-line activities such as sending explicit photos to children, while the remainder involved the so-called travellers. Of the FBI cases investigated, at the end of 1999 only two hundred men were in prison as the result of prosecution. Like most computer crime, which is often committed from long distances, quite probably using encrypted software, matching crimes to local laws reduces the likelihood of criminal charges.

The frustration of many parents is evidenced by the activities of Web watch groups which have been set up around the globe. One, founded in Australia, enlisted a group of thirty-five computer security experts to track sites peddling child pornography. They then contacted the Web hosting company or Internet service provider and provided details to the local police. If no action was taken, the team of experts hacked into the sites and, where possible, disabled them. The group launched its campaign in December 1999 and within a month had hacked into 115 websites, 90 of them in the United States. At least three other groups with the declared intention of hacking into and knocking out child porn sites were operating on the Web by January 2000. But the irony is that they themselves face prosecution. Legal experts in America have concluded that they are breaking the law by hacking into, damaging or removing material from websites that no court of law has yet ruled as obscene.

Not only that, but using illegal tactics in support of a prosecution would be thrown out of court. The hackers also run the risk of deleting information that might form the basis of a prosecution. Julie Posey, director of www.PedoWatch.org, founded to fight child pornography, says that shutting down a website that contains this material is not the solution: 'There are thousands of Internet service providers as well as free Web hosting services that are readily available to provide instant service. Shutting down a site is only a minor inconvenience to the person possessing and posting the child pornography, and the predator is still out there and is still able to continue harming and exploiting children.'

The Australia-linked team, however, was undeterred and its website proclaimed: 'The Condemned Network was created, and is now maintained, by a staff of unpaid individuals and volunteers from around the world, who refuse to accept the presence, creation and distribution of child pornography on the Internet.' Many joined up to give support and sponsorship to the team, including numerous companies which helped with expenses and software. Meanwhile, a special team at the United Nations in New York initiated a link with parent and anti-pornography groups to combat the growing menace and immediately highlighted another problem. To police pornographic sites properly would keep dozens of men and women glued to monitors for hours on end. Even the FBI's child protection group does not have the time to surf the Internet and operates by specific targeting of chat rooms and reported sites.

FRAUD, HACKERS AND FINANCIAL CRIME

Nor is it just child pornography that requires the ever-increasing attention of police forces worldwide. According to a United Nations-sponsored study, computer crime generally is widespread and getting worse by the month. Even the British Department of Trade and Industry, keen though it is to encourage small businesses and other UK enterprises to launch on to the Web, issues regular warnings about crime and security. In February 2000, its latest website update issued the following fairly basic advice, clearly aimed at some of the millions of newcomers who are expected to join the Internet fraternity in the first year of the new millennium:

> The Internet is inherently insecure because it is a public
> network that has no central management or control. A
> company [or individual] using the Internet is responsible for the
> security of its own network, systems and information.
> Companies cannot control the route which a message will take
> when it crosses the Internet, from say the UK to the USA. It is
> possible for messages to be read or modified. If you download

any information from the Internet, including e-mail and attachments, you are vulnerable to virus attacks. Unless properly encrypted, credit card payments can be intercepted and manipulated or stolen.

Across computerland and the Internet, a multitude of thieves, fraudsters, porn merchants, counterfeiters, credit card forgers, hackers and others with malicious intent are daily inflicting costly wounds on the general public, companies and governments. As 2000 dawned, lawyers for the European Union nations and North America were examining the implications of keeping watch on the Internet for criminal acts, and attempting to cut a path through the minefield of legal obstacles that are at present making prosecution of the perpetrators difficult. Again, the only figures available that put a perspective on this particular problem emanate from the USA. Computer crime in general is difficult to quantify. The best attempts have come from the 1999 ASIS survey which concluded that thefts of proprietary information at Fortune 1000 companies accounted for $45 billion in losses between January 1997 and June 1998. The survey also confirmed suspicions recorded in the UN manual that reported thefts are the tip of the iceberg – many crimes go unreported either because losses are undetected or because the company concerned does not wish to face public disclosure.

Loss of consumer confidence in a particular business and in its management can lead to even greater economic loss than that caused by the crime itself. In addition, many managers fear personal repercussions if responsibility for the infiltration is placed at their door. Company executives have also complained about the inconvenience of lengthy criminal investigations and have even questioned the ability of police to investigate what may be a highly complex crime, using manpower that is not fully conversant with the possibilities or the technology. Even if crimes are reported, obtaining tangible and admissible evidence can be virtually impossible (as will be detailed below). In 1998, federal attorneys in the USA refused to prosecute around 70 per cent of cases of computer-related crime for those reasons. Most cases which were found proved involved information theft or malicious damage by hackers. British Home Secretary Jack Straw and his counterparts in the European Union and the USA were all studying methods of increased surveillance, encryption-busting techniques and revision of laws for specific crimes as these words were being written.

Financial Crime

With the globalisation of the securities and commodities marketplace and an incredible boom in Internet share trading by people who have never previously done so, old investment fraud schemes have risen again. But securities offered over the Internet add an entirely new dimension to securities fraud investigations. Investors are able to research potential investments and invest over the Internet with ease, since it provides links to a number of services that offer stock and commodity quotations and critical financial information.

However, Wall Street and stock exchanges around the world recognise that the low cost of setting up a Web page and the anonymity that can be achieved have made the Internet vulnerable. In fact, it is the perfect vehicle for hype, rumour or degrading information about publicly quoted stocks. Chat rooms, e-mail messages sent en masse and newsletters are delivered with ease, leading to wholesale manipulation, pumping up prices and creating a frenzy of buying. Gangs of operators, especially in Wall Street and the City of London, have carried out numerous raids, buying cheap, forcing up prices and then selling, leaving the shares to founder.

The North American Securities Administrators' Association has estimated that Internet-related stock fraud is currently the second most common form of investment fraud. That source reckoned also that investors lose $10 billion per year (or $1 million per hour) to this type of fraud. Fraudulent schemes include 'Prime Bank' investments which are sold as if originating from financial instruments of well-known domestic or foreign financial institutions, the World Bank, or a country's central bank. The financial instruments may be sold as notes, letters of credit, debentures or guarantees. The schemes include false claims of high rates of return and being risk-free. In one example, investors were offered an annual return of 200 per cent on 'Prime Bank Instruments'. The security did not exist, but attracted funds of $3.5 million in a matter of days.

The Investor Protection and Securities Bureau of the New York

State Attorney's Office has also issued numerous warnings about high-pressure marketing of penny stocks. These are stocks defined as a publicly traded stock of less than $5 per share and not listed on any national securities exchange. The securities bureau identified what it termed Micro-Cap stocks, which are thinly traded, risky stocks in companies with little or no earnings or start-ups with no track record. Typically, they are hyped by high-pressure telephone techniques and flashy Internet websites touting risky and low-priced stock which become the subject of market manipulation using foreign bank and brokerage accounts. Then the stock collapses: in 1998 losses to Micro-Cap fraud in America alone exceeded $6 billion.

The FBI's various computer crime investigation units have faced a multiplicity of traditional financial crimes such as marketing frauds, investment frauds, stock manipulations, credit card frauds and multi-million-dollar copyright scams and counterfeit materials, which have simply found a new medium on the Internet. Investment frauds accounted for the majority. Crooked or illegal gambling is also emerging from sites all around the world. Two operations purporting to be located offshore were in fact being run from a site in the north-east where, in just one year, proceeds were $56 million. In Operation Cyberstrike, an FBI undercover operation in six cities trapped a gang running a highly lucrative business selling unlawful copies of copy-righted software through computer bulletin boards, Internet file transfer protocol sites and chat channels. The group had also cloned stolen credit cards and calling card numbers and were gearing up to spread destructive programs such as a computer virus for the purpose of black-mail.

In Britain, the Metropolitan Police Computer Crime Unit was founded in 1984 and is still the only UK unit dedicated to investigating computer crime. One of the team, Detective Constable Paul Cox, said they had no doubt about the possibilities of computer crime: 'As everyone knows, the data held on computers is crucial to the running of the country. Everything, from telephone systems to the national grid, relies on computers to function and it is vital that they are protected from people who might try to modify the system data ... or steal information or intelligence that could lead to information warfare. It is important that law enforcers and potential victims are aware of the issues surrounding this type of crime because it can impact on everyone who uses a computer.' Even so, in January 2000 the team comprised just ten officers who are confronted with complex investigations which have included British troubles due to the infamous Melissa virus, hackers tampering with government files, and unauthorised attempts to access national databases.

The activities of Leon Fitch, twenty-one, a vocal contributor to privacy debates, held the attentions of the unit for three years before he was arrested in 1997 and charged with nine separate violations of the Computer Misuse Act. A controversial figure in the electronics underground, Fitch had hosted several Web pages devoted to the technical workings of telephone exchanges. His escapades spanned hacking into educational sites to tapping into industrial and United States military sites before he was finally caught on-line, running cloned mobile phones. He was eventually convicted for these offences.

The ability of those who gain unauthorised access to computer systems continued to amaze investigators – as indeed does the cost of the fraud, which can run into many millions. In 1994, the US secret service uncovered a $50 million phone card fraud against the accounts of AT&T, MCI and Sprint customers. It was the same year that an organised crime group based in St. Petersburg, Russia, famously transferred $10.4 million from the international Citibank in New York into accounts all over the world. After surveillance and investigation by the FBI's New York field office, all but $400,000 of the funds were recovered. In another case, Carlos Felipe Salgado, Jr hacked into several Internet service providers in California and stole one hundred thousand credit card numbers with a combined limit of over $1 billion. Joe Majka, regional director for Visa risk management fraud control department in America, related the story to me in Las Vegas:

> The guy had hacked into a website and stole the credit card numbers, MasterCard, Visa, American Express. Like a lot of these hackers he liked to brag about his exploits, so in a chat room he's bragging he could hack into any site. 'I hacked into one site, got a hundred thousand credit card numbers.' The guy he's talking to is thinking: 'I need to tell somebody about this.' He calls the FBI, tells them. The FBI says: 'Ask if he'll sell

you some of the numbers.' They set it up so he buys some of the numbers, we [Visa] test them, sure enough, they're good numbers. Now they set up to buy all hundred thousand at a price of about $240,000. They met at the San Francisco airport. The criminal had all the numbers on disks that were protected with cryptography, gave them the keys to unlock and we bought a hundred thousand credit card numbers.
Fortunately none of those numbers got into any other criminal's hands and there was no fraud used on those. We did prosecute that individual. Imagine the potential for fraud on a hundred thousand numbers ... the loss potential on that case was very significant.

Joe explained that in the US in 1998, Visa banks alone lost about $475 million to fraud, including ATM fraud, debit fraud and credit card fraud. If MasterCard, American Express, Visa and Discover are included US losses are over a billion dollars.

There are also programs available on the Internet that allow you to generate account numbers, credit card and debit card numbers that can be used throughout the world.

The program can generate account numbers by the user inserting a valid account number into the program and requesting a list of nearly a thousand additional account numbers based on the original number. The program generates a number, thirteen or sixteen digits, that meets a very simple algorithm used in the banking industry to create a credit card number. The program can't determine if any of the numbers generated will be valid. However, as many banks issue their numbers sequentially, the chances are the program will generate quite a few usable numbers. Joe Majka explained:

We're seeing junior high [school] kids who are computer-savvy downloading this program on the Internet. We had a principal at a junior high in the state of Washington call us and say: 'I found three pages of what look like Visa account numbers.'
This kid got into the program, downloaded it, generated and printed about eight hundred Visa numbers that he was going to use for mail order telephone order fraud.'

However, criminals also use the program. They get hold of a merchant terminal, or compromise a merchant or terminal ID number and send through an authorisation test. They might also simply contact AOL and see if they can open an account. If they can open an account on AOL with that credit card number it's valid because AOL will send through an authorisation for them. Joe continued:

> Everything you need to know to commit fraud is on the Internet. You want information on a credit or calling card number capturing system? Assembled, new, $1950. You could probably get it cheaper than that, and can probably learn how to build the equipment for less . . . Magnetic stripe card reader/writer, $1500. This has a warning on it, which I really like. The warning says, 'Credit card fraud is felony' . . . 'Anyone who attempts to order using a stolen credit card number will be prosecuted to the full extent of the law.' This merchant on the Internet doesn't want you using a stolen credit card number to order his stuff, but what's he selling?

Perhaps Joe's most alarming story concerned a small Chinese restaurant in Oregon. It was e-mailing the credit card numbers of its customers to a client in Beijing who was buying merchandise with counterfeit cards based on the numbers. Joe explained:

> From a law enforcement perspective, how do you go after these criminals? We knew who the kid was in the restaurant skimming the cards. But he's not the guy in Beijing buying the merchandise with the counterfeit cards, so how do you go after this kid? We got the search warrant, got his computer, never located the device he was using, never located any numbers on his computer, had no evidence other than the fact that he handled every transaction at that restaurant where the numbers turned up in the fraud.

The vast industry in trading counterfeit and stolen credit cards has meant these stories are all too common. None demonstrates the vulnerability of on-line trading and e-commerce better than a hacking incident which occurred in January 2000. The hacker, who goes by the name of Maxim, tapped into an estimated 350,000 user names and credit cards from the Connecticut-based CD Universe and boasted in e-mails to newspapers that he had often hacked into commercial sites, which does nothing to help the basic premise of e-commerce that all is secure and consumers' details are safe. He then offered the numbers for sale via a site located in the former Soviet Union. The potential for fraud ran to tens of millions, and resulted in one of the biggest combat operations in the history of credit card fraud.

In November 1999, two members of a group dubbed the Phonemasters were sentenced after their conviction for theft, possession of unauthorised access devices and unauthorised access to a federal computer. The Phonemasters were, and possibly still are, an international group who penetrated the computer systems of MCI, Sprint, AT&T, Equifax and even the FBI's own National Crime Information Centre. Using surveillance orders issued by a federal judge, the FBI's Dallas Field Office made use of new data-intercept technology – which so far remains a secret – to monitor the calling activity and modem pulses of one of the suspects, Calvin Cantrell. Cantrell downloaded thousands of Sprint calling card numbers, which he sold to a Canadian who passed them on to someone in Ohio. These numbers made their way to a person in Switzerland and eventually ended up in the hands of crime groups in Italy. Cantrell was sentenced to two years while one of his associates, Cory Lindsay, was sentenced to forty-one months.

The Phonemasters' activities were based on a remarkably simple premise and, according to the FBI, ought to have acted as a 'wake-up call' to corporation security firms. Their methods included what is known in the trade as 'dumpster diving': gathering up old phone books and technical manuals for systems. They then used this information to trick employees into giving up their log-on and password information, with which they broke into victim systems. It demonstrated that many cybercrimes still rely on the old-fashioned guile of conmen, calling employees and tricking them into giving up passwords.

Police units engaged in long-running investigations are also coming under increasing pressure from more general and small-time crime incidents. In early 1996, the American National Consumers' League decided to expand its efforts to cover an increasing number of relatively minor fraud complaints on the Internet. Thus was born www.fraud.org and the NCL's Internet Fraud Watch section, which takes reports of fraud through on-line forms twenty-four hours a day, seven days a week. By December 1999, the website was receiving 120,000 visits and 1500 e-mails per week from consumers around the world. In less than two years, complaints had increased 600 per cent. On-line auction produced the highest category of scams in the first six months of 1999, accounting for 68 per cent of all Internet-related complaints. Amounts involved tended to be in the hundreds rather than thousands, and a surprising 98 per cent of consumers had paid for their goods by cheque because the seller had no facility for taking credit cards.

There was still what the NCL described as a 'healthy cross-section' of other computer crimes, especially in selling phoney travel packages. Fraud Watch warn:

> Anyone can put up a classy website and the average consumer has difficulty determining which sites are legitimate and which are scams. Plus, when you buy something on-line, you are essentially buying it sight unseen. If something goes wrong and you've purchased it from a legitimate company, then you can always return it for a refund or replacement. But, as the victims of travel scams on-line can tell you, it's not always so easy to get satisfaction from a company you've never really seen. And have you ever tried to get a refund from another continent? On the Internet, national boundaries are meaningless. Crooks can be located on the other side of the planet or right down the street. You may have certain rights here, but those rights may be impossible to enforce when the company is halfway around the globe or just north of our borders for that matter ... curiously, one of the most common locations for companies to be located was in the Canadian province of Ontario.

Increasingly, however, studies and surveys point to employee-related crime as the largest threat. One such study estimated that 90 per cent of economic computer crimes were committed by employees. It is not uncommon, says a United Nations manual on computer crime, for input operators, hardware technicians and other staff members to find themselves in positions of 'extraordinary privilege' in relation to the key functions and assets of their organisation. In addition, such personnel are often permitted, and sometimes encouraged, to perform these duties during non-prime shift periods, when demands on computer time are light. As a result, many of the most critical software development and maintenance functions are performed in an unsupervised environment. Situations in which junior staff are trusted implicitly and given a great deal of responsibility, without commensurate management control and accountability, occur frequently. Some fall to temptation.

Intangible assets represented in data format, such as money on deposit or hours of work, are the most common targets of computer-related fraud. Modern business is largely replacing cash with deposits transacted on computer systems, creating a considerable potential for theft. Credit card information, as well as personal and financial information on credit card clients, has been regularly targeted in company databases, and the sale of this information to counterfeiters of credit cards and travel documents has proved extremely lucrative. Improved remote access to digitally connected databases allows the criminal the opportunity to commit various types of fraud without ever physically entering the premises of the victim.

VIRUSES, WORMS, LOGIC BOMBS AND TROJAN HORSES

Fraud by the 'manipulation' of computer data at the input stage is another common crime, easily achieved and difficult to detect. It involves changing existing programs in the computer system or inserting new instructions or routines. Sophisticated viruses and devices such as 'logic bombs' and 'Trojan Horses' can be used to commit a variety of crimes, either with immediate effect or to be activated at a future date with minimal chance of detection. The Trojan Horse is a scam whereby instructions are covertly placed in a computer program so that it will perform a criminal function alongside its normal routine, as in the process of bank transfers. Trojan Horse programs can also be used to gain access to the contents of hard drives of even home or home-office PCs.

Many Internet users in chat rooms have been unaware that, while on-line, their PC hard drive has been searched and possibly ransacked for personal details. It is one of the growth areas of computer crime, and one that potentially holds great dangers even to the most modest Internet surfers. In November 1999, a Trojan Horse called Back Orifice 2000 was discovered for sale on the international black market and detected in a number of countries. It allows the operators to tamper with computers on-line and view files on the computer's hard drive, undetected by the users. Like most Trojan Horses it could be programmed to self-destruct, thus leaving no trace of its existence. Others are already appearing.

Potentially far more dangerous is the use of computer viruses, especially where they are designed for an extortion operation or by an activist or vandal working to cause as much damage as possible. Extortion cases are actually few and far between and, when they come along and end with an arrest, are generally hyped up by the law enforcement officers for publicity and by the media because it makes a good story. In early March 1999, a British newspaper reported that a UK Skynet 4D military communications satellite had been hijacked by an unknown band of extortionists. They wanted $500,000 to return control of the satellite to its rightful owners. Some credence was attached to the story when the British military dealt with inquiries in its usual tight-lipped fashion. In fact it was just a fanciful story that never happened.

A few others famously have. They are the result of viruses that stand out above the welter of those floating around the ether every day of every year and which many computer owners are foolhardy enough to ignore. A virus consists of a series of codes in a program that attaches itself to legitimate programs and propagates itself to other computer programs. Many viruses, compiled in back bedrooms and on university campuses, are harmless graffiti attached by hackers to the home pages of countless government and public organisations. Others may cause irreversible destruction of all data on a computer system. The first such virus experienced in Europe, in 1990, was used in an attempt to extort a large sum from a medical research company. The virus threatened to destroy data progressively if no ransom was paid for the antidote, and a very substantial amount of valuable medical data was indeed destroyed. Virus writers are posing an increasingly serious threat to networks and systems worldwide.

In 1999, there were international alerts for at least three major viruses: the Melissa Macro Virus, the Explore Zip Worm and the CIH (Chernobyl) Virus, the first two of which the US authorities claim have caused $7 billion worth of damage internationally, although their figures must be treated with some caution. None the less, Melissa seems to have had a particularly dangerous potential. Upon its discovery in March 1999, the FBI called in experts from the US Department of Defense and the national Computer Emergency Response Team at Carnegie-Mellon University to discover the source. Melissa was a self-replicating virus that is transmitted via e-mail, jamming e-mail servers all over the world and forcing the shut-down of many systems. Technically known as W97M-Melissa, it affects systems using Microsoft's Word 97 or 2000 and Outlook products. It is triggered when a user opens a Word attachment called list.doc. Because the virus affected systems throughout public offices and had international potential, the FBI also took the unusual step of issuing a public warning which helped to mitigate the damage by alerting computer users to the virus and informing them of the protective steps they could take.

The investigation team then received a tip-off from America Online via New Jersey State Police, which led to the arrest of David L. Smith on 1 April 1999. He became one of the first people to be prosecuted for creating a computer virus. Smith, a computer programmer, appeared in court in December 1999 and acknowledged that the virus caused damage by disrupting e-mail systems worldwide. He pleaded guilty to a state charge of computer theft and to a federal charge of sending a damaging computer program. In the federal plea, both sides agreed that the damage had cost more than $80 million. The virus was named after a topless dancer Smith knew. He said: 'I did not expect or anticipate the amount of damage that took place.'

A month before Smith's appearance in court other Macro viruses, the toadie.exe and the W97M/Thurs.A, struck around the globe. The latter was known to have infected over eight thousand systems and to have deleted files on victims' hard drives. The warnings, as ever, are these: never open an e-mail from an unidentified source, and always keep anti-virus software updated by constant visits to the software supplier's website.

The same applies to another nasty infiltration of systems known as a worm. These are created and distributed in much the same way as viruses, infecting legitimate data-processing programs and altering or destroying the data. A worm differs from a virus in that it does not have the ability to replicate itself, although the consequences of a worm attack can be just as serious. Examples included in the UN manual include that of a bank computer instructed by a worm program, that subsequently destroys itself, to transfer money continually to an illicit account.

A logic bomb, also known as a time bomb, is another technique by which computer sabotage can be perpetrated, but it is programmed to unleash its damage at a specific time in the future. Unlike viruses or worms, logic bombs are very difficult to detect before they blow up and they possess the greatest potential for damage. Detonation can be timed to cause maximum damage and to take place long after the departure of the perpetrator. The logic bomb may also be used as a tool of extortion, with a ransom being demanded in exchange for disclosure of the location of the bomb.

While the creation of viruses, worms and logic bombs is aimed at attacking computer data or programs and falls under the heading of computer sabotage, motives vary from sheer bravado in the case of (usually young) computer specialists, out to test their abilities against police, computer systems supervisors and Internet service providers, to determined criminal intent. Constant vigilance by corporate computer security specialists as well as home PC users is becoming a vital element in the battle.

INFORMATION THEFT

Law enforcement, meanwhile, still faces legal constraints regarding investigation and access to computer systems because of differing national laws concerning computer-related crimes. Many criminologists have condemned existing criminal law as an inefficient and ineffective weapon against the theft of information. In England and Wales, information does not constitute 'property' for the purposes of the Theft Act 1968 and cannot therefore be stolen. There is also, according to the UN, a blatant lack of international assistance treaties and this particularly affects the investigation of foreign industrial espionage.

As the ASIS survey demonstrated, the density of data stored means that the loss or theft of intellectual or trade information can be significant. In the summer of 1999, the Canadian Security Intelligence Service (CSIS) released documents on such incidents to draw attention to the increase of economic espionage. It warned that, as in the USA and the UK particularly, Canadian companies were experiencing a substantial loss of trade and pricing information, investment strategies, contact details, supplier lists and, perhaps most importantly of all, research and development data.

The CSIS stated that the most common method of acquiring such information was by recruiting an employee, contractor or consultant to copy data from company computers. Theft of laptop computers or hacker access to them while left, for example, in hotel rooms, was increasingly evident. The CSIS also warned of the need for vigilance when hosting visits from overseas businessmen, scientists, students and delegations. In one incident, two foreign exchange students copied a Canadian university professor's computer-stored work on applications for high-energy equipment. The technology was then reproduced in the students' home country.

Business travellers carrying laptops and modems are increasingly vulnerable. The CSIS had recorded incidents where telephones in hotel rooms were routinely tapped by local intelligence operatives or data thieves, and rooms were clandestinely entered and searched. Even hotel safes may be accessible to foreign intelligence services. Industrial espionage agents have also become adept at using traditional forms of electronic eavesdropping to exploit data-processing systems. A variation on wire tapping involves the illegal use of a minicomputer to intercept data communications and to generate false commands or responses to other system components.

CSIS cited two recent examples. In one, a foreign government ordered its intelligence service to obtain specific business intelligence. The intelligence service then recruited a team of computer hackers, whose work resulted in the theft of numerous computer systems, passwords, and personnel and research files from two companies. In the other case, a Canadian company's technology was compromised when the company, hoping to win a lucrative contract from a foreign government, found that its trade secrets had been stolen by a visiting national of that country. He had copied the technology from company computers.

The Russians and Chinese head a long list of nations actively sponsoring industrial and economic espionage, which, like most things associated with the IT age, is a growth industry. Washington meanwhile excuses its own operations in that direction by pointing out that, internationally, economic crime and corruption drain an estimated $260 billion a year out of US-based companies as well as $140 billion out of overseas operations.

Its economic police name twenty-three countries engaged in economic espionage against United States targets. The intelligence services of these countries steal ideas and give them, or in some cases sell them, to their own domestic companies to enable them to manufacture goods that compete with US products. They name as chief offenders Russia, which, according to the Defense Intelligence Agency, launched an economic spying blitz in 1998; Japan, which beat the United States in the microchip industry in the early 1980s; and France, a 'strong diplomatic ally that is very aggressive in its espionage efforts'. Japan and France, meanwhile, claim the CIA has been conducting economic espionage against them for years. The CIA offers the defence that this clandestinely collected intelligence was not intended to give an advantage to United States companies but was collected in pursuit of the national interest and was only to be used in inter-government trade negotiations.

As we have already seen, the industrialised nations of the West spy upon each other constantly. Their own intelligence services are more capable than most in the activities of bugging, burgling and getting into other people's computers. It is worth remembering that, like the NSA, the CIA, the CSIS and the rest, under the UK's own Intelligence Services Act MI5 is charged with 'protection against a threat to the economic wellbeing of the UK', while MI6 and GCHQ are concerned 'with obtaining and providing information in support of the UK's wellbeing'. This is jargon for economic espionage. GCHQ, meanwhile, is at the hub of all British interceptions, linked of course to the UKUSA nations and, latterly, to the databases of Europol. The UN manual points out in a forthright manner that state or privately sponsored adversaries 'with sufficient motivation, resources and ingenuity can compromise the most sophisticated security safeguards. Until recently, computer-related crime was concentrated in the economic environment. The law enforcement community responded by training existing commercial crime or fraud experts in the specialised area of computer crime investigation. Modern experience indicates that computer crime has progressed far beyond both the economic environment and legal capability.'

Clearly these thoughts had begun circulating among the upper echelons of law enforcement as the new century dawned. On 10 January 2000, in front of an audience of lawyers at Stanford University, US Attorney General Janet Reno rolled out her own plan to form an international around-the-clock anti-cybercrime force. She suggested the formation of teams of highly skilled computer crime prosecutors and investigators linked to forensic computer laboratories. She also proposed new laws to facilitate subpoenas and warrants stemming from Internet investigations.

With e-commerce expected to top the staggering figure of $1 trillion by the end of 2003, Reno reckoned action was urgent. She laid down her plans for what she called LawNet, a collection of information-sharing networks to beat computer crime, combined with new laws to overcome the confusing tapestry that confronts present investigators. Reno said LawNet would also need to focus on privacy issues, protecting consumers from dataveillance which renders computer users vulnerable to the disclosure of all their private details from bank accounts and tax records to book selections and movie choices. As New York Attorney General Eliot Spitzer told her: 'It's not so much Big Brother we should be worried about, but big browser. The aggregation of information, if it is misused, is terrifying.' Reno responded: 'If we aren't vigilant, cybercrime will turn the Internet into the Wild West of the twenty-first century. The Justice Department is determined to pursue cybercriminals at home and abroad.'

The same theme was pursed by Visa security expert Joe Majka in his vision of the future: 'We need cyberposses to track criminals through cyberspace. Security operations really need to get somebody on board who understands the Internet, how to track these individuals, how to do Internet investigations. Computer intruders are going to be hired as security consultants. That's not futuristic, it's already happening.'

First in America, and then across the globe ...

CHAPTER 16
HACK ATTACKS!: THE PROBLEM OF HACKERS AND CRACKERS

EARLY ONE MORNING IN THE SUMMER of 1998, an eighteen-year-old computer enthusiast, who uses the pseudonym of Chameleon, awoke at his home in Irvine, California, to discover a pistol sticking up his nose. He was told to get out of bed with his hands up and would he kindly spread-eagle while a search was made of his underpants and duvet. The federal agents running the show informed the young man that they had a dossier on him. This showed he was a cyber-terrorist, a hacker into secret government communications who had been selling US military secrets to one Khalid Ibrahim whom the FBI had reason to believe was running a Pakistani terrorist group known as Harkat Ansar – which was true, but only in part. He wasn't a hacker but a cracker, and those who do it know the difference; it is about degrees of seriousness. To the FBI they are all one breed – computer criminals – and Chameleon now faced a seven-hour grilling.

He had cracked military sites on occasions and had also received a cheque for $1000, supposedly from Ibrahim, along with a telephone number to call in Boston. He could have money, he had been told, if he passed on details of US government computer networks that he had charted during his career as an Internet traveller. Chameleon maintained that he had not passed on any information to Ibrahim, nor had he cashed the cheque. The FBI had rumbled Chameleon and had been keeping watch on him with electronic surveillance.

In the event, he was not charged with any criminal offence. Few of his kind ever are, either because they are never caught or because there is insufficient tangible evidence of a criminal act under existing law to bring them to trial. But there was good reason for the FBI's state of jitters.

US military sites are under constant attack from hackers. According to the US Deputy Secretary of Defense, John Hamre, his people were 'detecting eighty to a hundred [potential hacking] events' *every day* in the first quarter of 1999. The perpetrators are all officially classed as 'political hackers' and there is a huge contingent of intelligence agents and espionage chancers at work. But most attacks come from young computer buffs, often barely in their teens, pursuing what has become a worldwide obsession to crack the system, following what one hacker e-zine has described as 'an intellectual quest, a noble offshoot of scientific curiosity'.

That quest is supposedly the motivation of true hackers. Crackers are less serious about the knowledge, and are in it for the thrills which, in turn, often leads them into criminal activity. True hackers are particular about the distinction. Law enforcement does not agree; hacking in all its forms has reached epidemic proportions and the dedicated criminal element is still on a winning streak.

British and US caseloads for computer hacking and network intrusion cases doubled during each of the last two years of the 1990s. Undoubtedly, many of the 'events' reported by the Department of Defense are political, inspired by foreign organisations and governments, and they occur across the whole spectrum of US government and public offices. Even the White House and the Library of Congress sites were hacked into in the summer of 1999.

British government sites suffer the same problem to a lesser degree but they do not as a rule talk about it. There have been occasional spectacular successes, as when a hacker found a route into a British Telecom computer from which he downloaded top secret information about British government and intelligence departments. It detailed the telephone numbers and billing information of some of the most sensitive sites in Britain, including M15, M16 and GCHQ, as well as information on a number of US listening posts in the UK such as Menwith Hill. Among other data were secret telephone numbers from a government bunker which would be used in the event of war, and the names and home addresses of senior military personnel. The hundreds of pages of documents on which all this appeared were relayed by the hacker over the Internet to Scottish journalist Steve Fleming in July 1994, after he had posted a message asking for confirmation of rumours among the hacking fraternity that British Telecom had been compromised. It was believed that the passwords for entry to its systems had been gained from a temporary worker at a BT office. Fleming then decided to test out that possibility. He applied for temporary work through an employment agency and, sure enough, was soon walking into BT where he found 'to my amazement – just as my source had described – passwords openly distributed and a remarkable lack of supervision'.

STRATEGIC INFORMATION WARFARE

But the British experience was a minor event compared to a hacking scare in the USA during February and March 1998, a few months before the raid on Chameleon's home. During those two months, more than five hundred military, civilian government and private sector computer systems in the United States were attacked by hackers. The attacks appeared to be a concerted effort from a particular source, a group of very clever hackers. The alert went up in Washington that this could be the start of the first-ever outbreak of 'information warfare', because the intrusions occurred during the build-up of United States and British military personnel in the Gulf in response to tension with Iraq over United Nations weapons inspections.

British and American warplanes were already assembled in the Middle East and bombing raids over Iraq were under way. The Pentagon began to get seriously worried. President Clinton was informed. Chiefs of staff and heads of various sections of the US intelligence community were summoned to urgent meetings. The British, co-partners in the Iraqi bombing raids, were told of the situation and MI5 took lead responsibility fo overseeing the security of the British computer infrastructure. Meanwhile, the Pentagon set up constant liaison with the CIA, NSA and FBI as more penetrations were discovered: at least two hundred US military computer systems were attacked, including those at seven Air Force bases and four Navy installations, the Department of Energy National Laboratories, NASA sites and universities.

There was a specific reason for their concern which went beyond the scenario unfolding in the Gulf. The build-up sounded very similar to models prepared by the CIA on which the Center for Strategic and International Studies subsequently produced a warning document entitled *Cybercrime, Cyberterrorism, Cyberwarfare: Averting an Electronic Waterloo*. The ninety-page report outlined the possibility of information warfare being launched against the USA in which the nation's entire computer infrastructure might be attacked, possibly combined with the use of chemical or biological weapons.

Was such an attack now under way? The timing of the intrusions and links to some Internet service providers in the Gulf region caused a number of experts in the assessment team to believe that Iraq was behind the attacks. A combined top-level investigation was ordered, calling in the talents of a number of agencies including the FBI, the CIA, the Department of Defense, the Defense Information Systems Agency and the Department of Justice.

The investigation, however, had a startling outcome with a *Dr Strangelove* flavour, which revealed much about the ease with which hackers are able to break into not one or two but dozens of important government computer systems, and how little the government could do to halt it. Using a legally enforced FBI wire-tap of computer networks, the culprits were eventually identified as two juveniles in Cloverdale, California, and several individuals in Israel. It rammed home to those in high places the difficulties encountered in attempting to identify an intruder. The facts have to be gathered in an investigation involving a mass of electronic surveillance and all the other techniques at the disposal of the agencies concerned. It also vividly demonstrated the vulnerabilities of computer networks that allow 'root access' to defence systems.

The upshot of the scare was dramatic. President Clinton signed an immediate order for the formation of a new national crime-fighting unit and database specifically geared to the hacking problem: $64 million was committed to fund the creation of the National Infrastructure Protection Center, an anti-hacker investigation unit which came into being in February 1999 and would eventually be manned by five hundred of the country's best computer specialists seconded from the FBI, the CIA, the secret service, NSA, NASA, the Department of Defense, the State Department and the US Postal Service. Based in Washington, they were to have direct links to fifty-six FBI Field Offices across the USA. Squads of at least seven agents were additionally created in ten Field Offices in Washington, New York, San Francisco, Chicago, Dallas, Los Angeles, Atlanta, Charlotte, Boston and Seattle, with a further six key cities covered by squads of up to five agents.

In addition Clinton, by then armed with the report on information warfare produced by the Center for Strategic and International Studies, announced a $1.5 billion commitment to fight cybercrime: 'We already are seeing the first wave of deliberate cyber attacks – hackers break into government and business computers, stealing and destroying information, raiding bank accounts, running up credit card charges, extorting money by threats to unleash powerful computer viruses.'

The reaction had been swift – the Strategic Studies report had probably scared the President's men half to death. It dealt with various possible levels of information warfare that could be waged by small terrorist groups with the aid of a team of skilled hackers. The feasibility of such an event was described in no uncertain terms and mentioned the multi-platform Satan program, originally created by the KGB and sold on the hackers' black market in the 1990s. Satan, when combined with other software, creates an automated reconnaissance and intrusion package that leaves virtually no trail. An improved version called Saint arrived on the black market in mid-1998.

Strategic information warfare (SIW) could, according to the study, if successfully managed as part of an extended campaign, cripple economic, power and communications infrastructures. Additional features of an SIW attack, such as the use of biological or chemical weapons and the sabotage of water supplies by the same method, might be used to try to force the USA into compromise or acceding to a demand.

Finally, to demonstrate the reality of such a strike to members of government reluctant even to contemplate the possibility, an NSA team of thirty specialists, using only those programs available on hacker websites, proved beyond doubt that they could disable most of the US power grid as well as deny service to the entire Pacific military command and control systems. This more or less concurred with the results of similar exercises carried out on British military and government computer networks. In the UK, the defence community subjects its systems to regular mock attacks by 'tiger teams'. They may strike anywhere at any time and perform real-time hacking events against selected systems. The latest available figures showed that there was no room for complacency: of thirty-eight thousand probes made in a year, twenty-four thousand were successful to some extent, only nine thousand of those were detected and fewer than a hundred of these 'incidents' were reported.

But to return to the Strategic Studies report: briefly summarised, it called for immediate and stern measures:

- develop national security policies for the information revolution;

- make strategic information dominance a national security objective;

- adopt policies that ensure critical government services;

- understand and work with the private sector;

- prepare US DoD forces for an information age conflict; and

- prepare US intelligence agencies for information age threats.

WHO ARE THE HACKERS AND CRACKERS?

Most of these recommendations were accepted in Washington, although the hackers and crackers did not seem unduly perturbed. They had long since been branded as criminals, although there are still many who prefer to stick to the romantic image of network adventurers, an image created in the 1970s when remote intrusion into massive computers was a real feat given the expense and lack of technology. For those not familiar with the Internet, there are now many hacker-related sites, some of which are run in what they call a responsible manner and whose operators have been known to cooperate with the FBI.

The hackers and crackers come in many shapes and sizes, encompassing more or less all the conventional images. They range from spotty teenagers tapping away in their bedrooms in the dead of night, through to talented computer enthusiasts bent on cracking the code and passwords that get them into computer systems that are supposed to be the most safe and secure in the world. Many never get past the graffiti stage of hanging rude messages on to someone's carefully constructed home page or website. Equally, a good many are very capable technicians who manage to hack their way into sites whose owners would never believe it possible. And then there are the very serious political hackers, many employed by the state intelligence organisations of most nations, who are constantly trying to get into each other's knickers, as it were. It is a constant and ongoing battle.

Kevin Mitnick

The fact that few ever come to court is why the world's most famous hacker, Kevin Mitnick, has become a legend to those who indulge in the pursuits for which he became renowned. This is not entirely due to his capabilities as a hacker, but largely due to the treatment he has received from the law. On a scale of one to ten, his activities had a danger quotient of about two when compared to activities which are now recorded daily. In truth, Mitnick was a man of relatively modest talents as a programmer; but his hacking career, at a time when such things were a comparative rarity, was driven by a compulsion which began in his early teens when computers were new and few people had heard of modems.

He was first arrested in 1981 for stealing computer manuals. He had three other brushes with the law during the next five years and then in 1988, when he was twenty-five, he was arrested on charges of stealing software from a digital equipment company. He was refused bail during the eight months he was awaiting trial, and for most of that time was kept in solitary confinement. There were all kinds of rumours surrounding his computer antics and hacking abilities, including one that he had already broken into the Aerospace Defense Command system and could launch a nuclear missile by whistling down the telephone. This was apparently one of the reasons he was kept in seclusion. The scenario was copied for a film called *War Games*.

In 1989, after serving a prison sentence and with a probation order still in force, Mitnick went on the run and continued his hacking activities. In 1994, his notoriety was enhanced by a *New York Times* article by John Markoff, who described him as a computer hacker run amok and stated that the FBI had lost him. Markoff later wrote of the efforts of FBI computer specialists, in particular Tsutomu Shimomura of San Diego, to track him down. For Shimomura it became a personal quest which ended in the arrest of Mitnick in February 1995. Markoff got a bestselling book out of the story, called *Takedown*, which was made into a film with Tom Berenger and Skeet Ulrich, reportedly earning the writer $750,000. Mitnick, who said he didn't recognise himself in the book, was in the meantime sentenced to twenty-two months for his earlier probation violation and possession of unauthorised access devices and then, additionally, spent over two years in prison awaiting trial on charges of breaking into computers.

David Schindler, an assistant US attorney, worked on the Mitnick case from 1991 and relentlessly pushed the argument that the hacker had jeopardised research and development that cost tens of millions. To prove it, the prosecution filed a massive nine gigabytes of electronic evidence – more than the memory of most modern home computers – which it had accumulated while Mitnick was on the run. He was initially refused a laptop computer with which to read the prosecution case while in prison for fear that, even without a modem, he might cause havoc.

With their client facing a ten-year sentence called for by the prosecution, Mitnick's lawyers eventually negotiated a plea bargain which kept him inside until February 2000, much to the chagrin of his supporters. He also agreed to be the subject of a three-year supervision order when he came out and to provide a written undertaking not to go near a computer. The prosecutors had submitted that Mitnick had copied computer and cellphone source codes from Motorola, Nokia and Sun Systems, property worth $80 million. Mitnick acknowledged $10 million worth in his plea but his lawyers said the figure was misleading because he never sold it or redistributed the information, in other words never profited from it in any way. He is the only hacker to have been seriously punished, and to some extent it backfired. Websites dedicated to him proliferated. Mitnick became the hacker's hero. In the wake of his case, some commentators could not help noticing that a degree of paranoia had crept into Washington life.

POLITICAL HACK ATTACKS

Meanwhile, the new National Infrastructure Protection Center was up and running. Its mission was to prevent attacks, not to respond to them: the latter task, according to the NIPC's first director, Michael Vatis, would 'typically be for the other bodies, such as the Army or Air Force, since it is likely that such an attack would be combined with biological warfare'.

If there were any doubts that the FBI and the Pentagon were deadly serious about these thoughts, they were dispelled in October 1999 when Vatis was called before a Senate Judiciary Committee to give a progress report on the organisation's work and his own wide assessment of cyber-warfare and America's readiness to fight it. His report makes stark reading. Vatis immediately revealed that hackers and possibly foreign-based intruders had, since NIPC's formation, successfully accessed US government networks and downloaded large amounts of unclassified but sensitive information:

> It is important that the Congress understands the very real threat that we are facing in the cyber-realm, not in the future, but now. Perhaps the greatest potential threat to our national security is the prospect of information warfare by foreign militaries against our critical infrastructures. We know that several foreign nations are already developing an information warfare doctrine, programmes and capabilities for use against each other and the United States or other nations.
>
> Some are doing so because they see that they cannot defeat the United States in a head-to-head military encounter and they believe that information operations are a way to

strike at what they perceive as America's Achilles' heel – our reliance on information technology to control critical government and private sector systems. For example, two Chinese military officers recently published a book that called for the use of unconventional measures, including the propagation of computer viruses, to counterbalance the military power of the United States.

More recently, Vatis reported, worrying hacking events had occurred during the combined NATO bombing raids on Serbia during the Kosovo crisis. From the very beginning of the conflict, hackers around the world who were either anti-American or sympathetic to the Serbian cause began to launch 'ping' attacks against NATO Web servers. Russian and Chinese computer experts were believed to have joined several other group formations and a large number of individuals supporting the Serbs in launching hack attacks on military and government websites in NATO countries, including Britain and the United States, using virus-infected e-mail and other hacking procedures. Over a hundred US government sites in the United States had received these e-mails. A similar number were delivered to the UK, and a number of British organisations had lost files and databases. The attacks did not cause serious disruption to the military effort but were judged by intelligence analysts in Washington and London to be portents of much more serious attacks that might be expected in future conflicts as technology progresses.

According to Michael Vatis, foreign intelligence services had adapted to using cyber-tools as part of their information gathering and espionage. In a case dubbed The Cuckoo's Egg a ring of German hackers had penetrated numerous military, scientific and industrial computers in the United States, western Europe and Japan, stealing passwords, programs, and other information which they had sold to the Russians. Intelligence services increasingly viewed computer intrusions as a method of acquiring sensitive government and private sector information.

In his document to the Senate committee, Vatis highlighted some cases reported around the world:

Terrorists are known to use information technology and the Internet to formulate plans, raise funds, spread propaganda and to communicate securely. For example, convicted terrorist Ramzi Yousef, mastermind of the World Trade Center bombing, stored detailed plans to destroy United States airliners on encrypted files on his laptop computer. Some groups have already used cyber-attacks to inflict damage on their enemies' information systems. For example, a group calling itself the Internet Black Tigers conducted a successful 'denial of service' attack on servers of Sri Lankan government embassies. Italian sympathisers of the Mexican Zapatista rebels attacked Web pages of Mexican financial institutions. And a Canadian government report indicates that the IRA considered the use of information warfare techniques against British interests. We are also concerned that Aum Shinrikyo, which launched the deadly Sarin gas attack in the Tokyo subway system, could use its growing expertise in computer manufacturing and Internet technology to develop cyberterrorism weapons for use against Japanese and US interests. Thus, while we have yet to see a significant instance of cyberterrorism with widespread disruption of critical infrastructures, all of these facts portend the use of cyber-attacks by terrorists to cause pain to targeted governments or civilian populations by disrupting critical systems.

The rise in what has been dubbed hacktivism by US, British and Canadian intelligence services, who are at the forefront of the attacks, adds another element to the IT phenomenon. The intelligence services believe that terrorist and foreign espionage attempts to break into their national computers are being deliberately targeted in areas of the infrastructure such as defence and government sites, where hundreds of hacking and cracking attempts are made by eager young computer enthusiasts. Thus the investigators cannot see the wood for the trees because the investigations are long and complex and, in spite of modern technology, it is virtually impossible to track the source of the hacking events even when they are in progress.

There has been sharp a rise in the number of known hack attacks by political groups, quasi-political organisations or those pursuing a particular cause, such as animal rights, on publicly accessible Web pages or e-mail servers. In recent years, more and more groups and individuals have found ways to overload e-mail servers and hack into websites to send a political message. One such group, the Electronic Disturbance Theatre, promotes civil disobedience on-line in support of the Zapatista movement in Mexico. In the spring of 1999, it called for worldwide electronic civil disobedience and took what it termed 'protest hacking' actions against the White House and Department of Defense servers. Supporters of Kevin Mitnick, prior to his release from prison, hacked into the Senate Web page and left some graffiti to make sure everyone knew they had got in.

In fact, the hackers themselves have excellent networking facilities. There are many websites where hackers and crackers can record their exploits in what has become a highly competitive environment. While remote cracking once required a degree of skill or computer knowledge, today's interloper can now download attack scripts and protocols from numerous websites. The tools of attack may have become more sophisticated, but they have also become easier to use.

HACK EFFECTS

Unskilled teenage crackers, however, can cause more trouble than they ever imagined possible, sometimes with potentially fatal consequences. One fifteen-year-old, who hacked into the Bell Atlantic telephone system using his personal computer and modem, shut down the telephone service to six hundred customers in one community. The disruption affected all the local police and fire emergency services in Worcester, Massachusetts, and at the same time knocked out runway lights for incoming aircraft at the local airport. The telephone service was out of action at the airport control tower for six hours. The upside of the investigation of the case by the US secret service was that it discovered vulnerability in twenty-two thousand telephone switches nationwide that could be taken out by hackers with four keyboard strokes. Because he was a juvenile, this hacker was sentenced to two years' probation and 250 hours' community service. He was also ordered to forfeit his computer equipment and pay $5000 damages to the phone company.

In another attack on public services, a disgruntled former employee of the US Coastguard performed a slick hacking job that had dire consequences. Shakuntla Devi Singla used her insider knowledge and another employee's password and log-on identification to delete data from the Coastguard personnel database system. It took 115 agency employees over 1800 working hours to recover or re-enter the lost data. Singla was convicted and sentenced to five months in prison and five months' home detention, as well as being ordered to pay $35,000 in restitution.

These are just two of many such cases which demonstrate once again that attacks on critical communications hubs can have cascading effects on several infrastructures. They highlight the potential for skilled intelligence agents working with high-tech gear.

HOW HACKERS ACCESS SYSTEMS

So how is it done? How is it that one kid, sitting alone at a home computer, can cause so much mayhem? Access is invariably achieved from a remote location along a telecommunication network by one of several means. The hacker may be able to take advantage of lax security measures to gain access, or may find loopholes in existing security measures or system procedures. Hackers may impersonate legitimate system users, especially in systems where users employ common passwords or maintenance passwords found in the system itself. Modern hackers can also easily bypass password protection using one of several common methods. If a hacker is able to discover a password allowing access, then a Trojan Horse program can be put in place to capture the other passwords of legitimate users. The hacker can later retrieve the program containing the stolen passwords by remote access and can trawl about the system as he wishes.

Password protection can also be bypassed successfully by several password-cracking routines. For example, legitimate security software has been developed that allows access to data only after it checks encrypted passwords against a dictionary of common passwords so as to alert system administrators of a potential weakness in security. The same security process can be imitated for illegitimate purposes. A variety of system-specific encryption routines can be obtained from hacker bulletin boards around the world, which are regularly updated as security technology develops.

Another method of gaining unauthorised access is known as the trapdoor, achieved through access points created for legitimate purposes such as maintenance of the system. The international hacker community then uses electronic bulletin boards to network its methods. In one case, details of a Canadian attempt to access a system were found on suspects in an unrelated matter in England; they had removed the material from a bulletin board in Germany. International sharing of information is commonplace and aids system intrusions from around the globe, often resulting in staggering telecommunication charges to the victim.

The latest developments in telecoms and mobile phone systems and their integration with computer-based communications have also helped, not hindered, the hackers, who have responded to these advances by duplicating the microchip technology. Once one system is accessed, a computer operator with sufficient skill can infiltrate the entire telecommunications network of a city.

Determining that an intrusion is under way is virtually impossible, particularly in the early stages. It could begin with a 'probe' to find vulnerabilities or entry points in the target system, the planting of a Trojan Horse or malicious code, or an attack to disrupt the system. Nor is it possible to establish the type of intrusion because the methods used are principally the same, whether it is a simple back-bedroom hacking job, a terrorist attack, foreign intelligence gathering or criminal activity to steal data.

TRACKING THE HACKER

Identification is similarly fraught. One of the few routes for law enforcement is to use electronic surveillance methods to determine the size and nature of the intrusion; how many systems are affected; what techniques are being used; and what the purpose of the intrusions is – disruption, espionage, theft of money or a hacker just having a look around. The NIPC can call on the FBI for electronic surveillance, but ostensibly only if the attack is from a foreign source; elsewhere permission for surveillance has to be applied for to a federal judge.

The first known case in which electronic surveillance was used against a hacker came to court in May 1998. It involved an Argentine computer hacker who was tracked down with the aid of an FBI wire-tap on a computer network. The investigation actually began in the summer of 1995 when the US Department of Defense detected intrusions into a number of military and university computer systems containing secret information about government research on satellites, radiation and energy. The activity was traced to a set of misappropriated accounts on an Internet host computer at Harvard University. The investigation team put together an electronic profile of the intruder, using keywords such as unique names the intruder gave to files and Internet protocol addresses of systems being targeted by him.

This profile was used as the basis for a federal application for a wire-tap order, the first ever obtained to search communications over a computer network. It was also used to configure a monitoring computer, adapted to enable the complex and high-speed searches necessary to track the hacker's activities while he was on-line.

Barry Mawn, an FBI special agent from Boston, ran the investigation and enlisted the aid of Argentine intelligence officers. The joint surveillance ended with the arrest of Julio Cesar Ardito from Buenos Aires. Although the USA had no extradition agreement with Argentina, he returned voluntarily to the United States after his defence counsel organised a plea bargain deal. Ardito agreed to plead guilty to charges of unlawfully intercepting electronic communications over a military computer and damaging files on a second military computer. The agreement negotiated with the prosecution was that he would accept a sentence of three years' probation and a $5000 fine. The only other condition was that he cooperated fully with the law enforcement team; be spent two weeks being debriefed on his methods, which were apparently of great interest to the Naval Criminal Investigative Service which had kept a watching brief.

Sensitive naval websites were being hacked at the rate of around two hundred actual or attempted intrusions a week. One site alone, the Naval

Surface Warfare Center, was being attacked about forty times per week, according to the head of its intrusion detection unit, Stephen Northcutt: 'If we really want to catch the people attacking our sites we have to employ some pretty sophisticated Internet forensics. In practice, this process would involve installing surveillance sensors on high-profile websites that are commonly targeted by crackers. That information could be stored and later analysed. If a bank is robbed at 2 p.m., the police will go back and examine the videotape and see who had been casing the joint that morning. Well, it's the same with the Internet. When a hacker breaks into a site and steals information, it's likely that he has been in casing the joint before.'

The Navy's hacking estimates do not, incidentally, include virus attacks. The Naval Computer Incident Response Team discovered that over 1208 of its systems had been infected with viruses in the first quarter of 1999. It took 1118 man-hours to clear them.

When the National Infrastructure Protection Centre (NIPC) was set up it was placed at the core of the government's warning of attacks under way. The methods of discovering them remain classified, but between January and September 1999 the NIPC issued twenty-two alerts or warnings, which constituted a tiny percentage of the hacking activity that occurred in that period. According to CIA boss George Tenet in a 1999 speech at the Georgia Institute of Technology in Atlanta, in 1995 – the year that the Argentine hacker was operating – the Defense Department had been attacked 250,000 times.

Some experts dispute the figures and believe that, along with such buzzwords as cyberterrorists, paedophiles and organised crime, they are exaggerated in order to arouse concern in Washington, so that eventually any action taken by law enforcement is condoned by the public; one writer on hacker issues compared it to the situation at the time of McCarthy and his committee on un-American activities. John Vranesevich, a security specialist and founder of AntiOnline, a popular news site for hackers and security people alike, actually welcomes the formation of the NIPC but suggests that the government should create awareness campaigns about the dangers of cracking in the same way that it conducts drug awareness campaigns: 'Some of these guys hacking the Pentagon's website are just kids and it's a game to them. Chameleon, for example, is a talented programmer and I don't believe he knew that he would get caught up with terrorists. The last I heard of him, he'd gone ligit. He was working in Internet security.'

Even so, in the early summer, FBI chief Louis Freeh was back in front of a senate committee investigating the proliferation of cyber-crime. He produced results of a new survey from the US Computer Security Institute which revealed that 74 per cent of the companies which responded had experienced security breaches in the previous 12 months. They had suffered multi-billion dollar losses from fraudsters, thefts of proprietory information and denial of service through attacks on computer infrastructure by hackers, crackers and computer hitmen.

Then came the news that by the beginning of August 2000 the number of attacks of a potentially serious nature on US Department of Defense computer installations and general US national computer infra-structure had reached record levels – almost 15,000 incidents were recorded in the case of the DoD, close to the figure for the whole of 1999. Another US security study by research group IDC confirmed the trend and estimated that malicious hacking, viruses and organised cyber crime would increase by a staggering 1400 per cent by 2004.

Of course, Internet security is not always crime-related and often has more to do with the fallibility of computer systems. In August, 2000 Britain's Barclays Bank famously hit snags with its new online banking set-up which allowed customers to read details of other accounts. The system was shut down while modifications were made, but rising fears about Internet security were merely heightened by Bruce Schneider, a cryptographer and chief technology officer at Counterpane Internet Security writing in the *Mail on Sunday*'s financial pages. He warned that in many cases, Internet security was 'fatally flawed' and that the Barclays incident were merely the 'tip of the iceberg'.

As we have been warned by Britain's own Trade and Industry website, the Web is inherently insecure. Secret lives become an open book to those with the will and tenacity to break through even the toughest security barriers. And that, apparently, does not require the brain of the man who cracked Enigma. The above statistics show that if young kids can launch attacks on highly secure government websites or break into databases that hold credit card details then surely nothing is secure from highly trained professionals.

Big Brother today has the capability of appearing in many guises, on both sides of the legal divide.

EPILOGUE
PARANOIA AND REALITY

SO ... **WHAT ARE WE** to make of it all? Writers on the topic of surveillance invariably turn to George Orwell. Yet his biographer Bernard Crick has, over the years, regularly told us that *1984* was not intended as a prophetic portrait of life in the future. It was, he said, a dark satire based more upon conditions existing in Orwell's own time, notably evident in Stalin's brutally repressive regime in Soviet Russia, combined with snatches of post-war Europe and a bomb-site society hammered down by austerity, rationing and the rising threat of a Third World War which might be atomic. Orwell's vision may well have been based upon what was already the norm for many millions of people, coloured by the extremes of the Soviets, the hypotensive state of the intelligence services of the West and events such as the hearings of the House Committee on un-American activities which we have glimpsed in these pages.

Orwell's deepest engagement on his novel, *1984*, coincided with this uneasy international climate – and with the summoning in September 1947 of forty-three witnesses to appear for HCUA hearings in Washington during an investigation into Communist influence in the film industry. Famously, the 'Hollywood Ten' were given prison sentences for their refusal to answer the committee's questions about their personal political beliefs. The year was 1948. Orwell simply transposed the last two digits to create the title for his novel. His book was published the following year, a few months before tuberculosis claimed the author's life.

Despite Crick's suggestions to the contrary, futurologists and Orwell fans have persisted with their claims that the novel is a classic work of prophetic wisdom. Indeed, in the fiftieth year of the anniversary of his death, an American science fiction writer, David Ross, claimed that he had identified 137 'total-surveillance predictions' in *1984*, of which 100 had come true.

Orwell's vision of totalitarianism arrived in various forms. Ministers of Truth or Ministers of Internal Repression certainly did turn up, in all but name, in various guises under both Communist and right-wing regimes around the globe. In the free world, they mutated in other forms, with spin doctors pumping out propaganda, newspeak appearing as soundbytes, successive governments and their ministers introducing Orwellian measures by stealth and big business demonstrating its determination to achieve its own controls over the very society on which it feeds.

On route, those who warned of the onset of a Big Brother society were generally dismissed by those in high places as cranks, treacherous alarmists, irresponsible conspiracy theorists or held to be suffering from a severe case of paranoia. In the year 2000 it is impossible to use such arguments. How could anyone, whose life and secrets are packaged in electronic dossiers available to all and sundry, be accused of paranoia? How can eavesdropping upon millions of people, whether at work, at home or simply walking down the High Street, be considered a benign development? And can we really accept as 'necessary' such innovations as the British Environment Agency's revelation that it had hidden a £3,500 mini-camera in an old drinks can to catch illegal rubbish dumpers? Paranoia, if such it ever was, has been replaced by well-based concern as privacy and civil rights become eroded under the combined activities law enforcement and criminals.

Examples of increasing levels of surveillance arrive almost daily. Indeed, one of the great difficulties I experienced in researching and collating material for this book has been keeping up with developments. On virtually every front, information has been constantly overtaken either by new spy tactics in both state and private sectors, or by the revelation of the latest misdemeanours that required their attention.

In Britain, for example, as these pages were being written, the new Regulation of Investigatory Powers Bill was rushed into print by Home Secretary Jack Straw to update and replace the old Interception of Communications Act. MI5, as we have seen, was also revealed to be ahead of the game by drawing up plans for a major new facility to intercept Britain's Internet traffic. Not far behind this news came some disturbing and dramatic events which the authorities could point to as specific examples of why such tactics were needed. They included renewed outbreaks of soccer violence across Europe involving British fans and the most devastating computer viruses ever transmitted over the World Wide Web.

In spring 2000 Jack Straw pledged another £30 million to increase the UK's CCTV coverage, in addition to the £150 million he had promised only four months earlier. This extended the number of cameras installed to 500,000 across the nation. Results of general surveillance experiments with the latest digital CCTV technology trialled in six Cornish towns were also revealed in the early summer of 2000. The demonstrations were applauded by the police for the clarity of captured images, whether the subjects were innocent or guilty. The next step in these experiments is trials with a digital system that will allow police helicopters to beam clear pictures to stations or police cars on the ground. Even the police were worried, however, about one of the benefits of digital technology, which allows the enhancement of photographs. It would lay them open to accusations of alteration of the actual image.

And then came ILOVEYOU, the e-mail transmitted virus created by a truant Filipino student. It was pounced upon by the security agencies as another example of the need for constant vigilance. The fact that a kid armed only with cheap equipment could bring widespread disruption to computer systems across the world in fact represents one more nail in the coffin of privacy. Global systems were hit as the virus spread from Manila to Hong Kong and then moved swiftly across time zones to Europe. In Britain, Parliament was affected, as were major conglomerates such as Barclays Bank, News International, the BBC and British Telecom. The Swiss government and several banks closed their computer systems down until the virus could be eliminated. The virus moved on to America where Congress was forced to shut down its e-mail system and many businesses were affected. The cost was counted in billions. Barely had the scare died down when a new strain – even more devastating in its ability to multiply – appeared and Louis Freeh, head of the FBI, was soon back on the campaign trail, to reassert all the warnings that have been covered in these pages. In his armoury was another new case, unearthed in Britain. Two teenagers, both under eighteen, sparked an international investigation involving the British authorities, the FBI and Canadian law enforcement. They were alleged to have hacked into several e-commerce websites to steal credit card information relating to twenty-six thousand accounts in America, Canada, Thailand, Japan and the United Kingdom. The projected value of possible losses through the intrusions was put at $3,000,000.

This and the Love viruses once again prompted the thought that if a few determined teenagers could create so much mayhem within global computer systems, the potential for sabotage by experienced professionals must surely be considerable. As yet, no such major incident has been reported. The possibilities – as displayed by the accidental closure of the London Stock Exchange through computer failure for just eight hours in April 2000 – are seemingly limitless in a world now so dependent on electronic communication and its beating heart, the Internet. Only in very recent times have nations begun to wake up to the vulnerability of major national computer infrastructures – and the solutions ultimately will lead to even more surveillance.

On a more individual level, the possibilities of interception and invasion of personal computers by hostile websites is no less worrying. Vulnerabilities are identified on a daily basis. SecuritySearch.Net, whose chief executive Simon Johnson has provided an appendix to this book, produces a weekly summary of potential problems. For example, in May 2000 SecuritySearch.Net reported that a vulnerability in Microsoft Office 2000 allowed a malicious website owner to gain access to files on the visitor's computer system. Although Microsoft identified the problem and the fault was corrected such reports are frequent and often alarming to the user.

For the individual, however, perhaps the most worrying aspect remains the huge amount of information which is collected from each of us every time we buy a product or use a service. The boundaries are being pushed ever outward. In May 2000 the American bank Morgan

Stanley invited selected householders throughout Britain – myself included – to take up a platinum credit card. The small print, if one bothered to read it, contained the clause: 'In processing transactions, we may incidentally collect some limited personal data about your racial or ethnic origin, political opinions, religious or other similar beliefs, physical or mental health, sexual life or criminal record. You agree that we may use, disclose and transfer those personal data as described in this Condition.' Britain's new Data Protection Act provides the clause for any citizen to stop companies from using any information stored on computer. But to invoke that right might prejudice or delay the individual obtaining a loan, a credit card and perhaps even a job, such is the reliance of big business upon the information they can gather about us via lists and databases.

In the end, it is left to the individual to either play along or opt out. That really is the nub of the debate: what level of being spied upon does modern society require for its own protection and, entrepreneurs would argue, for its economic benefit. For the perpetrators, there is only one answer: more.

Picture, for a moment, a motor car produced in 1905 and compare it to a Rolls-Royce coming off the production line at the end of the century. Now, replace that image with the computer and the Internet. It has been calculated that in the year 2000, on-line connectivity is at the same stage as the car industry was in 1905. As the new century got under way, the incredible power and potential of the Internet and computer networks became apparent to the ordinary individual. At the same time the power of home computers expanded tenfold in the space of a couple of years. So did the on-line capabilities of business, commerce, law enforcement and crime. As these chapters have demonstrated, in virtually every area imaginable information is flowing freely through computer databases, e-mailed or file-transferred across the Internet, Intranet, Ethernet, telephone lines, cellular telephones, fax machines and pagers, most of which have security problems somewhere along the line. The facility for misuse and abuse arrived ahead of laws that might at least have saved the uninitiated and the innocent from serious trouble and guided the world on a more orderly journey along the information superhighway.

In the early days of the Internet, as those who signed up to lumbering Compuserve will recall, there was a strict, self-regulating code of practice which was promoted as necessary for all who entered through the electronic portal. The basis was free speech, free expression and good manners. There were rules to be followed and etiquette to be remembered. Commerce was frowned upon. That lasted about five minutes after the money-making possibilities of the Internet were realised and the whole thing exploded into an out-of-control electronic Wild West show where Mammon ruled. The original serious-minded concepts of free and forthright exchanges of views, study, research and educational possibilities were overwhelmed by commerce and crooks so that law enforcement also had to get heavily into the act, really in the space of less than two years.

Far from being controlled by society the Internet is itself becoming the controller and, in one respect, another incarnation of Big Brother. The Internet has had such a major impact upon civilisation on this planet that our very future seems to revolve around it. In spite of all its undoubted benefits, there remain concerns that it is much more personally invasive than any other creation in the twentieth century.

The Internet and computer power combined have led to clear problems. They revolve largely around issues of privacy and, bit by bit, year by year, actually losing control of certain aspects of our lives. In these pages, we have examined the electronic interception capabilities of the NSA, GCHQ and other similar organisations; we have witnessed the human intelligence advances of the likes of the CIA, MI5, the ex-KGB and law enforcement agencies. Surveillance from the state is now more extensive and all-embracing than at any time in history, more so, even, than during the infamous post-war years when J. Edgar Hoover was out of control, the CIA was dominated by cowboys and its dirty tricks department and MI5/MI6 was ruled by dogma, arrogance and an undoubted disregard for the rights of man. Old habits die hard and when computer power arrived, the facilities and the capability for creating lists of people and assets became even greater.

Readers must form their own views on the need for such extensive surveillance. In the end, it comes down to a personal view: are politicians and agencies chiefs right in reminding us that state interception is necessary to combat terrorists, paedophiles, the drug barons and others engaged in criminal enterprise? Or is there deliberate scare-mongering on their part to create the 'climate of fear' from which the public will accept any form of surveillance in the name of protection and law enforcement? And do businesses and corporations really have the right to collect such extensive information on us under the guise of providing a more efficient service and more effective marketing?

The intelligence agencies, the law enforcers and big business will press on; expansion is their keyword and it is a certainty. Although there is no sign of it as yet, public reaction may force a re-examination of their powers of interception, monitoring and information gathering. Until then, the standard response to complaints of human rights abuses remains the same: law-abiding individuals have nothing to fear. Yet, if we continue to accept the demands of the law enforcers and businesses without question or challenge, 'they' are gradually gaining control.

Society has already lost the battle for personal privacy. The amount of information that can now be freely acquired on our individual possessions, debt, aspirations and habits is seemingly limitless. There is yet some grappling to be done to harness this monster and, fortunately, the rise of intrusion has been matched by the growth of independent groups whose concern is our privacy in thought, deed and life, and others who are helping to guard our basic human rights. They are in no doubt . . .

Big Brother has to be watched!

APPENDIX
A GUIDE TO SAFETY, SECURITY AND PRIVACY ON THE WEB

By Simon Johnson, Chief Executive Officer,
SecuritySearch.Net
http://www.securitysearch.net/

SECURING YOUR COMPUTER

Hostile Web users and sites are becoming increasingly proficient at downloading files from a visitor's computer system without their knowledge.

One of the most common ways to hack into a computer system is via exploiting a flaw in the operating system.

Keeping up to date with the latest security patches and fixes for your software is critical. Many security problems could have been avoided if users had upgraded their software to the latest version or installed the latest security fixes from their software vendor. This is especially important for Web browsers which have many vulnerabilities. Apart from installing the latest security patches, users should install a PC Firewall. This will protect your PC from service attacks, port scanners and probes from hackers and crackers.

Passwords

There are various ways you can protect yourself from password crackers. A strong password should be at least eight digits in length and include mixed case (upper and lower case), alphanumeric and special characters. A password should not be a dictionary word, the name of your pet cat or your ex-partner's name.

EAVESDROPPING

When you send an e-mail message on the Internet it will travel through a number of nodes (gateways) until it reaches its destination. At each node your Internet provider or a hacker or cracker, using the Internet provider's network, can read everything you download or send via e-mail. What steps can you take to stop this from happening? The key to protecting yourself from eavesdropping is encryption.

Some encryption codes can be easily broken. However, algorithms such as Blowfish and programs such as PGP (Pretty Good Privacy) are built to withstand sophisticated attacks and have a high level of encryption. To date, nobody has succeeded in breaking a message that has been encrypted using PGP. You can access PGP via software such as Outlook and Eudora. PGP uses public and private keys to encrypt and decrypt information. Anyone wanting to send you an e-mail message must have your public key. You decrypt a PGP message by using your private key and a pass phrase. This form of encryption is called public key encryption and is stronger than conventional methods because the keys used for encryption and decryption are different. This means you can give out your public key to anyone without compromising your decryption (secret) key.

PGP encryption is also available for encrypting your hard and floppy disks. If your PC or laptop are stolen, then PGP will prevent the thief from accessing your confidential information.

SPAM

There are many robots on the Internet that are in place to scan and store e-mail addresses when surfers log on to newsgroups, bulletin boards and websites. The addresses are then sold to marketing companies and software developers that create bulk junk e-mail programs. These junk e-mail programs are called spammers. If you post a message to a newsgroup, there is a high probability that your e-mail address will end up in the database of a spammer. So how can you stop the barrage of junk e-mail? There are a number of blacklists of known spammers. If your Internet service provider subscribes to a blacklist then they can prevent you from receiving the e-mail in the first place. However, a number of service providers do not have the software, knowledge or the will to filter incoming e-mail. A cheaper alternative is to use the sophisticated mail filtering in your e-mail software. Such software as Eudora or Microsoft Outlook allow you to set rules that are applied when you receive an e-mail message. For example, if you have received an e-mail with the subject line of 'Download Adult XXX Images', you can place a rule in your e-mail software which automatically moves these messages to your Trash Bin.

PRIVACY: WEB BROWSING

Websites can obtain a wide spectrum of information on their visitors for their own statistical and marketing purposes, without the visitor's knowledge. That information will include your Internet provider address, country, Web browser name, operating system and even your monitor resolution. Many Internet advertising companies have been scrutinised for profiling users and targeting them with specific on-line advertising. How would you feel if you confided in one website and they shared the information with another website that you didn't trust?

Many users are turning to companies that offer anonymous Web services. Companies such as Anonymizer and Zero Knowledge Systems offer paid subscription services that can protect your on-line identity. When you want to access a particular site, the software uses a proxy server or a gateway to download the information and then send it on to you. This 'man in the middle' approach protects your privacy because the site that you are visiting sees the proxy server or gateway as the visitor and not you.

JavaScript and Active-X Controls

JavaScript and Active-X Controls are engines that run within your Web browser. They can pose a security risk as they can allow access to other information. Consult your Internet service provider about disabling these controls on your Web browser.

A Word on Cookies

Contrary to popular belief, cookies used by many Internet sites are not malicious in nature. Cookies store information on your computer system when you visit a website. Many sites use them to identify the current status of an on-line transaction or uniquely identify repeat visitors to a website. Cookies can only be read by the site that provides them. Cookies cannot read information from your hard disk, nor can they obtain your e-mail address or compromise your computer, however it is advisable to set your browser to warn you that you are accepting a cookie by browsing the website.

PRIVACY POLICY

If you must submit personal information to a website then read their privacy policy beforehand. Try to find out the data-sharing relationships that the site has with other companies. Does the site have any other ways to gather information about you? For example: if you participate in an on-line survey, will this information be included in a user profile? Will you be entitled to see or update your user profile? Many companies share information with their subsidiaries or other entities. Consequently you may find yourself receiving large amounts of junk mail by providing your e-mail address or other contact details.

Companies such as TRUSTe provide a seal of approval to websites that comply with their privacy policies and data collection practices. Unfortunately these policies have holes in them that various companies have exploited. In November 1999, it was revealed that RealNetworks was gathering information about the music-listening habits of people using its RealJukeBox software despite the fact that RealNetworks displayed the TRUSTe 'trustmark'. This resulted in a major public outcry and TRUSTe was forced to revise its policies.

SUMMARY: TOP TWELVE TIPS FOR THE INTERNET USER

1. Update your Web browser and operating system software constantly.
2. Install a PC Firewall.
3. Install a good anti-virus scanner and set it to update itself automatically each day.
4. Disable JavaScript in your Web browser.
5. Disable Active-X Controls in your Web browser.
6. Set cookies to 'Warn me before accepting a cookie'.
7. If you receive an e-mail message containing a suspicious file attachment, do not click on the file attachment. Delete the e-mail message.
8. Avoid posting e-mail messages to newsgroups.
9. Encrypt your e-mail messages.
10. Encrypt your hard disk, floppy disks and any confidential files.
11. Do not write down your password or stick it on a 'post-it note' on your monitor.
12. Turn on your screen saver and set its password to something unique.

ABOUT SECURITYSEARCH.NET

SecuritySearch.Net (http:/www.securitysearch.net) is the world's leading IT security search engine, directory and community portal, containing thousands of links to products, companies, white papers, tools, underground sites, and much more. Security managers and consultants from around the world visit SecuritySearch.Net daily to view the latest security news and learn about tools, products and resources they can use to protect their companies and clients. SecuritySearch.Net also publishes free weekly newsletters including the SecuritySearch.Net Vulnerability Report, which provides subscribers with information about critical security vulnerabilities and news. Subscribe on-line at http://www.securitysearch.net/.

SURVEILLANCE GLOSSARY

ASIS	American Society for Industrial Security
CALEA	Communications Assistance to Law Enforcement Act
CCTV	Closed circuit television
CDT	Centre for Democracy and Technology
CESA	Cyberspace Electronic Security Act
CESG	Communications Electronics Security Group
CIA	Central Intelligence Agency
Comint	Communications Intelligence
CRIS	Crime Report Information System
CSE	Communications Security Establishment
CSIS	Canadian Security Intelligence Service
DIAL	Direct Intelligence Access Listening
DMA	Direct Marketing Association
DSD	Defence Signals Directorate
FBI	Federal Bureau of Investigation
FCC	Federal Communications Commission
FISA	Foreign Intelligence Surveillance Act
FRU	Force Research Unit
FSB	Successor to the KGB

GCHQ	Government Communications Headquarters
GCSB	Government Communications Security Bureau
Humint	Human Intelligence
ILETS	International Law Enforcement Seminar
IPLD	Individual Position Locator Device
ISDN	Integrated Services Digital Network
IT	Information technology
JIU	Joint Intelligence Unit
KGB	Soviet Intelligence Agency
MI5	British counterintelligence unit
MI6	British intelligence unit
Mossad	Israeli intelligence
NCI	National Credit Information
NCIS	National Criminal Intelligence Service
NIPC	National Infrastructure Protection Centre
OCU	Operational Command Unit
PNC	Police National Computer
NCL	National Consumers League
NSA	National Security Agency
Sigint	Signals Intelligence
SIS	Schengen Information System (P29) also – Secret Intelligence Service
SID	Systems for Intelligence and Detection
SIW	Strategic information warfare
SSI	Strategic Studies Institute
STOA	Scientific and Technological Options Assessment
WMD	Weapons of mass destruction

SELECT BIBLIOGRAPHY AND SOURCES

In addition to contact with more than 80 experts in their particular field by way of interviews, correspondence, e-mail exchanges and lecture notes, the following published works, documents and Internet archives were also consulted:

Abbott, John, Director of the UK National Crime Intelligence Service, on British involvement with Europol, the first EU Criminal Intelligence Agency, 30 September 1998: www.ncis.co.uk

American Management Association, 'Survey on Electronic Monitoring and Surveillance', published 1997

American Employment Law Council, 'Electronic Interaction in the Workplace: Monitoring, Retrieving and Storing Employee Communications in the Internet Age', October, 1996

ASIS International with PricewaterhouseCoopers, 'Intellectual Property Loss Survey', Report, September 1999: www.asisonline.org

APB: G-files and attempts to secure NSA 'Diana and Dodi' documents under the US Freedom of Information Act: www.apbonline.com

Bamford, James, *The Puzzle Palace: America's Most Secret Agency*, Houghton and Mifflin, 1982

Barr, Congressman Bob, former CIA official and current campaigner on privacy issues, and seeking to enforce public statements on Echelon by the NSA: www.house.gov/barr

Bickford, David, former legal adviser to MI5, evidence to Commons Select Committee on Home Affairs, Third Report, 'Accountability of the Security Service', published 14 June 1999

Bridge, Lord, Chairman of the Security Commission: 'Investigation and Report into the Michael Bettaney Affair', May 1985

Bogonikolos, Nick, Zeus EEIG, 'Development of Surveillance Technology and Risk of Abuse of Economic Information' edited by Dick Holdsworth, Head of Scientific and Technical Options Assessment Unit, European Parliament, May 1999 as part of a technology assessment project on this theme initiated by STOA in 1998 at the request of the Committee on Civil Liberties and Internal Affairs of the European Parliament

Burrows, William, *Deep Black: Space Espionage and National Security*, Random House, New York, 1986; soft cover version Berkeley Books consulted: pages 167–191 and 358–362

Campaign for Nuclear Disarmament, Yorkshire, and their long running campaign to close Menwith Hill: www.gn.apc.org/cndyorks

Campbell, Duncan, 'Interception Capabilities 2000', report to the Director General for Research of the European Parliament in the Scientific and Technical Options Assessment programme office on the development of surveillance technology and risk of abuse of economic information; an excellent technical report, available on Duncan Campbell's home page at www.gn.apc.org/duncan; and at www.iptvreports.mcmail.com/ic2kreport.htm

Campbell, Duncan, 'Somebody's Listening', *New Statesman*, 12 August 1988

CCTV on the London underground: 'Watching them watching us' and other surveillance updates: www.spy.org.uk/tube.htm

Chicago Hospitals, University of, 'At Forefront of Medicine *and* Security technology,' Andover Controls report to American Society for Industrial Security International, Convention, Las Vegas, September 1999

Clarke, Roger, 'A History of Privacy in Australia', Canberra, 31 December 1998: www.anu.edu.au/people/Roger.Clarke/DV/OzHistory.html

Clinton, President Bill, statement on 'Cyberspace Electronic Security Act of 1999' (CESA), 16 September 1999

Cohen, William, US Secretary of Defense with Janet Reno, Attorney General, William Daley, Secretary of Commerce, 'A Report to the President: Preserving America's Privacy and Security in the Next Century; A strategy for America in Cyberspace', 16 September 1999

CommerceNet, with Nielsen Media Research, 'Internet Habits of British Adults' – CommerceNet/Nielsen Internet and Ecommerce Survey (UK)

Coultarh, Ross, Channel Nine Australia, correspondence with Martin Brady, Director of the Defence Signals Directorate, Australia on Echelon and related matters: www.echelonwatch.org

Cyber-Rights and Cyber-Liberties (UK), founder Yaman Akdeniz, Centre for Criminal Justice Studies, University of Leeds: various archive items consulted at www.cyber-rights.org

Davies, Nick, 'M15's Surveillance machine', *Sunday Times*, 10 March 1985

Davies, Simon, 'Spies Like Us', *Daily Telegraph*, 16 December 1997; 'EU Simmers over listening post', 16 July 1998 or www.electronictelegraph.co.uk

Dempsey, James, Senior Staff Counsel for Centre for Democracy and Technology, testimony to the US House of Representatives Committee on the Communications Assistance for Law Enforcement Act 1994, before the Subcommittee on Crime; October 1997: www.fas.org/irp/congress/1997-hr/index.html

EchelonWatch in conjuction with the Free Congress Foundation, Electronic Privacy Information Centre, Cyber-Rights, Cyber-Right (UK) and the Omega Foundation; many links and sites to all aspects of electronic interception and privacy issues: www.echelonwatch.org

Elcock, Ward, director of the Canadian Security and Intelligence Service, submission to Senate Committee, Ottawa, 24 June 1998: www.csis-scrs.gc.ca/index.html

Electronic Frontier Foundation, articles and updates across the whole field of electronic communications and intelligence: www.eff.org

Electronic Privacy Information Centre, Surfer Beware III: Privacy Policies without Privacy Protection, Report, December 1999: www.epic.org

Europol, 'Tasks and Powers': www.minjust.nl:8080/a_belied/fact/europol.htm

Federation of American Scientists; vast current and archive site on intelligence and defence, maps and imagery (including Menwith Hill) maintained by John Pike: www.fas.org

Freeh, Louis, Director Federal Bureau of Investigation, speech July 1999, and other speeches, 1996–99: www.fbi.gov/pressrm/dirspch/dirspch99.htm

Freeh, Louis, 'Impact of Encryption on Publish Safety': statement of Louis Freeh before the Permanent Select Committee on Intelligence, US House of Representatives, Washington, 9 September, 1997

Frost, Michael and Michael Gratton, *Spyworld*, Doubleday, Toronto, 1994

Government Communications Headquarters; home page: www.gchq.gov.uk

Hagar, Nicky, *Secret Power: New Zealand's Role In The International Network*, Craig Potton Publishing, New Zealand, 1996, 2nd edn

Hansard written answers, House of Commons to questions on Menwith Hill and Interception of Communications, 14 July 1997 and 20 January 1998: www.statewatch.org/search

Hasting, Max, 'What a pity MI5 don't know more', *The Standard*, 4 March 1985

Home Office, 'Interception of Communications in the United Kingdom: A Consultative paper, foreword by Home Secretary Jack Straw: www:homeoffice.gov.uk/oicd/interint.htm

Hersh, Seymour, Pulitzer prizewinning US journalist; various reports, *New York Times*, 1975–81

'The Hill', *Despatches*, Channel 4, transmitted 8 October 1993

Ikonos Satellite, launch, projections and download imagery: www.spaceimaging.com

ILETS: International Law Enforcement Telecommunications Seminar, 'International Requirements for Interception: www.dcita.gov.au/nsapi-text/?MIval=dca_dispdoc&ID=529

Kent, Bruce, writing in the *Guardian*, 22 September 1999

Kitchen, Jay, President, Personal Communications Industry Association, testimony to the US House of Representatives Committee on the Communications Assistance for Law Enforcement Act 1994, Subcommittee on Crime, October 1997

Leigh, David, 'Churchill pressed over Wilson plot', *Observer*, 21 December 1986

MacKay, Niall, 'Did EU Scuttle Echelon Debate', *Electronic Telegraph*, 9 October 1998

Majka, W. Joseph, 'Financial Crimes: The Globalisation of Fraud', lecture to ASIS International Convention, Las Vegas, September 1999

Matchett, Alan, Eye See U! Security Enterprises, 'New Era: Digital Video Recording and Storage', lecture to ASIS International Convention, Las Vegas, September 1999

Massiter, Cathy, 'MI5's official secrets', Channel 4 television, transcripted in the *Guardian* after IBA banned the showing of the film, 1 March 1985

Mathiesen, Thomas, Professor of Law, University of Oslo, 'On Globalisation of Control: Towards an Integrated Surveillance System in Europe', published by Statewatch, November 1999

Mecham, Leonidas Ralph, Director of the Administrative Office of the United States Courts, Applications for Orders Authorising or Approving Interception of Wire, Oral or Electronic Communication, report and statistics for the US, 1999

Menwith Women's Peace Camp, 'A history, various arrests, court hearings and imprisonment of protestors': www.apc.org/cndyorks/mhs/wpcinfo.htm

Metropolitan Police, 'Aspects of Criminal Investigation and Metcrime Units': www.met.police.uk

MI5: 'A History of the Security Service' and official website: www.MI5.gov.uk

National Army Security Association: http://nasaa.npoint.net

National Security Agency, home page: www.nsa.gov:8080

National Counterintelligence Centre, 'Foreign Economic and Industrial Espionage, 1999', report and recommendations: www.nacic.gov

Olson, Daniel, Cryptanalyst Forensic Examiner, Racketeering Records Analysis Unit Federal Bureau of Investigation, Washington, 'Analysis of Criminal Codes and Ciphers', published January 2000, downloaded from FBI website

Operation Opt-Out:Centre for Democracy and Technology Washington, campaign against multiple-link data bases, profiling, junk mail and marketing: www.cdt.org

Owens, Charles, head of FBI Financial Crimes Unit, in evidence to US Senate Committee on the Judiciary, 19 March 1997: www.fbi.gov/homepage.htm

Pierce, Charles, LRC Electronics, 'Digital CCTV', lecture to ASIS International Convention, Las Vegas, September 1999

Poole, Patrick S., 'America's Spy in the Sky': http://capo.org/opeds/pp0615.htm

Privacy, Echelon and the UKUSA Resources: http://civilliberties.tqn.com

Privacy and Human Rights, 1999, 'An international survey of privacy laws and developments; and Technologies of Privacy Invasion', survey and reports jointly performed and published by Privacy International and Electronic Privacy Information Centre, 1999: www.privacyinternational.org/survey/summary

Richelson, Jeffrey T., *The US Intelligence Community*, Ballinger, New York, 1989, pages 167–197. And fourth edition, 1999, pages 185–191

Shane, Scott, 'Mixing Business with Spying', *Baltimore Sun*, 1 November 1998

Shayler, David, 'The case that made me quit', *Mail on Sunday*, 24 August 1997

Shelley, Professor Louise, Congressional Testimony before the House Committee on International Relations, 'Threat from International Organised Crime and Terrorism', 1 October, 1997

Statewatch: 'EU and FBI Launch global telecommunications surveillance', Statewatch Bulletin, Vol 7 No 1, January–February 1997. 'UK Spying on EU Partners', Statewatch Bulletin, Vol 8 No 1, January–February 1998. Statewatch (holder of the 1999 Champion of Privacy award by the London School of Economics) publishes its bulletin six times a year and maintains a vast searchable archive at: www.statewatch.org

Thirteenth USAFA Field Station. This was formed in 1991 as a contact organisation for operatives stationed at Menwith Hill between its inception in 1958 and its turnover to the civilians in June 1966. Website contains chat, information, convention dates and members' personal recollections: www.sni.net/menwith/

United Nations, 'Manual on the prevention and control of computer-related crime', UN Crime and Justice Information Network: www.uncjin.org

US Intelligence Community, 'Who we are, What we do': www.odci.gov

US Electronic Espionage, *A Memoir*, source Columbia University Library, Ramparts V11; 1–12 July 1972. And additional links to NSA electronic interception documents and accounts at: http://jya.com/echelon.htm

Vanunu, Mordechai, author's personal recollections

Vatis, Michael, Director, National Infrastructure Protection Centre, 'Cyber Threat Assessment' to Senate Judiciary Committee, Washington, October 1999: www.fbi.gov/nipc/index/htm

Vest, Jason, 'Listening In', *Village Voice*, New York, 12 August 1998

Washington Post, 'US Tapes Russia Car Phones', 5 December 1977, *Newsweek*, 12 July 1977

Wright, Steve, Omega Foundation, Manchester, 'An Appraisal of the Technology of Political Control' presented to the Scientific and Technological Options Assessment Unit of the European Parliament in December 1997, Summary and Options, 1999: www.europarl.eu.int/dg4/stoa/en/publi/166499/execsum.htm

INDEX